MILITARY ETHICS

WHAT EVERYONE NEEDS TO KNOW®

T0055156

"Professor Lucas has constructed a gem of a book. It is a true innovation in the complex and challenging field of military ethics. His approach is engaging and unique in that he tackles the major themes through a process of incisive questions and comprehensive answers. His analysis of the issues ranges from the influence of the Greeks, just war theory, St Thomas Aquinas, and Kant through to the contemporary challenges of private security contractors, drones, cyber, and robotics. This is highly recommended for field commanders, military educators, and general readers alike."—Jamie Cullens, Colonel, ADF (retired) and Director, Centre for Defence Leadership and Ethics, Australian Defence College, Canberra

"George Lucas, in *Military Ethics: What Everyone Needs to Know*, offers us an excellent, compact, and highly readable account. Interest in military ethics has exploded in recent years, and Lucas here constructs a masterful introduction which is both easy-to-read and filled with helpful real-world examples. In the first part, he details the foundations of professional military ethics, which range from ancient custom through just war theory and into international law. In the second, Lucas applies the established practices of military ethics to such cutting-edge issues as: private security companies, drones, cyber-warfare, and using military force in aid of humanitarian crises. This is highly recommended for anyone interested in professional military ethics."—Brian Orend, author of *The Morality of War*

"With scholarly erudition and a deep understanding of the military milieu, Professor Lucas explores the myriad ethical challenges facing soldiers and provides a clear basis for how to think about them. This work takes on ancient issues of just war theory as well as challenges presented by emerging technologies. It should be a required reading for all, military and civilian alike."—Major General Robert H. Latiff, PhD (US Air Force, retired) and Research Professor and Director of the Intelligence and Security Research Center at George Mason University in Fairfax, Virginia

"George Lucas has written the ideal introduction to military ethics. The book is engaging, comprehensive, and deeply erudite. From ancient sources to the battlefield frontiers of military robots and cyber-war, Lucas ranges across different traditions and historical periods to show how we can make sense of the ethical problems of war. Whether citizen or serviceman, the need to reflect on the ethics of military action has never been greater. This is the perfect guide."—David Rodin, Co-Director and Senior Research Fellow, Oxford Institute for Ethics, Law, and Armed Conflict, University of Oxford

MILITARY ETHICS
WHAT EVERYONE NEEDS TO KNOW®

GEORGE LUCAS

FOREWORD BY
GENERAL JOHN R. ALLEN, U.S. M.C.

OXFORD
UNIVERSITY PRESS

OXFORD

UNIVERSITY PRESS

Oxford University Press is a department of the University of Oxford. It furthers the University's objective of excellence in research, scholarship, and education by publishing worldwide. Oxford is a registered trademark of Oxford University Press in the UK and certain other countries.

Published in the United States of America by Oxford University Press 198 Madison Avenue, New York, NY 10016, United States of America

"What Everyone Needs to Know" is a registered trademark of Oxford University Press.

Library of Congress Cataloging-in-Publication Data
Lucas, George.
Military ethics / George Lucas.
pages cm.—(What everyone needs to know)
Includes index.
ISBN 978-0-19-933688-3 (pbk.: alk. paper)—ISBN 978-0-19-933689-0 (cloth: alk. paper)   1. Military ethics.   I. Title.
U22.L78 2015
174'.9355—dc23
2015009184

1 3 5 7 9 8 6 4 2
Printed in the United States of America
on acid-free paper

For my favorite US Marine Corps trinity

General James N. Mattis, USMC (retired)
General John R. Allen, USMC (retired)
and
Col. Arthur J. Athens, USMCR (retired), Director, Vice Admiral
James B. Stockdale Center for Ethical Leadership

Semper Fidelis!

No matter how clearly we see the citizens and the soldier as [one and the same] man, [or] how strongly we conceive of war as the business of the entire nation . . . the business of war will always remain individual and distinct . . . [And] for as long as they practice this activity, soldiers *will think of themselves as members of a kind of guild,* in whose *regulations, laws, and customs* the spirit of war is given pride of place. . . . No matter how much one may be inclined to take the most sophisticated view of war, it would be a serious *mistake to underrate professional pride (esprit de corps)* as something that may and must be present in an army to greater or lesser degree. Professional pride is the bond between the various natural forces that activate the *military virtues*; in the context of this *professional pride* they crystalize more readily.

—Karl von Clausewitz, *On War*, 1830,
book 3, chap. 5

CONTENTS

Part 2 Ethical Challenges Facing the Military Profession

FOREWORD

GENERAL JOHN R. ALLEN
US MARINE CORPS (RETIRED)[1]

Early on, I learned from my father, a Navy officer and veteran of two wars, that the pervasive and persistent ingredient in all his stories about the military and combat was the essential dimension of ethics in war. For generations, my family has been dramatically shaped by war: my grandfather was gassed on the western front in World War I, and my father's destroyer was torpedoed by a German U-boat in the North Atlantic. My own experiences of war began in Sarajevo in 1995, and, a decade later, intensified in Iraq and Afghanistan. In all these transformative experiences of war and conflict, a single theme was prominent: ethics.

War is the most demanding undertaking of humankind. Indeed, in the perennial debate about the nature and character of war, the one unchanging aspect of the nature of war is the centrality of humanity. In fact, war and conflict have provided us examples of the loftiest moments of the human endeavor, alongside examples of its most reprehensible conduct. The two extremes frequently exist at the same time and in the same place, and the moral contrasts are often vivid and horrifying. Unconstrained, the dark side of humanity can find its worst, most repugnant expression in war. We are witness to it now, as the so-called Islamic State heaps one unparalleled depredation upon another, in the most graphic and repulsive ways conceivable.

From the earliest of times, humans have sought to restrain their baser instincts by seeking to govern them during the use of force: limiting its destructiveness and, in particular, the cruelty of its effects on innocents. These limits have been codified over time into a body of international law and professional military conduct that seeks to guide and limit the use of force and violence. And herein is the paradox: as we visit violence and destruction upon the enemy in war, we must do it with a moderation that acknowledges the necessity of its use, offering the means of discriminating between and among the participants, and admonishing us to apply proportionality.

For any nation, but in particular for the United States, reconciling the necessity of violence and killing in war with our moral values has been one of the most demanding challenges we have faced as a nation, particularly as we've prepared our young troops for the essential nature of war and the reality of the battlefields we've faced throughout our history, and certainly during more than a decade of armed conflict in Afghanistan and Iraq. My view is that there can be no reconciliation of this dichotomy without *understanding and embracing a set of moral principles that guide every aspect of the life of the warrior.* These principles, these "ethical standards of the military profession," create an imperative—a moral redoubt and a spiritual shock absorber—essential to the institutions that wage war and to the men and women who carry it out.

Unchecked, human savagery in war delivers our young troops to the edge of an abyss within which is found indescribable deprivation. We have seen this savagery in al-Qaeda, among the Taliban, and most recently in the horrendous movement ISIL. These groups—these miscreants—fight from their own set of moral principles. Their leaders and religious scholars engage in tortuous justifications and rationalizations to try to legitimize their acts of abject brutality. This creates an ever

greater imperative for us and for our nation not only to condemn the falsehood of their ethics, but also to redouble our
efforts to inculcate our young military personnel with our own
moral and professional principles. This sets us above and apart
from these groups and creates for us, in battle, a clarity and
certainty that we fight from the right place and from a higher
moral plane.

Ethics, however, does not only consist in the professional
moral code that binds us in battle. It guides our everyday existence and gives us purpose and strength of character to make
the right choices in every dimension of our personal and professional lives. Indeed, being guided by ethics in peace directly
influences our performance in battle. In his landmark book
The Anatomy of Courage, Lord Moran provides us one of the
most profound means of linking our daily ethics with our ethics in battle by explaining that ethics—the choice of right over
wrong—is indeed the wellspring of one's acts in battle:

> Man's fate in battle is worked out before war begins.
> For his acts in war are dictated not by courage, nor by
> fear, but by conscience, of which war is the final test. The
> man whose quick conscience is the secret of his success
> in battle has the same clear cut feelings about right and
> wrong [even] before war makes them obvious to all. If
> you know a man in peace, you know him in war. The
> thing a man does practically believe—if you tell me what
> that is, you tell me to a very great extent what the man is,
> what the kind of thing he will do is.[2]

In this important book, *Military Ethics: What Everyone Needs
to Know*, George Lucas has, in turn, given us a comprehensive
treatment of ethics—of the ethics of the military profession,
not just in war, but in peace. It will not only contribute to our
individual efforts at ethical development, but will also find
an esteemed place among military ethicists and in our military classrooms as well. As we emerge from thirteen years of

war and crisis, and as we confront yet another challenge in the form of ISIL, our nation will continue to be tested. Those serving on the front lines—our troops—will bear this test more profoundly than the rest of us. This seminal work readies us for that test, and Professor Lucas has done us all good service.

Mount Vernon, Virginia
July 4, 2015

Notes

1. General Allen retired from the US Marine Corps in April 2013, after having served for two years as Commander of the International Security Assistance Force (ISAF) in Afghanistan. For the three years prior he was Deputy Commander of the US Central Command. He is currently serving under appointment by the US President as Special Envoy for the Global Coalition against ISIL (Islamic State of Iraq and the Levant).
2. Charles McMoran Wilson (Lord Moran), *The Anatomy of Courage* (Garden City, NY: Avery Publishing Group, Inc., 1987): 160.

ACKNOWLEDGMENTS

I would like to thank the following US and international military service personnel who read drafts of this book and commented on its suitability for both a military and a civilian audience, as well as addressing concerns of citizens and military personnel from other nations facing similar questions and challenges. In particular:

Commander (JG) Andreas Bauer, German Armed Forces
Lt. Col. Iryna Bystrova, General Staff, Armed Forces of Ukraine
Squadron Ldr. Faisal Nadeem, Pakistani Air Force
Major Ejaz Nazir, Pakistan Army
Major Budi Setiawan, Indonesian Navy
Mr. Kiril Ognyanov Angelov, Bulgarian Ministry of Defense
Col. Eris Jemadi Tajudin, Turkish Army
Capt. Tomas Cayia, US Army
LCDR Victor Cunningham, US Navy
LT Paul Ortiz, US Navy
Capt. Anthony Grusich, US Marine Corps
LCDR Krysten Pelstring, US Navy
LT Daniel F. Stayton, US Navy
LCDR Mark Webb, US Navy
LCDR Michael Winters, US Navy

Most especially, I would like to thank my wife, Professor Patricia J. Cook, who also teaches ethics at the Naval Postgraduate School and (formerly) at the US Naval Academy, for carefully reading and commenting on this manuscript. We share a hope that it will (thanks largely to her and to my students) prove understandable and helpful to the wonderful young men and women whom we have been privileged to teach over the years, as well as to interested and concerned members of the general public who worry about war, pray for peace, and often express heartfelt concern for the health and welfare (along with their gratitude for the selfless service) of these same young men and women.

INTRODUCTION

Why Military Ethics?

In 2003, during the first year of the American-led military intervention in Iraq, a contingent of reserve army personnel in charge of the Abu Ghraib prison was discovered to have engaged in numerous acts of torture and abuse of prisoners. Torture and abuse of prisoners is widely held to be immoral and certainly a violation of international law. These discoveries and others similar to them (e.g., the "enhanced interrogation" of detainees at the Guantánamo Prison in Cuba) are often cited as *moral failings* by US military and security personnel that were sanctioned, if not encouraged, by top officials in the US government. US Army Major General Anthony Taguba, subsequently appointed to head the official investigation of the Abu Ghraib incident, characterized it as a massive failure of ethics, leadership, and military professionalism.[1]

On November 6, 2013, a high-ranking US Navy officer was arrested for conspiring with other officers and at least one corrupt member of the Naval Criminal Investigative Service (NCIS) for accepting cash bribes, prostitutes, and Lady Gaga tickets, in exchange for steering classified information concerning multi-million-dollar ship maintenance and reprovisioning requirements to a private military contractor headquartered in Singapore, nicknamed "Fat Leonard." The contractor was presumably successful in landing lucrative contracts in which he and his firm grossly overcharged the Navy for these goods and services, while key military figures charged with the oversight and accountability for these contracts turned a blind eye.[2] Ultimately, three admirals were censured and face possible criminal indictment for their alleged roles in the scandal, including a recent superintendent of the US Naval Academy, generating an enormous black eye for the US naval service.[3]

These are only isolated samples of what many inside and outside the US military see as grave ethical crises and moral failings. From the operational, war-fighting side: torture and abuse of prisoners, deliberate targeting and killing of civilians—for example, by Marines in Haditha, or during a drug-fueled rampage in Kandahar by Army Staff Sergeant Robert Bales, or by remotely piloted "drones" over the sovereign airspace of allied nations. Even some of the wars themselves in which the military fights, such as Iraq, are deemed to be illegal under international law, as well as morally unjustified under what is widely known as "just war" doctrine (discussed in chapter 4). Meanwhile, from the individual and organizational side, and quite apart from the just or unjust conduct of warfare, military personnel (as above) have been found to engage in corruption, sexual harassment, and assault on subordinates and new recruits, embezzlement of travel funds, conflicts of interest, and gross ethical violations of standing regulations. General Taguba's citation of failures in ethics, leadership, and military professionalism seem to apply to these actions as well. As in any other realm of professional practice (e.g., medicine, law, government, or business) in which such misconduct is found to occur, these scandals seem to point to problems in what we might term "military ethics."

Quite a few people, however, including some military personnel themselves, believe that the phrase "military *ethics*" is either a meaningless contradiction or a wildly inconsistent term—an "oxymoron." How could ethics (concerning right and wrong conduct) have anything to do with war (the use of deadly force, ostensibly to kill large numbers of people and destroy their property)? Persons with experience of war and combat, in particular, wonder if there can ever be anything ethical about the death, destruction, and widespread misery they observe as a consequence of war, even when they themselves otherwise agree that military personnel are and should be held to a very high standard of personal conduct in their daily lives.

And yet "ethics" (however we define it) does seem to factor into combat, into the declaring and the waging of war, as well as into the personal lives and individual careers of military personnel in service to their country in many nations around the world. There are wars that seem, on balance, justifiable, and others that seem wrong to wage. And there are ways to go about fighting those wars that seem "right" or permissible, and other forms of conduct during war that seem egregiously wrong and sufficiently outrageous for us to label them "war crimes." And without doubt in any case, no one approves of military personnel engaging in graft, corruption, or fraud, or the abuse or harassment of their uniformed subordinates.

Where do we come by such "moral intuitions" about right and wrong, both when deciding to declare war, and when choosing among alternative methods to wage it? And how is it that we hold the military personnel charged with waging our wars—indeed, how is it that they hold themselves—accountable for an especially high degree of moral rectitude and professionalism in their personal lives in these other respects?

Dr. David Whetham teaches military ethics at the Staff and Command College at the UK Defense Academy in Shrivenham, England. Recently, he described his "expeditionary" experiences of being frequently asked (or "tasked," as they say in the military) to travel to foreign military bases and academies throughout the world to lecture on and teach the topic of military ethics. The demand for his services is quite high, and the interest in ethics quite keen in the many nations of Latin America, Africa, the Balkans, and the Middle East to which he has been invited. Sometimes he suspects, however, that this keen interest on the part of a military's leadership seems phony: a feigned interest, just for show. But just as often, he reports, the concern on the part of military personnel and their leaders to understand and improve the ethical quality of their conduct seems genuine and urgent.[4]

In the United States, Professor Martin L. Cook holds the Vice Admiral James B. Stockdale Chair in Ethics at the US Naval War College in Newport, Rhode Island. His elective course in ethics and moral philosophy, the "Stockdale Course" (also named after this famous naval war hero and Medal of Honor recipient), is one of the most popular elective courses at this institution. The interest in ethics, and in "military ethics," seems both genuine and intense on the part of the midcareer officers who are chosen to study there prior to assuming senior positions of military command. Ethics and military ethics are required courses, taught at all US federal service academies: West Point, Annapolis, the Coast Guard Academy, and the Air Force Academy. The same is apparently true among the many reserve officer training units scattered across US colleges and universities nationwide. And the same is true at military educational institutions in many other countries, ranging from Japan, South Korea, and Australia to France, Canada, Norway, the Netherlands, and the United Kingdom.

At the very same time, General Martin Dempsey (US Army), the present chairman of the Joint Chiefs of Staff (the senior military commander in the US Department of Defense) laments (as did his predecessor, Admiral Michael Mullen) that "ethical lapses" and "moral failures" among individual members of the General Staff and senior officer corps, coupled with incidents of sexual assault and harassment among the troops, both officers and enlisted, constitute one of the most grave crises he faces daily. Indeed, he ranks these "ethical failures" right alongside the activities of the Islamic State in Syria and Iraq, the incursions of the Russian army in Ukraine, the difficulties of winding down the war in Afghanistan, or mediating the testy dispute between Japan and China over the Senkaku/Diaoyu islands.[5]

How can it be that "ethics" is mentioned as constituting a grave and important concern, equal in urgency to these other ongoing and persistent military crises? And how is it that these "ethical lapses" seem to be so frequently in the news headlines? Don't the military services and their personnel pride themselves on setting and maintaining the highest standards of personal conduct? Don't they likewise appear to go to great efforts to engage in "professional ethics education" and "character development"? How does this strong organizational push for ethics square with the widespread incidence (or public perception) of moral failure?

Perhaps these efforts to instill and ensure widespread ethical behavior are simply not working. Or perhaps, despite such efforts, a certain degree of moral failure is simply to be expected among members of a large, complex, diverse organization. Perhaps we the public, and perhaps military leaders themselves, set too high an expectation of exemplary conduct and are accordingly humiliated when that standard is not fully met by all members. Or perhaps we in the wider public expect more of military personnel in this respect than we do of the members of other occupations (e.g., politicians and business leaders).

Whatever it is, something seems very odd, very confused, and very wrong about this topsy-turvy picture. And it only gets worse when we try to probe below the surface and examine the wide range of views and contrasting understandings of what ethics *is* in a military setting.

The intense public discussions that often accompany the new release of films and cinema—such as *Hurt Locker*, *Zero Dark Thirty*, or *Lone Survivor*—depicting military ethics issues on and off the battlefield, provide an insight into just how perplexing, and sometimes convoluted, those public perceptions can be. Consider the current debate about the morality of snipers in the wake of the Clint Eastwood film *American Sniper*, portraying the life and death of Navy SEAL Chris Kyle.

Initial reactions to Kyle's autobiography and the movie were very positive, especially in the "American heartland" and among military personnel, who felt their lives, views, and experiences are often overlooked by Hollywood. Then came the negative reactions to the SEAL's activities as portrayed there, with critics denouncing Special Forces snipers as "cowards" and "cold-blooded murders" rather than "American heroes."[6]

Which view is correct? Kyle himself comments on the value and moral courage of police snipers in urban settings. And there were no such negative remarks about military snipers being cowards when three of Kyle's SEAL colleagues precisely shot and killed three pirates who were holding the *Maersk Alabama*'s captain, Richard Phillips, for ransom off the coast of Somalia in 2009. (The public moral debate in that case focused instead on whether Captain Phillips himself had behaved like a hero, or instead recklessly risked his ship's crew against their wishes by sailing too close to the Somali coastline in the first place.)[7]

On the other hand, if critics are right, and there is something distasteful or morally repugnant about human snipers in (all?) such situations, would not that judgment carry over to our moral evaluation of "targeted killings," accomplished by remotely piloted vehicles, or "drones"? How is this better or worse, or even morally distinguishable, from killing by sniping?

Consistency and coherence do not seem to play a large role in these heated public debates about military ethics. Yet somehow we all must consider carefully our views on such matters, and link them up, in turn, with our perspectives on graft, corruption, sexual harassment, and "proper professional decorum" (or its absence) by military personnel off the battlefield as well. This is a daunting task, but it is clearly something about which all of us—both military and civilian—need to know a great deal more than we do.

As teachers, my colleagues and I assign our midcareer "students" to write papers on the moral dilemmas they have faced on deployment, and on their own understanding of ethics and military ethics that result. The results span a wide spectrum of experiences, as well as of sophistication in describing them. But the takeaway is invariably that, despite

a college degree that usually included one or more ethics
courses, and despite some remarkable and painful experiences in combat, veterans with several years' military experience collectively have very little in the way of a coherent or
shared view of military ethics. There is a lot that they don't
know that they should know, and that they urgently need to
know about this topic. Indeed, there is a lot that it would help
military personnel immensely to know when going about the
performance of their duties, especially if such knowledge
replaced the highly overexposed and shopworn inspirational
speeches and training sessions that currently pass for ethics
training in the military.

It is a challenge to say what ethics means to military personnel in the different branches of military service, whether
in the United States, Canada, and Great Britain or globally.
Is there anything in common between military personnel in
India, China, Pakistan, or is there any content to the views
of ethics in a military context that would span the vast cultural and situational differences of armed forces in Africa,
Latin America, and the Middle East, and link them to military
service and principles of ethical practice among the military
forces of NATO in Europe, or the United States, Canada, and
Australia, beyond the bare minimum of wearing a uniform
and carrying a rifle?

This may all seem to constitute one giant headache, or in
slightly more frank military jargon, "one big [bleeping] mess!"
But notice that if we were to change the context and ask a
similar range of questions about the core ethical values and
moral practices of, for example, doctors, lawyers, or members
of other, reasonably well-defined communities of professional
practice (clergy, journalists, educators), that would not seem
so strange or unreasonable. At the very least, we expect physicians and healthcare professionals, for example, to exhibit a
vast range of cultural differences in the manner in which they
practice healthcare while still holding some things in common
(like putting the welfare of their patients first and resolving to

"do no harm"). We might also expect educators the world over to be united in their fundamental dedication to teaching vital areas of significant knowledge to the next generation, while refraining from abusing their power and influence, or otherwise exploiting or abusing their students. And despite the vast differences of cultural beliefs and practices, we might likewise find it possible to determine when a doctor or nurse (or a wayward teacher) was engaging in malpractice, or deliberately violating or forsaking the common core of shared professional values and practices.

Could we do something similar with soldiers, sailors, and Marines? It is our task in this book to examine such questions in a question-and-answer format, to sort all this out, and finally to help discern "what everyone needs to know" about military ethics. In order to do that, it will help to take seriously the commonly used phrase "profession of arms" and to imagine military service itself as a kind of profession, similar to medicine or law or education. Just what that means, how it might work, and particularly how ethics comes to play a central role in the profession of arms is what we will explore together.

How should we define the central terms of this book?

A few words of caution about this project, regarding two central terms: "ethics" and "professions."

First, the terms "profession" and "professional" have been widely but indiscriminately applied over the past few centuries to everything from defining respectable vocations for the offspring of a culture's nobility, all the way to the right and expectation of individuals to receive a salary and make their living through the exercise of their specialized knowledge and expertise (thus everything from auto repair to pipe fitting, plumbing, and masonry would qualify as a profession rather than a specialized skill).

In this book, however, I have intentionally used the terms "profession" and "professional" in a very specific sense, encompassing many of the common uses of the terms today. A profession constitutes

- A *distinctive practice*, or set of social practices, that in turn requires
  - *Mastery of specialized knowledge and techniques* through education and intensive training
  - Acquaintance with *a language, vocabulary, and set of technical assumptions* unique to those practices that enable their common mastery and performance, and (perhaps most importantly) that ultimately provide
  - A shared understanding among the members that they and their profession are dedicated to providing a unique and urgently needed *service to the wider public or the civil society within which those professions are* practiced.

"Professional" then denotes either one who belongs, or claims to belong, to one of the recognized professions defined in this sense, or else it is a laudatory adjective, attributing excellence or proficiency in practice to one of a recognized profession's individual members (as in "She is a true professional, in every sense of the word!"). The great New York sportswriter Bill Heinz (d. 2008) used to define "professionalism" as "a basic code of life," when "you can sleep because you did what you had to do."[8]

In our historical era, *professions exist to serve the public*, and it is their dimension of *public service* (and often sacrifice or dedication) that results in the conception of professional ethics, encompassing both the

- *Aspirations, ideals, and core values* of a profession in terms of the ends or goods it provides to the wider public, and the
- *Limits on acceptable practice and professional probity* that together circumscribe proper or acceptable professional behavior and decorum.

A second and final word of caution concerning the term "ethics," which is subject to a wide range of interpretations. This word of caution and clarification is especially important for military personnel, who are routinely bombarded with the "E-word," in ways that are frequently punitive and accusatory, as well as unflattering and unhelpful.

In this book, I generally use the terms "ethics" and "morality" interchangeably, as is the practice in ordinary language. This common usage represents the origins of these words as, respectively, Greek and Latin terms denoting essentially the same set of urgent questions: namely, how should we live, what ideals should we strive to attain, and how are we obliged to treat one another in the pursuit of these goals? (Importantly, these understandings bear very little resemblance to the routine citation of laws and regulations that is equated with "ethics training" in the military.)

Careful readers will note a subtle distinction, however, in which "morality" is applied more frequently to the *basic rules or principles* by which individuals or social groups guide their choices and evaluate their behavior (somewhat more akin to laws and regulations), while "ethics" sometimes refers to the *comparative and critical examination of these moral principles.* The term "professional ethics," however, always applies specifically to a distinctive body of moral principles that guide the practices and evaluate the behavior of members of a discrete community of professional practice, and which are largely self-generated and voluntarily self-imposed, quite distinct from the law (as in "medical ethics," or in this case, "military ethics"). While all this closely tracks normal usage, normal usage can sometimes prove a bit confusing on these matters, and I hope this brief statement will help prevent such confusions.

Notes

1. See Antonio M. Taguba, "Ethical Leadership: Your Challenge, Your Responsibility," Annual Stutt Lecture on Ethics, US Naval

Academy, Annapolis, MD, 2006: http://www.usna.edu/Ethics/_
files/documents/TagubaPg1-24_Final-1.pdf. Public expression of
this concern subsequently cost General Taguba his army career.
2. Lee Feran, "'Massive' Navy Bribery, Hooker Scandal Grows: Third
Officer Charged," *ABC News*, November 6, 2013: http://abcnews.
go.com/Blotter/massive-navy-bribery-hooker-scandal-grows-
officer-charged/story?id=20809942.
3. Christopher P. Cavas, "3 Admirals Censured in 'Fat Leonard'
Scandal," *Defense News*, February 11, 2015: http://www.defensenews.
com/story/defense/naval/navy/2015/02/10/navy-admirals-
scandal-fat-leonard-gdma-flags-corruption-bribery-carrier-reagan-
deployment-singapore/23167837/.
4. See David Whetham, "Expeditionary Ethics," in *The Routledge
Handbook of Military Ethics*, ed. George Lucas (London: Routledge,
2015), 123–132.
5. See Jim Garamone, "Chairman Stresses Professionalism to
Combat Ethical Lapses," *Department of Defense News*, March 10,
2014: http://www.defense.gov/news/newsarticle.aspx?id=121806;
Charles S. Clark, "Pentagon Going Full Speed Ahead to Improve
Ethics," *Government Executive*, February 10, 2014: http://www.
govexec.com/oversight/2014/02/pentagon-going-full-speed-ah
ead-improve-ethics/78563/. See also General Dempsey's foreword to
Lucas, *Routledge Handbook of Military Ethics*.
6. Kyle's own reflections on such charges are revealing: "Kyle heard peo
ple call snipers cowards. He would point out that snipers, especially
in urban warfare, decrease the number of civilian casualties. Plus, he
said, 'I will reach out and get you however I can if you're threatening American lives.'" On the "moral justification" for what he did,
Kyle also remarked: "You don't think of the people you kill as people.
They're just targets. You can't think of them as people with families
and jobs. They rule by putting terror in the hearts of innocent people.
The things they would do—beheadings, dragging Americans through
the streets alive, the things they would do to little boys and women
just to keep them terrified and quiet—that part is easy. I definitely
don't have any regrets about that." Excerpts from Michael J. Mooney,
"The Legend of Chris Kyle," *Dallas Magazine*, April 2013: http://
www.dmagazine.com/publications/d-magazine/2013/april/
the-legend-of-chris-kyle-01?single=1.
7. Once again, this public debate arose after the release of the Tom
Hanks film *Captain Phillips* in 2013: see Tricia Escobedo, "Controversy

Surrounds Release of New Tom Hanks Film, 'Captain Phillips,' " *CNN News*, October 8, 2013: http://www.cnn.com/2013/10/08/showbiz/captain-phillips-movie-controversy/.
8. Nathan Ward, in a memorial essay for the op-ed page of the *Wall Street Journal*, February 7, 2014, A11.

Further Reading

Clausewitz, Karl von. *On War*. Edited and translated by Michael Howard and Peter Paret. Princeton, NJ: Princeton University Press, 1976.

Coleman, Stephen. *Military Ethics: An Introduction with Case Studies*. Oxford: Oxford University Press, 2013.

Cook, Martin L. *The Moral Warrior: Ethics and Service in the U.S. Military*. Albany: State University of New York Press, 2004.

Cook, Patricia J. "A Profession Like No Other." In *The Routledge Handbook of Military Ethics*, edited by George Lucas, 32–43. London: Routledge, 2015.

Lucas, George, and W. Rick Rubel, eds. *Case Studies in Military Ethics*. 4th edition. New York: Pearson, 2014.

Lucas, George, and W. Rick Rubel, eds. *Ethics and the Military Profession: The Moral Foundations of Leadership*. 3rd edition. New York: Pearson, 2012.

MacIntyre, Alasdair. "Military Ethics: A Discipline in Crisis." In *Routledge Handbook of Military Ethics*, edited by George Lucas, 3–14. London: Routledge, 2015.

Part 1

THE MORAL FOUNDATIONS
OF THE MILITARY PROFESSION

1

ETHICS AND THE PROFESSION OF ARMS

How can we talk about ethics in war, when people are killing each other and deliberately inflicting destruction and misery on one another?

This question expresses a common misconception that has a grain of truth. Of course killing people and destroying property are morally wrong in virtually all societies, under normal conditions.

The only way we would not categorically condemn these actions is if they were an unavoidable part of our attempts to *stop something that was even worse*. Simply put, the use of lethal force is morally justifiable only if war is *the only remaining way* we have available to us to prevent or avoid something even more terrible.

Put slightly differently: if there is something really terrible we are trying to avoid (genocide, extermination, enslavement?) and we have tried everything else we can reasonably think of to prevent it, *only then* may we resort to lethal force and armed conflict. (That, incidentally, is a very important consideration called the "principle of last resort." We'll return to it in greater detail in chapter 4.)

Almost immediately, however, there will be some persons who raise an important objection, known as "pacifism," the moral opposition on principle to any resort to armed conflict and lethal force (even as a last resort). Pacifists in effect either deny that there is anything worse than war itself as a *matter of fact*, or else claim as a *matter of moral principle* that it is always and everywhere wrong to use violence for any purpose whatsoever, even when others threaten to do so, and even to avoid a "fate worse than death."

When stated clearly in this fashion, pacifism is a pretty radical position: even if forceful resistance were the only way to prevent some atrocity, the pacifist is nevertheless committed to allowing that evil to triumph.

The premise of ethics as pertaining to warfare, by contrast, is that war is waged only as the last remaining alternative to an even worse atrocity. But this basic recognition also provides a source of moral boundaries, somewhat different from the boundary observed by the radical pacifist. That is, if our justification for going to war is to avoid an even greater atrocity or evil, then *we ourselves cannot inflict more harm than we are trying to rectify or prevent.*

And here we encounter yet another important moral principle, known as the "principle of lesser evil" or more commonly, the "principle of proportionality." That is to say, very quickly in considering whether to wage war (and in arguing the point with those opposed in principle to doing so) we are forced to invoke moral considerations. We need *a really compelling reason* (like avoiding genocide or enslavement); we need to have first tried other, less "evil" alternatives than war (and presumably failed); and even then, we need to be reasonably sure our decision won't bring about even more harm than we are trying to avoid or prevent.

That is how ethics comes to play a role in something even as terrible as violence and warfare. The ethics comes in through the questions we are forced to pose and answer that explain why it is both necessary and reasonable to sometimes fight, rather than surrender and put up with whatever terrible circumstances we are facing. The ethics comes in when we are forced to explain ourselves to pacifists, or even to more moderate fellow citizens who quite rightly think that war itself is an evil that we ought to try to avoid at (almost) any cost.

As a result, one finds these kinds of questions and these moral considerations (good reasons, last resort, and proportionality) being evoked in all sorts of settings throughout history. In Thucydides's great work of history, *The Peloponnesian War*, for example, the Spartan king and military general Archidamus opposes going to war with Athens precisely because (he says in effect): "No one *wants* war. It will cause great misery and suffering, which we will bequeath to our children." That is to say, even though Archidamus was the leader of a civilization that supposedly glorified war and military virtues, he nonetheless demanded a *justification* for fighting in one and worried about the "disproportionate harm" war invariably brings on its perpetrators. (Some readers who are familiar with that particular war will remember that the other members of the Peloponnesian League thought Athenians had become so arrogant, dangerous, and unreasonable that they simply had no choice but to oppose them with military force.)

This exemplifies what the great contemporary political philosopher Michael Walzer terms "the moral reality of war." Moral considerations, he writes, have always and everywhere played a central role in the debate about war.

But once we do finally decide to go to war, isn't the goal to win by whatever means required?

This is a variation of a famous moral question: do the *ends* (winning the war, in this instance) justify the *means* (doing whatever is required, however awful that may be)? Remember in this instance that our strategic goal, purpose, or "end" in declaring war was to *avoid something even worse*. And so we were obliged (even if we didn't believe in, or know much about, ethics) to make a moral case for the need to resort to war.

But once decided upon, if the end goal is now to win the war we have justifiably declared, wouldn't that permit us to use any tactics available to us that would make us successful in pursuing this end? Indeed, if the point is for the winner to prevail, *wouldn't it be foolish to introduce moral scruples* into the process?

This was the view of General Karl von Clausewitz, a famous 19th-century Prussian soldier and theorist of warfare. He thought that moral sentiments (like benevolence or pity) were not merely irrelevant but also dangerously out of place in the midst of armed conflict. Once begun, war should be prosecuted with a kind of ruthless, mechanical efficiency.

In very sharp contrast to pacifism, Clausewitz espoused a political view known broadly as "realism." Realists like Clausewitz maintain (contrary to what we just discovered above) that moral considerations play no role either in deciding to go to war or in carrying out warfare tactics thereafter.

It is all too easy to give a superficial view, or caricature, of sophisticated and nuanced views concerning war, such as realism and pacifism. Let's try to avoid doing that, because both perspectives raise thoughtful and important considerations for us to ponder.

Clausewitz had good reasons for his concerns. He thought wars were fought for reasons of state, in pursuit of the political interests of states, and that ethics played no meaningful role in those considerations. (And that seems quite true, historically, in wars from the Peloponnesian League to World War I, at least, even though that does not thereby prevent us from questioning or offering a critique of those decisions, and those many resulting instances of war, on moral grounds.)

Just as importantly, Clausewitz also believed that once a nation had set upon this course, it was best to pursue it relentlessly and efficiently to the quickest possible conclusion. But notice that this hard-nosed realistic advice from him seems to embody an underlying *moral* concern: namely, to avoid prolonging the harm and suffering caused by war. War is a terrible thing, a blunt, powerful, and often brutal instrument of the state. So, if we do decide to use that blunt instrument, we must do so quickly, effectively, and efficiently lest the suffering and misery be prolonged and turn out to be much worse than they need have been.

Suppose we accept this hard-nosed advice: does it matter whom we target, whom we kill, or how we kill them during combat?

Granted, it is often maintained that we may fight a war by any means at our disposal, without limitation (other than those perhaps imposed by good sense or political prudence). In particular, this means that concepts like "ethics in the conduct of war" or laws pertaining to how a war can be fought are patently absurd or seriously misconceived.

But here is an example, an actual instance or case study, that shows that soldiers themselves do not always think this way.

Early in 2013, a platoon of highly trained army troops from Botswana were deployed, along with troops from the South African National Defence Force (SANDF), to the Central African Republic in response to a request for aid from its beleaguered president, François Bozizé (who was subsequently ousted by Seleka rebels). The troops were asked to provide security and to repel a loosely organized band of insurgents laying siege to the capital city, Bangui. The platoon engaged and took fire from the rebels, returned their fire, and eventually drove them away from the outskirts of the city.

When the platoon returned to base, however, it was discovered that they had taken a surprisingly high rate of casualties: 13 troops were killed in the action, and many others had been wounded. The Botswana Defence Force commanders were shocked that their highly trained and well-equipped soldiers, among the most proficient on the African continent,[1] had encountered such effective and deadly resistance from a poorly trained, disorganized, and lightly armed insurgent force.

What had happened? That "resistance force," it turned out, had consisted mostly of child soldiers, upon whom the surprised Botswanans were reluctant to fire. Some of the children behaved like hardened soldiers, the returning troops reported. This was why so many of their own forces had been wounded or killed. But some of the armed children were obviously terrified, sobbing, crying for their mothers. "This is not what we came here to do," the soldiers reportedly objected. "We didn't come here to shoot children."[2]

This vignette illustrates something elementary, and yet profound, about military ethics. The Botswanan soldiers, and those who would commend them for showing restraint, are quite prone to think in moral terms about wartime activities.

But wouldn't other soldiers who were less scrupulous or less sentimental than the Botswanans simply have fired on the children?

Very possibly, and, in any case, one single story doesn't prove a point. But this case reminds us that not all soldiers are simply mercenary "murderers for hire," who unreflectively "kill people and break things" without the slightest concern or regret. Remember that these Botswanan soldiers are among the most highly trained and proficient professional armies in present-day Africa. And their instinctive reaction *does* tell us something about what dedicated, highly trained and proficient professionals are willing and (perhaps even more importantly) *unwilling* to do.

In fact, the questions raised here exemplify basic questions of military ethics. Questions about what the Botswanan soldiers should do, what other military personnel might do under similar circumstances, and what still others might think about it afterward are precisely *questions about ethics*, and specifically about *military ethics*. They force us to test the limits and explore the boundaries of acceptable moral conduct under extremely difficult and gut-wrenching circumstances. In any given community of shared practice, this narrating of experiences (what are termed "case studies"), and subsequent discussion or debate by the members of that community on what should or should not have been done, constitute the beginning of reflection upon the ethical standards of that profession, and the core values and beliefs that define it.

Those considerations are somewhat different from the "ethics of war" discussions with which we began. We might say that the questions about whether and when to go to war are everybody's business, including soldiers. None of us should fight, or order others to fight, in wars that are unnecessary or unjustifiable.

But when ordered to fight by his or her nation, the soldier incurs some additional responsibilities. *These are among the considerations of military ethics*, as distinguished from discussions of political philosophy regarding the ethics of war and peace generally. These specific questions of military ethics arise amid the routine practices of the profession of arms.

That is important, in turn, because most of the principles now enshrined in international humanitarian law, or the so-called law of armed conflict (as we will discover in the very next chapter) *arose first as questions regarding proper professional military conduct*. Only when various military services in the United States and Europe, during discussions taking place in the 19th century, had adopted an informal code of professional conduct for the profession of arms, did many elements of that code find their way into what became the first Geneva and Hague conventions of the late 19th and early 20th centuries.

Even if ethics has a place in war-fighting, what do we say about soldiers who are ordered to do horrendous things? Does military ethics apply to them?

Some people believe that military personnel, whether officers or enlisted, are little more than mercenaries or armed thugs in the service of some "political elite." We see today in Syria and certain African nations that dictators, strongmen, or totalitarian regimes can use their military forces to oppress and intimidate their own citizens. Certainly in such situations, ethics plays no role in the behavior of those sorts of militaries, nor is their activity properly described as "professional," and the killing they do is therefore hardly different from murder.

Others believe that the military itself, in most countries, at least, constitutes merely an obedient bureaucracy in service to the interests of the state, whatever those interests may be. It is the state and its leaders who behave morally or immorally. Soldiers and sailors strictly do as they are told in enforcing the prevailing political will. In this paradigm, military personnel are indistinguishable from robots, machines, or the guns and armaments troops wield: both the soldier and his weapon are merely instruments of killing, and whether that killing is justified homicide, or murder, depends upon what orders the state gives and what policies it is pursuing.

Neither view seems to account for the Botswanan situation. But there is a third model that more adequately describes their reluctance to kill child soldiers. That third view holds that military personnel are members of a profession, the profession of arms. As such, and like members of other traditional professions (healthcare, law, journalism, education, police and firefighters, the clergy), the members of this profession serve their society. Professionals belong to organizations that serve an essential social purpose. They are defined by their commitment to sacrificial service, putting the public good ahead of their own. The professions embody values that redound to the benefit of the public, which the members of the profession serve and protect.

The professions adhere to certain explicit standards that are derived from the different goals, ends, or goods that each profession aims to serve. In the case of the medical profession, the goal is health; this yields professional precepts such as

"Do no harm." For attorneys at law, the good is justice, which produces standards such as confidentiality and the zealous representation of clients. In general, members of a profession are expected to understand the purpose of the profession to which they belong, "the good" that their profession embodies, and the responsibilities—both for aspiring to the highest ideals of professional practice and for respecting the limits on acceptable professional practice—that their membership imposes upon them.

Something like that attitude appears to be incorporated in the reactions of the Botswanan military to this tragic situation and explains their view of themselves, which didn't include the deliberate killing of children, even (at first) when the children were deployed as armed enemy combatants. This may come as a surprise to those who see soldiers merely as trained killers with little compunction about killing, even when this involves the killing of children.

If there truly is a profession of arms, does this mean there are rules for that profession regarding when, and against whom, to use deadly force?

Yes, that is exactly what it means: there are rules of professional practice, which deal directly with ethics. Some of them are codified in law (which we'll take up in the next chapter). But many rules of the military professional cannot be specified with code-like precision. They have to be thought of as internal matters of professional honor and responsibility. Here is a second good illustration of how this works.

A tragic case involving American Special Forces personnel took place in southern Afghanistan in the summer of 2005. In 2014, the release of the movie *Lone Survivor*, based on a book by the sole survivor of the incident, prompted renewed public discussion of this tragedy. This story of the fate of four Navy SEALs (three of whom were killed during the reconnaissance mission) has now become a required ethics case study for military students and personnel. It was even more intensely discussed after the sole survivor, former Navy Petty Officer Marcus Luttrell, published his account of the incident (also entitled *Lone Survivor*) in 2007.

This case, like the Botswanan case above, involves profound questions about whom soldiers may or may not kill, and when they may or may not do so. The issue here was not child soldiers, but so-called innocent bystanders or noncombatants. The moral dilemma arose when the four-member SEAL team, on the trail of a dangerous Taliban leader and his militia, inadvertently stumbled upon three local villagers (one of whom appeared to be little more than 14 years old). They were goatherds, tending their flock. Unlike the child soldiers in the Central African Republic, the three goatherds were unarmed. If allowed to go on their way, these local villagers would almost certainly alert the villagers of the SEALs' presence, and the local Taliban forces were then almost certain to find out as well.

Readers who have seen the movie, or otherwise know of this story, will probably have very strong opinions, and not necessarily agree with one another about what the four SEALs should have done next. But first let's note: If ethical considerations play no role in warfare, *we would not be having this discussion!* After all, if military personnel are little more than trained killers in a struggle for survival of the fittest, there would be nothing to discuss: the soldiers in Africa in our previous case study should have shot the children, and the SEALs in this present case should have killed the goatherds. End of story! Killing those who pose a threat would be a means for soldiers to ensure their own safety. Wouldn't any of us—civilians, that is—kill those who posed a threat to our safety?

But, of course, that is the point: in neither case did the military personnel do what "anybody" would have done when confronted with this choice. "Moral considerations"—and considerations of "professional ethics"—played a role in military decision-making in both cases.

*How can we say something is ethical if it results in our own
soldiers getting killed? Were there no other ethical
or professional choices in these situations?*

To be sure, in both cases mentioned above, other military
personnel might have chosen differently. And these are two
especially difficult cases for moral reasoning. Some persons
who study the two accounts may think the military personnel
in each instance would have been right (or at least justified)
in killing the child soldiers and the goatherds, while others think that, under both sets of circumstances, the soldiers
might have at least been excused, and not blamed, for having
done so. After all, the child soldiers were armed, and at least
some of them were shooting at the Botswanan army personnel. Don't soldiers have a right to defend themselves? And
Petty Officer Luttrell, who says he voted with the SEAL team
commander to spare the lives of the goatherds and let them
go at the time, does indeed now say he was mistaken. Luttrell
believes he should have voted to kill them instead and blames
himself for what he sees as the resulting deaths of three close
comrades-in-arms.

It is always tricky to second-guess decisions made in the
heat of the moment, in part because we are no longer in that
moment, but also because later we possess additional information. Both we and Luttrell now possess information that the
SEAL team did not have at the time: namely, what *did* in fact
happen, rather than their best guess at the time about what
might happen. In the case of SEAL Team 10, Taliban soldiers
later attacked and killed three of the four team members,
while Luttrell himself escaped. He was seriously wounded in
the firefight and (he admits gratefully) would probably not be
alive today were it not for other Afghan villagers who found
him, cared for his wounds, and hid him from the Taliban.

If we go back into the moment, we see the problem
starkly: how can the four SEALs infallibly know *which Afghan
villager was which*, and how could they guess what the goatherds

would do? Especially when you lack sufficient knowledge to predict the future reliably, you are usually required to rely on established principles, including professional principles, to guide your choices. And that seems to be, in the end, precisely what the SEALs did in that case. With guidance from their commanding officer, Lieutenant Michael Murphy, they agreed to let the goatherds go on their way.[3]

Doesn't the resulting disagreement in this case demonstrate that there is nothing authoritative in military ethics, that it is finally just a matter of opinion?

There *are* objective standards in military ethics. Disagreement and debate do not imply otherwise. Notice, for example, there is debate in the scientific community about whether humans have caused global warming. But this debate does not indicate that there is no truth of the matter. The debate, we assume, is iterating toward that truth. In military ethics, as in ethics in general, disagreements are usually about applications of principles, rather than about principles themselves. This is what we are witnessing in the discussion about Marcus Luttrell and the SEAL team.

Subsequently, during my own career, I had the honor of teaching these topics with two other members of that same military community in our required military ethics classes at the US Naval Academy. Both of these SEALs, a senior captain and the SEAL Command Master Chief, related accounts of the heated debates among the members of the especially tight-knit SEAL community about this case. At one point, they reported, the admiral who commanded the SEALs at the time angrily declared, at the conclusion of one such discussion, that he would personally court-martial any member of the SEAL community who espoused or defended the idea of deliberately killing civilian noncombatants.

Of course, neither that admiral, my two SEAL colleagues, or any of us outsiders were present on that hill in southern

Afghanistan. Perhaps none of us therefore has a right to speak, or hold an opinion, not even this admiral. What the admiral was doing, however, was invoking his right as a senior commander to pronounce judgment on this case. He is the most senior and experienced member of the organization, as well as the person charged to exercise that judgment. We might think that, in a hierarchy like the military, such a conclusion emanating from the senior commanding officer would therefore settle the matter once and for all.

But this is not what happened, and brief reflection shows this foreclosure of opinion, this pronouncement from authority, cannot by itself be infallibly correct in moral matters. *Moral standards* themselves also exercise some sort of authority in the decision-making of military personnel, independently of command authority. Simply suppressing dissenting views, even with a direct order from the senior commanding officer, is not finally valid as an argument, and obviously it has not made the underlying question or moral dilemma disappear. So apparently, SEALs themselves, and people who have read the book and seen the movie, do not grant either the lone surviving eyewitness or the senior commanding officer the right to settle on a final decision.

The admiral in command at that moment, however, did do something that may turn out to be far more important. In the midst of widespread anger, uncertainty, and contentious debate within his organization following the occurrence of this terrible event, he emphatically underscored and defended with no uncertainty a *profound professional principle* that is at issue in the SEAL case. That principle goes by various names in military ethics and in international law: the "principle of distinction," sometimes also called the "principle of discrimination," or the "principle of noncombatant immunity." That principle basically holds that there are no circumstances under which a member of the military profession may deliberately and intentionally harm civilian noncombatants. And (just as LT Murphy apparently did with his team), it is sometimes important for the senior person in charge to remind everyone of their professional responsibilities and moral commitments, in no uncertain terms.

For my part, I preferred the more subtle instructional approach of the same two SEALs mentioned above, whom I frequently observed teaching and discussing this case with midshipmen and cadets (you will find them acknowledged and thanked by name at the end of this book). They would review the circumstances, and then allow their respective classes (composed of midshipmen 3rd class—i.e., sophomores—whom they jokingly referred to as "battle-hardened teen-agers") to debate and discuss, and finally vote themselves on what they thought should be done in these difficult circumstances.

Invariably there were sharp differences of opinion. To the group of midshipmen who voted in favor of a "hard-nosed, realist" position—namely, that, however unpleasant, the killing had to be done—their military instructor would then hand a large combat knife to the group leader. "Okay," they would say. "You win. You start with the 14-year-old."

The argument would suddenly cease, and the classroom would grow silent. It was not merely that the next step would be personally repugnant and unpleasant. Instead, it dawned on all the members of the class, despite their earlier opinions, that the next step would be *wrong*. The majority of midshipmen examining this case intuitively see what the SEALs themselves probably recognized in the moment—a simple but hard truth that the Botswanan soldiers neatly summarized in their own case as well: "We didn't come here to do this."

But aren't there other examples of unethical behavior by soldiers that demonstrate that ethics dissolve during wartime?

There are certainly cases of terrible or tragic behavior during war that many ordinary citizens, and most members of the profession of arms themselves, do not remember with pride or approval: the My Lai massacre during the US war in Vietnam; prisoner abuse at the Abu Ghraib prison in Iraq; "saturation" or "terror bombing" of German cities by Allied forces toward the end of World War II; the use of nuclear weapons against civilian targets in Japan; the killing or severe mistreatment of prisoners of war by all sides in the Atlantic and Pacific theaters during World War II; the Holocaust itself. The list is not a short one.

The question is what to make of these events. If we label them "atrocities," we are implicitly recognizing that certain kinds of acts are morally repugnant, even in the midst of war. The examples themselves, like the My Lai massacre, provide us with illustrations of behavior that is *morally inexcusable*, even in war. This, in effect, certifies that there really is such a thing as military ethics.

Even if we refrain from harsh judgments or condemnation, we thereby acknowledge that we believe that there were choices that might have been made between the atrocities that were committed and other less morally unworthy alternatives. Likewise, if we denounce these activities as "war crimes" (as is often done, presumably with reference to international law), then we are once again recognizing that such activities are not to be approved of or tolerated.

During the Vietnam War, in one infamous example, US Army Lieutenant William Calley's platoon went on an infamous killing rampage in My Lai in 1968. More recently, US Army Staff Sergeant Robert Bales went on a midnight "killing spree" and murdered some 17 Afghan villagers as they slept, during what is now known as the "Kandahar Massacre" of March 11, 2012. We may wonder, especially in the latter case, *what happened to these individuals* to make them do such terrible things. But we do not attempt to condone them, or justify them, or simply dismiss these actions as the sort of thing that happens in war, even though such things *do* happen in the midst of war all the time.

In Sergeant Bales's case, he himself later apologized and denounced his actions as "cowardly"[4]—although many worried that he had suffered some kind of psychological break-down following multiple deployments to combat while struggling through severe family problems at home.

The My Lai massacre was halted through the efforts of an American soldier with a very strong intuitive sense of the importance of ethics on the battlefield. US Army Chief Warrant Officer Hugh Thompson landed his reconnaissance helicopter in the midst of the chaos, pointed his rifle at his fellow American soldiers in the village, and ordered them to halt the killing of civilians. When later asked why he did this, he replied simply, just like the Botswanan soldiers: "This was not what we came here to do."[5]

Notes

1. The US African Command (AFRICOM) considers the Botswana Defence Force "one of the most professional militaries on the [African] continent": see http://www.africom.mil/about-africa/southern-africa/botswana#.
2. This story of the Botswanan soldiers' dilemma was subsequently related and discussed the individual later asked to help the Bostwanan army personnel understand and cope with what happened to them, Dr. Ibanga B. Ikpe, a professor of philosophy at the University of Botswana (Gabarone) and an adjunct professor at the newly created Botswana Defence Command and Staff College. His report, and the discussion it provoked, occurred amidst a gathering of military officers, enlisted personnel, and civilian teachers from around the world, assembled for the annual meeting of the International Society of Military Ethics at Notre Dame University (October 10–12, 2013). Dr. Ikpe's task was to assist the army personnel to understand their professional responsibilities, and the limits on responsible and permissible professional behavior in such a confusing, morally ambiguous, and heart-rending situation. See Ibanga Ipke, "Military Ethics and the Dilemma of Irregular Combatants," Military Virtues and Contemporary Challenges, 2013 ISME Conference, Notre Dame, IN, October 15, 2013: http://reilly.nd.edu/news-and-events/conferences/isme-conference-2013/. This paper is not yet published or available, but an earlier essay illustrates the author's perspectives on

such problems: "Being Human and Being Armed: A Reassessment of Duty and Commitment in the Military": http://volgograd2007.goldenideashome.com/ikpe_paper.htm.

3. The movie version fails to clarify what Luttrell himself originally reported in numerous news interviews after the event, as well as in his 2007 book: namely, that the SEAL team for some reason deployed without carrying the routine passive restraints (such as plastic handcuffs) that otherwise might have offered a third, less stark alternative solution to this dilemma. Instead, in the movie version, the goatherds are first tied up, and then (fearing they might die of exposure), LT Murphy orders them released and the mission aborted.

4. http://www.cnn.com/2013/08/22/us/robert-bales-afghan-killings/.

5. The case of Hugh Thompson and the My Lai massacre can be found in George Lucas and Rick Rubel, eds., *Case Studies in Military Ethics*, 3rd ed. (New York: Pearson Publishers, 2010). The book itself is dedicated to CWO Thompson's memory.

Further Reading

Coleman, Stephen. *Military Ethics: An Introduction with Case Studies.* Oxford: Oxford University Press, 2013. See especially "Operation Redwings."

Lucas, George. "War." In *The Bloomsbury Companion to Political Philosophy*, edited by Andrew Fialla, 109–125. London: Bloomsbury, 2015.

Luttrell, Marcus. *Lone Survivor: The Eyewitness Account of Operation Redwing and the Lost Heroes of SEAL Team 10.* New York: Little, Brown, 2007.

Orend, Brian. *The Morality of War.* 2nd edition. Petersboro, Ontario: Broadview Press, 2013.

Walzer, Michael. *Just and Unjust Wars: A Moral Argument with Historical Illustrations.* 5th edition. New York: Basic Books, 2006.

2

MILITARY ETHICS
AND INTERNATIONAL LAW

If, as the cliché goes, "All's fair in love and war,"
then how can there be laws or rules in combat?

The idea that warfare is chaotic, lawless strife was captured by
the famous remark of the Roman senator and orator Cicero,
in the first century BCE: "In time of war, the Law is silent."
The breakdown of normal law and order, especially the laws
against killing, seems to be the chief characteristic of war.
Obviously, those engaging in combat are doing things that are
normally unlawful (and, like killing, are almost always considered immoral as well).

As we discovered in the preceding chapter, however,
this does not mean that all moral principles are suspended.
Despite appearances to the contrary, important moral principles remain in place and demand respect, even in the midst of
armed conflict. Law—an extensive body of international law—
is also operative in war, as has been increasingly recognized
and respected in our era.

But what is this law, and where is it found?

In the SEAL team case from the preceding chapter,
Petty Officer Luttrell later testified that, during the team's
heated discussion over how to deal with the goatherds,
the commanding officer, Lieutenant Michael Murphy, cau-
tioned that the SEALs' deliberate killing of unarmed local

villagers would constitute "a violation of international law." If so, Lieutenant Murphy was almost certainly invoking his understanding of the so-called law of armed conflict (LOAC). These rules and principles governing the behavior of combatants during war are embodied in a series of treaty agreements, or "conventions," adopted over the past century by international bodies of state representatives, meeting in European cities like The Hague and Geneva (and named accordingly).

The Hague Conventions tend to focus on the proper conduct of armed hostilities by opposing military forces: their provisions place limits on the amount of force used in specific combat operations, and prohibit the use of certain kinds of weapons. Force is only to be used to achieve legitimate and reasonable military objectives ("military necessity"), and only as much as is required to attain those objectives ("proportionality").

Thus, if a village housed a group of insurgents, it might be deemed necessary from a military standpoint to capture the village and kill or imprison the insurgents. But it would not be reasonable to firebomb the entire village, let alone to use a nuclear weapon to achieve this military objective. Such an excessive use of force would be deemed all out of proportion to the significance of the military's purpose in capturing the village. In addition, use of certain prohibited weapons, like poison gas or exploding bullets, has been found to inflict "superfluous injuries" or cause cruel and unnecessary suffering, neither of which furthers the legitimate military objective. Poison gas and nuclear weapons, moreover, are examples of weapons of mass destruction (WMDs), which fail to distinguish between enemy combatants and civilian noncombatants, and so are prohibited on those grounds as well. The Hague Conventions thus primarily address the weapons and tactics of warfare itself, as practiced between opposing military forces, and constitute what is termed the law of armed conflict.

The Geneva Conventions, somewhat in contrast, are written declarations resulting from assemblies usually convened
by the International Committee of the Red Cross (ICRC),
headquartered in Geneva. These deliberations approach the
problem of war from the standpoint of its inevitable victims,
caught between those opposing armies: that is, refugees, civilian noncombatants, and prisoners of war. These conventions
attempt to define and establish certain rights and protections
to be afforded those victims (such as not being deliberately
subject to attack by competing militaries). They also afford
recognition and protection to medical personnel attempting
to render aid to these victims. By affording specific rights and
protections to each of these groups, the Geneva Conventions
require that military personnel recognize their protected status
in the midst of hostilities. This fundamental principle goes by
many equivalent names: the so-called principle of distinction
(in law), or of noncombatant immunity, is also called the "principle of discrimination" in the earlier historical deliberations
concerning the morality of warfare that we take up in chapter
4. These conventions (plus some customary protocols and precepts) are referred to collectively as "international humanitarian law" (IHL).

While not identical, the two bodies of international legislation invoke similar underlying principles, such as the principle
of distinction, or noncombatant immunity. That principle was
also mentioned at the end of the last chapter as an important
moral principle in the customary code of conduct of the profession of arms. International lawyers tend to prefer the "IHL"
label for these collective bodies of law, while the military personnel whose conduct is directly governed by these laws tend
to refer to them as the "law of armed conflict." In either case,
this was what Lieutenant Murphy was specifically invoking
as a guide to the SEAL team's choices as they deliberated on
the fate of the local goatherds who had inadvertently stumbled
upon ("stepped on") their location.

All of these laws seem to pertain to the conduct of soldiers, but aren't there also laws determining the behavior of their respective state governments, as to when the government can order its soldiers to fight?

Indeed there are entirely separate bodies of international legislation governing the behavior of state governments, or "nation-states." Let's first explain the meaning of that hyphenated term in international law, because, with a kind of deceptive innocence, it represents the source of much of the conflict that leads to wars in the first place. That simmering, ongoing conflict, in turn, requires some international agreements that aim to hold that conflict in check and prevent the outbreak of war.

To begin with, not every nation is a state, and not every state is equivalent to a single nation. The Navajo in America, and the Kurds in central Asia, are both nations bound by a common history, language, and culture, but neither controls its own state. States like the United States, the Russian Federation, and Iraq, by contrast, are political entities with recognized borders and governments within which there may be many different nations.

Conflicts may arise when a nation (such as the Kurdish people) find themselves scattered across many distinct states, and subject to different bodies of domestic law, restrictions on travel or immigration, or religious persecution as ethnic minorities within their respective states (e.g., in Turkey or Iraq). This leads the members of the nation to aspire instead to control their own destiny within the sovereign borders of their own state. But the recognized governments of currently existing states in which the members of this nation reside are reluctant simply to cede territory, natural resources, or political sovereignty to the members of a nation within their present borders for a variety of reasons ranging from security concerns to loss of revenue or prestige (and also, perhaps, due to long-standing enmity, contempt for, and hatred of the members of that nation and their political aspirations). Kurds in northern Iraq, for example, control a sizable portion of that state's oil reserves, while, for security reasons (among other considerations) Turkey is reluctant to have the Kurds on its side of the border join with Iraq's Kurds to form an independent state. It is not difficult to see how such political tensions and their resulting conflict can lead to war.

Internally, the states suffering from such conflict can resolve some of the tension by granting regional autonomy and greater self-determination to the disaffected members of their minority nations. The United Kingdom has granted regional autonomy of a sort to Scotland, for example, while Canada offers an enormous latitude in governance to its French-speaking peoples living in the province of Quebec. Both Canada and the United States have granted increasing autonomy over the past century to indigenous "First Nations" (like the Navajo, Hopi, Sioux, and Apache) within their sovereign borders.

Such legal arrangements and good-faith political compromises can help stave off more severe conflict that, in previous eras, almost surely would have resulted in war. But there are practical limits on how far these kinds of legal arrangements can go toward resolving the underlying conflicts. It would prove extremely awkward and impractical if the indigenous nations within the sovereign states of Canada and the United States, for example, were granted full sovereignty, autonomy, and independent status as states. Intense discussions leading up to the recent referendum on full independence for Scotland—a proposed political "divorce" of sorts from the current United Kingdom—illustrates the enormous range of complexities and practical difficulties generated by such aspirations, even given the best of intentions and good faith on all sides (as in that instance) to resolve their differences without resorting to violence.

But such good faith and best intentions are quite frequently absent in such disputes. Instead, these conflicts lead states to resort to armed conflict and war in order to resolve them.

In 2008, Russian-speaking people in the northern province of Ossetia complained of their treatment and status under the government of the state of Georgia. The Russian Federation resorted to what turned out to be a nasty and destructive military intervention in an effort to force Georgia to relinquish political control of Ossetia. Neither the breakaway province nor the state of Georgia itself has fully recovered from the harmful consequences of that military conflict. The Russian Federation, meanwhile, has offered its support and assistance to Russian-speaking peoples in the Crimean peninsula and eastern mainland portions of the neighboring state of Ukraine, allegedly seeking their independence from the Ukrainian government in Kiev. In the months during which this book was being written, that regional military conflict has resulted in grave loss of life, economic disruption and hardship, and serious political instability in the region that some fear might lead to a widening of the war.

Such political conflict, it seems, is relentless and unceasing, and consequently, over the centuries, the resort to armed conflict to resolve these conflicts among states and nations has likewise seemed unending. Following two massive and unimaginably destructive world wars in the 20th century, however, the surviving states, nations, and their populations collectively resolved to construct legal arrangements that might curb this unceasing resort to violence and warfare. The United Nations Charter was adopted in San Francisco on June 26, 1945 by international delegates from war-weary nations around the world. Certain specific provisions of the UN Charter pertain to conditions and restraints on the declaration of, and resort to, war itself, at least among member states of the United Nations. These are contained in specific chapters (e.g., Chapter 7), sections (e.g., Section 51), and articles (e.g., Article 2.4), which collectively provide a mutually agreeable legal framework governing the rights of individual states to deploy their military forces. (We will discuss this distinct body of law, together with the so-called just war tradition in ethics, in a later chapter.)

For the moment, suffice it to say that the historical account of the origins and development of international law and emerging norms of state conduct is, in itself, an important story. Readers of the conventions and the UN Charter will find in these documents a record of what ordinary, sensible people have wrestled with over centuries in trying to limit the suffering inflicted by armed conflict. These documents reflect a dismal history during which states and governments have been all too eager and ready to resort to war to settle their disputes. The UN Charter, and the Hague and Geneva Conventions, represent a collective, ongoing effort to set bounds on the destruction and anguish that war itself can inflict. These conventions and resolutions, which eventually acquired the force of law, seek to limit the resort to war, as well as to make war itself less savage than it might otherwise be.

It is worth pointing out that reading and studying these documents is a required exercise in the curriculum of the military schools, academies, and reserve-officer training programs of most of the world's nations, including India, China, Russia and the countries of Eastern Europe, some countries (like Egypt and Israel) in the Middle East, as well as the United States, Australia, Canada, and the member states of the North Atlantic Treaty Organization (NATO). It was through such required education that Lieutenant Murphy came to be familiar with their provisions regarding the treatment of noncombatants.

Military educators for their part lament an absence of such required education in the military training of other states (e.g., Syria, Libya, and many African states) and seek to inculcate that education as part of the proper "professional military education" of the military forces of those states. US Army General Anthony Taguba, who (as noted earlier) led the 2004 official investigation into prisoner abuse by National Guard reserve units placed in charge of the Abu Ghraib prison in Iraq, identified the absence of any such training for the members of that unit as an important contributing factor to their subsequent outrageous behavior, and went so far as to post copies of the Geneva Conventions pertaining to treatment of prisoners of war on the walls of the prison itself.

To summarize this account of the international law pertaining to war: we have identified two distinct bodies of legislation. One, grounded in the provisions of the UN Charter, defines the limits placed upon its signatory states in ordering their military forces into war. That large problem is what we will take up next. Meanwhile, the provisions of law to which the leader of SEAL Team 10 referred are largely encompassed within the Hague and Geneva Conventions, which aim to codify and legislate protections for prisoners of war, refugees, and civilian noncombatants from death and injury at the hands of military forces. Here are some specific examples of international humanitarian law:

- Those not posing a threat in combat must be treated humanely.
- It is forbidden to harm an enemy who is surrendering.
- No one may be subjected to torture.
- Civilians may not be targeted.
- Captured combatants must be treated humanely, cared for if injured, and allowed to correspond with their families.
- Production and use of nerve gas (or hollow "exploding" bullets) is prohibited.

What authority, if any, do such laws have, especially when some combatants seem to ignore them without penalty?

We often think that the law's authority comes from the power of its enforcement. Laws control us, in other words, because if we don't follow them, we will be punished. If a law were not accompanied by severe consequences for disobeying it, we would say that it had no teeth. Because Interpol and international courts are not nearly as effective at law enforcement as we would like, it is sometimes said that international law, unlike most jurisdictions of domestic law, has no teeth.

Philosophers have long recognized, however, that the threat of punishment is not the only thing that makes people comply with the law. External enforcement may not even be the main thing that makes most of us respect the law. Instead, law can carry a separate kind of authority. This is particularly significant with international "humanitarian" law. The best way to explain this is with another story: a piece of historical fiction from Shakespeare's famous play, *Henry V*.

This play, written around 1599, offers an account of the Battle of Agincourt in 1415, during England's so-called Hundred Years' War with France. There are numerous well-known scenes and speeches, perhaps none so well known as King Henry's inspirational "St. Crispin's Day Speech" (act 4, scene 3: 18–67), urging his soldiers to fight enthusiastically as "a band of brothers." As you might expect, this play, and especially this speech, are also frequently on the reading list for cadets and midshipmen at military academies in the United Kingdom, United States, Canada, Australia, and elsewhere as well.

The key scene occurs shortly after King Henry's famous speech. Henry's soldiers had routed the French army and taken a large number of prisoners, both young warriors and boys ("pages") who assisted in carrying their gear and supplies. Henry thinks the French forces are regrouping to counterattack. He thereupon *orders that the prisoners being held behind the lines should be put to death,* so that they cannot turn and fight against the English from the rear. This order is discussed by two of Henry's infantry captains, who are expected to supervise this execution. Here is a portion of their dialogue (act 4, scene 7):

First Infantry Captain (angrily): Kill the prisoners? 'Tis expressly against the law of arms, as errant a piece of knavery, mark you now, as can be offer't.

Second Infantry Captain (sarcastically): 'Tis the King himself hath ordered it . . . O, 'tis a gallant king!
First Captain (disgustedly): Aye! And the cowards that fled
the fight before, now eagerly comply!

Note the complaint that describes the killing of prisoners (of
war) as "against the law of arms," and also suggests that it is
the sort of thing that would willingly be done only by cowards,
and not by those who were earlier engaged in legitimate combat with their enemies. This appears to be a criticism lodged
against an otherwise popular monarch, that his command in
this instance is. . . . well, how should we put it? Dishonorable?
Immoral? Illegal? A violation of military custom and tradition?
Perhaps all of the above?

What is of particular interest to us is that this passage is
explicitly repudiating the "lawfulness" of the king's command.
The second infantry captain even dares to remark sarcastically,
in derogatory fashion, on the tarnished honor and even questionable moral character of the king himself for having issued
such a command.

*What sense does it make for Shakespeare's character
to describe this custom or tradition among rival combatants
as a violation of the law of arms?*

Obviously, this play, and the historical events it is dramatizing,
transpired centuries before the Hague or Geneva Conventions
were enacted. Shakespeare's characters are not referring to any
actual legislation, or to the kinds of treaties and conventions
formulated by the international organizations and institutions
we have today. So what would Shakespeare's audience have
thought the characters were talking about?

The real King Henry ("Prince Hal") was a well-known
and well-liked figure in English history. And the historical
details of this battle, over a century before, were probably still
well known to Shakespeare's audiences (as the details of the

American Civil War are known to American audiences, or the horrors of World War I and World War II to British and French audiences today). We have to assume that Shakespeare was appealing to common knowledge and widespread assumptions, shared by both commoners and the literate nobility, about things like the law of arms. The members of those audiences were expected to know intuitively *what the two infantry captains meant*. And it looks like the audience was expected to agree that this one command by an otherwise-respected king and military leader to kill unarmed prisoners of war was, as the first soldier remarks, "as errant an act of knavery . . . as could be offer't."

What Shakespeare is invoking is an *unwritten* law. Far in advance of the 20th century, people were aware of this unwritten law of arms. We also find references to the unwritten "law of war" in our intellectual history. At just about the same time that Shakespeare was writing his dramas, the Italian jurist Alberico Gentili had fled to England on account of his Protestant beliefs and was teaching and writing at Oxford University on a topic he called "the law of war" (*de jure belli*) in 1589. Prior to Gentili, the same phrase had been used by the Spanish Dominican priest Francisco di Vitoria in lectures at the University of Salamanca (c. 1539) that criticized the Spanish conquistadors for their harsh military treatment of indigenous peoples in the New World. Vitoria outlined what he termed *ius gentium*, "the habits and customs of civilized peoples and nations," and described the wars of Spanish military forces against "the Barbarians" as at least sometimes constituting a serious violation of these laws, which reflect civilized, lawlike customs and practices.

So we have a historical antecedent to international humanitarian law and the law of armed conflict in this unwritten law of war. The "law of war" here refers to habitual practice, understanding, custom, and the conventions implicitly observed among and between warring nations and militaries concerning appropriate limits on their behavior. Even when engaged in war against enemies, it is not the case that "anything goes" and all the rules are set aside. Military forces and their nations attempt to establish, practice, and enforce certain kinds of rules and constraints, designed to limit the damage done by war and to limit the suffering inflicted by war on combatants and noncombatants alike. Principal among those unwritten laws of arms or laws of war are prohibitions on the killing of unarmed prisoners of war (POWs) and bans on the deliberate and intentional targeting and killing of noncombatants.[1] It is our heritage of these unwritten laws that, in the end, gives written, ratified, international law its underlying authority.

But what good does it do to point to a law of war when history is littered with violations of it?

Violations themselves do not nullify the laws. If anything, it is the reverse: violations *highlight* the relevant laws. This, too, is illustrated in Shakespeare's *Henry V*. Right after the reference to the law of arms, in the very next scene, a marauding band of French soldiers sacks the English camp and kills the pages (young, unarmed male attendants). This provokes anger and moral outrage, in turn, on the part of Henry as well as his troops. So *both* acts—Henry's initial order to kill the French prisoners, and the French killing of unarmed pages—appear to be moral atrocities of some sort. They are cowardly and morally despicable acts of the sort from which "real" soldiers and military forces ought presumably to refrain. Once again, this doesn't mean that military forces and individual military personnel don't commit such atrocities all the time. Rather, it means that, *when they do, they are engaged in wrongdoing*.[2]

Such killings, we say, are *unjustified*. The reluctance and unwillingness of well-trained military professionals to undertake the killing of unarmed and defenseless civilians (or even of child soldiers, as described in the preceding chapter) illustrates the widespread intuition that such killings, unlike the normal killing of enemy combatants during armed conflict, are *unethical* from the standpoint of *customary professional practice.* These intuitions have the force of law: nowhere written or legislated, but fully understood and more or less accepted by all those engaged in conflict against one another.

So what does this unwritten law of war have to do with the international humanitarian law, formally codified only during the 19th and 20th centuries?

This raises what is likely the most fascinating and complicated feature regarding the authority of law, and of international law in particular. Lawyers often say somewhat circularly that the authority of the law stems from the fact that it is the law, yet in the same breath maintain that "international law" consists largely in what nations do, or tolerate being done. Critics of international law in particular respond that the authority of law generally is grounded in the power of a government to enforce it with police, courts, and other institutions of law enforcement. Consequently, since there is no world-state or robust international institutions of government exercising power and legitimate jurisdiction, international law, as a result, has no teeth. It is not really law at all.

All of these claims and counterclaims seem to miss the point. It is extremely important to recognize that there are, and were, venerable, widely practiced, and virtually universal customs and traditions that formed the prior basis of the treaties, conventions, and laws of the past century or more. It is not the legislation, the promulgated law, that defines these military practices. Instead, there are unwritten laws, discoverable by ordinary reason and enshrined in traditions and customs of the profession of arms, that have then served as the foundation for the specific content of present-day international law.

The "jurisdictional authority" of international law governing the conduct of armed hostilities is not grounded in the relatively weak sanctions or punishments that might be threatened by a loosely organized "international community." Much more significantly, the authority of this body of law is derived from the best traditions, customs, and the core ethical principles of the profession of arms itself.

This offers a sharp contrast to the cynical view, widespread among both military personnel and the wider public, that over recent decades, a bunch of international diplomats and delegates meeting in grand ballrooms in Geneva have vainly tried to impose arbitrary, idealistic, and ultimately meaningless constraints upon the behavior of military personnel in wartime. That is not really the full story. Instead, in a very real sense, these "laws of war," including the law of armed conflict and international humanitarian law, are rules discerned over centuries by opposing combatants themselves. These "rules" began as custom, as the unwritten law to which Shakespeare's infantry captains refer. The law of arms, as they call it in *Henry V*, has gradually been imposed on armed forces, and upheld as a matter of high professional principle, *by members of the armed forces themselves.* And that, in turn, is why the two infantry captains are so outraged at the king's order: he has ordered them to betray their most fundamental professional principles, and to engage instead in what we might rightly term *professional malfeasance*.

It is as if King Henry had ordered his physicians to deliberately kill their patients. *This sort of thing is simply not done.* And if it is done nevertheless, it is recognized as a moral atrocity, an outrage, or as professional malfeasance. As the Botswanan soldiers and Chief Warrant Officer Hugh Thompson summed up the matter so eloquently: "This [the killing of children, prisoners, or civilian noncombatants] is *not* what we came here to do."

How did these so-called professional principles find their way into actual international law?

As we noted earlier, the modern or contemporary era of international law dates to the founding international conventions in the late 19th and early 20th centuries in Geneva and The Hague. The authors formulated the inaugural treaty conventions from provisions of professional practice taught at the Prussian Military Academy (for which General Clausewitz, toward the end of his career in the early 19th century, had served as rector). Thus they were codified, elaborated, and put in writing for the first time.

Just to be clear: although the Prussian Military Academy's teachings were immediate references for the Hague and Geneva Conventions, they were not the original sources for these practices. The substance of the conventions were themselves adopted, with only minor alterations, from a historic document known as "General Orders 100," written by a former Prussian soldier who fought in the Napoleonic Wars, and was familiar with the military curriculum at Clausewitz's Prussian Academy before marrying and emigrating to America. Francis Lieber was teaching law, history, and political science at Columbia University when President Abraham Lincoln asked him to convene a working group of senior military officers in order to draft professional military guidance, or "standing orders," governing the conduct of Union Army officers during the American Civil War.

It was that widely admired and emulated document, also known as the Lieber Code, that first set forth, in written form, the principles of military necessity, proportionality, command responsibility, and proper treatment of enemy prisoners, thus explicitly using legal language to remind Union Army officers of their professional military responsibilities. And it is that historical document, more than even the later European conventions, which scholars of international law identify as the original written repository of these ideas. Discrimination and proportionality are the underlying principles in all of these documents: only bona fide military objectives should be targeted and attacked by military forces, and when doing so, only as much deadly force should be expended as is found necessary to achieve the legitimate military objective.

These principles may sound like straightforward common sense—and, according to the Confucian general and military strategist Sun-Tzu (who also advocated a version of these same principles), "common sense" and prudence in professional practice are exactly what mandate such guidelines. But taken together, these two important principles of warfare also perform a moral function, by establishing a limit on violence and destruction (such as the wholesale slaughtering of opposing forces, and laying waste to the surrounding countryside) that militaries might otherwise senselessly inflict on their enemy.[3]

So treaty conventions merely formalized the common-sense consensus of their international signatories that the use of military force in the pursuit of wanton, purposeless, or non-military intentions (such as exacting punishment or revenge for the death of comrades) must be prohibited. Noncombatant "distinction" and proper (i.e., "honorable") treatment of POWs were also included among these sensible restraints. These are, as we have been arguing, pieces of age-old prudential reasoning. Indeed, over two millennia ago, we find a former Athenian infantryman from the Peloponnesian War, better known as the philosopher Socrates, abjuring, for his students, precisely such military excesses, on the grounds that slaughtering the enemy's defenseless citizens and laying waste to fields and forests serve no useful purpose, make no sense, and in fact, make the ultimate goal of ending the war and establishing peace all the more difficult to attain.[4]

If this is all basically prudence, ordinary intuition, and common sense, why do we need treaties and conventions? Why doesn't everyone simply do what is right?

Given the venerable origins in the long history of reflection on military practice, we still might think that writing laws merely to clarify and codify customary prudent and professional behavior does not add much to their authority.

What codification does do, however, is emphasize what philosophers term "normative force." Law and morality have *normative force* in the sense that they lay significant claims upon us and impose burdens upon us, by defining strict and powerful constraints on acceptable behavior. Sometimes, but not always, failing to honor these constraints (especially in the case of law) is followed by punishment. Merely being invited to act in accordance with common sense doesn't carry the same weight, gravity, or burden of compliance as do specific, black-and-white principles of law or morality.

Of course, we shouldn't need to be commanded or exhorted (nor threatened with punishment for failing) to do what simple common sense would dictate. The issue here is that what seems like prudence or common sense on the battlefield can actually be *expediency*. There is a big difference between the two. Expediency denotes a kind of a short-term, easy path of least resistance. Prudence is practical, but concerned with long-term goals and consequences. So what is expedient may not be prudent, and vice versa.

It may be prudent for a commander to restrain troops from using excessive force or engaging in atrocities in the interest of achieving legitimate military objectives, but it is seldom easy, convenient, or expedient, especially if the troops under command are raw recruits or conscripts. Troops might feel like exacting revenge for comrades killed in action; they might even be tempted to loot and pillage. In such scenarios, it might even seem expedient for a commander to allow his or her troops the freedom or license to act on these desires. It might seem like common sense that they should be allowed to vent these feelings, or "finish the job."

Notice, however, that engaging in such senseless atrocities is in no one's long-term interests. Military actions are undertaken for the sake of a restoring a just peace. Doing "extra" harm can only escalate the conflict, prolong it, and inflame it.

Moreover, this is precisely the kind of thing that damages the psyches of those who engage in it. King Henry's infantry captains were being ordered to disgrace the customs of their profession. Doing so, they apparently believed, would cost them their professional honor and their moral authority. So it would emphatically *not* be prudent to allow this.

Accordingly, we find among the Prussian professional principles, and later the legal conventions, an important professional principle known as "command responsibility." The commanding officer must keep a rein on the behavior of forces under his command, and he (or she) will be held accountable for any breaches of ethics and professional decorum of which those troops may be guilty. The written law, in other words, can be a hedge on the battlefield against confusing the Confucian or Aristotelian virtues of "prudence" (and wisdom) with mere convenience or expediency.[5] Command responsibility was finally the principle exercised so admirably, and at such great personal cost, by Lieutenant Michael Murphy, the commanding officer of SEAL Team 10.

One concrete effect that establishing and signing the legal conventions had was to formally criminalize these breaches of professional ethics. Specific "black-letter" or "bright-line" statutes introduce criminal, not just professional, sanctions. The conventions also became a sort of fund of disastrous experience. New weapons are constantly being found to inflict "superfluous injury or unnecessary suffering." Weapons such as hollow, exploding bullets or poison gas (and more recently, land mines and "blinding" lasers) inflict cruel and terrible injury and suffering, without providing any discernable military benefit. With "superfluous injury" and "unnecessary suffering" as a legal touchstone, we have added specific conventions to outlaw the use of such weapons.

None of this is to say that laws have authority because of enforcement. Before there was an International Criminal Court, before there were even war crimes tribunals, there were penalties associated with violating the law of arms. Violating principles of prudence can exact real penalties in the form of misery, unhappiness, and even death, often based on what we term quid pro quo: "You use prohibited chemical weapons upon me, now I will use them on you!" Or, "You killed your POWs who were our troops, now we will kill our POWs . . . including you!" But the main normative force of such rules, in the absence of strict external sanctions and punishment, is that such violations make no sense, are unsustainable, and come to make an already-bad situation much worse for everyone (including the violators).

Still, there is always collateral damage. These casualties would not have occurred if we had not gone to war in the first place, so is it really possible to distinguish these deaths from true atrocities?

It is true that collateral damage is atrocious, horrific, and one of many ways in which war is hell. The very term "collateral damage" is itself morally offensive—a bland euphemism disguising the horrors of war. There is nevertheless a moral difference between such damage, done accidentally or inadvertently, and the deliberate and willful committing of wartime atrocities.

To see how this is so, suppose we try to *defend* the "atrocities." The commanders of Allied forces during and after World War II did something of this sort. They did so by invoking the principle we earlier labeled "military necessity." They claimed that the firebombings and the dropping of nuclear weapons on defenseless civilian cities, although truly terrible campaigns, were *necessary* to bring about the swift end of the wars in Europe and Japan. While unfortunate and regrettable, such actions are an unavoidable feature of warfare, they claimed. Similar explanations are often given for what appear to be atrocities or war crimes committed during a conflict: that they are necessary, *and in any case, seemingly inevitable* features of war.

There is a hidden fallacy in such reasoning. Notice first that when a person offers such an explanation, it is usually not meant as a blanket explanation for all such events. The attempt to explain the need for terror bombing, for example, does not seem to apply to the My Lai massacre, nor would it exonerate the wanton slaughter of Afghan villagers by Staff Sergeant Bales. So we seem to distinguish between what we might call "justified atrocities" (for which some kind of excuse, or an exculpatory account might be given), and other atrocities, like the My Lai or Kandahar massacres, which simply can't be justified on any grounds.

Once we have fallen into doing this, however, we are no longer consistently maintaining that all such actions are "necessary and inevitable" features of war. None are inevitable, as there are always other choices. And some of the choices made can, or might be justified, while others (such as killing defenseless children) cannot be justified.

Simply engaging in this discussion, let alone engaging in or evaluating these kinds of actions directly, is engaging precisely in ethical debate about military behavior: it is the "doing" of military ethics. So we can hardly deny that ethics has an important role to play in military decision-making (or in the postconflict evaluation of military tactics). Significantly, our attempt to describe some (but not all) actions as "regrettable but necessary" during war, involves attempting (at least) to offer *a kind of moral justification* for those acts (acts such as the use of nuclear weapons on civilian targets). By saying they are "necessary," we are claiming that those who ordered or carried out the bombing raids should not be denounced or blamed as war criminals, *because these actions were justified* by the greater good they were intended to attain (the swift ending of the war). Here, we say, the ends or ultimate purposes were morally worthy, and so justified the use of extraordinary and seemingly terrible means to achieve those ends.

But, of course, we wonder to this day if those exculpatory accounts or justifications are valid. On the 70th anniversary of those terrible events, we still find ourselves arguing whether the use of nuclear weapons on the cities of Hiroshima and Nagasaki was *absolutely necessary* to bring a swift end to the war in the Pacific? Was this the *only* way to avoid the need to send hundreds of thousands of troops to attempt an invasion (and even more bloody conquest) of the Japanese islands? And if so, did that end or goal justify the use of what were otherwise immoral and criminal methods to achieve it? Here, as in many such exceptional cases, we have a well-known moral principle, coupled with an international law, against deliberately targeting and killing noncombatants. But some argue that the rule or principle or law had to be overridden or ignored, or deliberately violated, in order to achieve a greater good.

But that, too, is a question of ethics: specifically, of military ethics. Indeed, this seems precisely the same *kind* of question that the members of SEAL Team 10 were debating: "We know we cannot and must not kill civilians deliberately, but perhaps we may have to do so, in order to achieve a greater good." (In military ethics, this claim is sometimes labeled "the argument for supreme emergency"—and it is extremely controversial.) All this would at least indicate that the claim that there is no such thing as "military ethics" (let alone that ethics has no place in the midst of war) seems seriously mistaken.

Notes

1. In what is arguably the 20th-century's premier work on this topic, Michael Walzer describes these features as essential components of what he terms "the War Convention." The War Convention is not a written document. Instead, it consists of a set of shared working assumptions among nations and their military forces, more or less practiced and consistently upheld, regarding combatants—licensed to use deadly force against one another in the interests of the state, and hence also liable to be killed by their adversaries under the same convention—and those who are not combatants, to include women and children (presumably who are not armed, wearing uniforms, or otherwise serving in the military), the elderly, and unarmed nonpartisans, presumably from countries not involved in the fighting, who may be caught in the crossfire. The noncombatants also include, by custom, enemy combatants who have been injured or captured, and

so rendered *hors de combat*—out of the conflict, and unable themselves to fight. None of the latter are liable to being deliberately targeted, injured, or killed. See *Just and Unjust Wars* (New York: Basic Books, 1977), chap. 3.

2. An eminent colleague in philosophy, Jeff McMahan (Rutgers University), observes that, in such instances, the soldiers are killing persons who have done nothing to make themselves liable to attack (McMahan 2009: 7–36).

3. Perceptive readers who are historically knowledgeable might object here that such wanton destruction was deliberately practiced by the Union general William Tecumseh Sherman, in his infamous scorched-earth march "from Atlanta to the sea." We will return to this event several times in subsequent chapters, as well as in more recent, deliberate acts of wanton destruction (like the firebombing of Tokyo and Dresden, or the use of nuclear weapons on Hiroshima and Nagasaki). The ethical question these admittedly horrific and excep-tional cases pose is always, "Were these individual incidents *justifiable exceptions* to the moral principles generally prohibiting such actions?" Clearly Sherman ignored the most central provisions of professional conduct enshrined in the Lieber Code in this instance. Was he justified in doing so? He himself responded to the pleas for leniency from the citizens of Atlanta by harshly condemning them, and their breakaway nation, for having "brought down this scourge of war on us all." Was this a sufficient justification for the punishment he exacted? Did it end the Civil War more quickly? Did it serve to reunify and pacify the rebellious factions? Grave questions about the wisdom and morality (as well as of the military necessity) of these acts have been raised ever since. The same kind of moral critiques are raised concerning more recent forays into clear-cut violations of the customary ethics of the profession of arms in the interest of achieving a quick or uncondi-tional victory.

4. We will consider the teachings about military professional practice from "literary legends" like Sun-Tzu, Thucydides, Socrates, Homer, and Plato in greater detail in the next chapter. The specific discus-sion among Socrates and his pupils referenced here can be found in Plato's *Republic*, at the end of Book IV [469c–471c]; see also George Lucas, "Forgetful Warriors: Neglected Lessons on Leadership from Plato's Republic," in *The Ashgate Companion to Modern Warfare*, ed. George Kassimeris and John Buckley (London: Ashgate, 2010): 329–342.

5. It is well to point out that philosophers like Socrates and Aristotle held that morality was largely a matter of prudence and the lifelong "getting of wisdom," while the law was designed to clarify expectations and establish limitations on minimally acceptable social behavior for folks who just "didn't get it," or who were either so ignorant or so lacking in moral character that they could not be trusted to act on the basis of virtue alone. For those (according to Aristotle) who lack the prospect for even "a tincture of virtue," there is the law and punishment to restrain criminal and antisocial behavior. This observation occurs in Aristotle's book, the *Nichomachean Ethics*, allegedly written for his principal pupil, Alexander the Great—providing an interesting (if not altogether successful or happy) example of a civilian academic attempting to discern and teach the guiding principles of proper professional practice to a future military leader.

Further Reading

McMahan, Jeff. *Killing in War.* New York: Oxford University Press, 2009.

Conventions

Charter of the United Nations and Statutes of the International Court of Justice. https://treaties.un.org/doc/publication/ctc/uncharter.pdf.

Geneva Conventions of 1949 and Their Additional Protocols. http://www.icrc.org/eng/war-and-law/treaties-customary-law/geneva-conventions/.

Hague Conventions of 1899 and 1907. http://www.icrc.org/ihl.nsf/INTRO/195.

Classics on War and Ethics

Aristotle. *The Nichomachean Ethics.* http://catdir.loc.gov/catdir/samples/cam032/99036947.pdf.

Grotius, Hugo. *On the Law of War and Peace.* 1625. http://www.lonang.com/exlibris/grotius/.

Shakespeare, William. *Henry V.* http://shakespeare.mit.edu/henryv/full.html.

3

THE ANCIENT ORIGINS
OF MILITARY ETHICS

Isn't this idea of ethics and professional conduct in war
a relatively recent concept?

It is certainly reasonable to conclude that the moral concerns
and moral sensibilities enshrined in relatively recent international conventions to protect the rights of war's vulnerable
victims (discussed in the preceding chapter) are, by definition,
recent phenomena. But we did notice that the concerns embed-
ded in those documents for proper professional decorum considerably predate those legal conventions by several centuries.
Still, a few centuries are only a drop in the bucket of human history. At first glance, formidable and fearsome military adversaries from earlier historical eras, such as "Vlad the Impaler,"
and Attila the Hun, don't conjure up images of moderation
or moral discernment in combat, whether in the treatment of
POWs or the distinction of combatants from noncombatants.

War is often portrayed as a violent and perpetual curse
inflicted endlessly upon the human population, bringing
death, destruction, famine, pestilence, and misery in its wake
as the first of the Four Horsemen of the Apocalypse. A statistic
(attributed to the historian and philosopher Will Durant) suggests that during some 25,000 years of human history, there are
only about 250 or so years in which peace was universal. It is
only comparatively recently (according to this line of thought)
that human beings have moved beyond tribalism and brutality

and begun to civilize, tame, and limit war's destruction through laws limiting the recourse to violence, and through the gradual recognition of basic human rights.

The first of those two claims is beyond dispute. War is a miserable business. It is hell, according to the American Union Army general William Tecumseh Sherman (who, as we noticed in a note in chapter 2, practiced it as such). And perhaps it is a good thing that it *is* such a dreadful business, according to his Confederate army counterpart, General Robert E. Lee, "lest we come to love it too much." Lee was no doubt thinking (as would the philosopher J. Glenn Gray a century later) about some of the positive aspects of war, calling forth the "military virtues" that Karl von Clausewitz also celebrated: honor, valor, courage, loyalty, camaraderie, and heroic sacrifice. Gen. Sherman, by contrast, was dwelling on the misery inflicted—perhaps by those like himself, who thought instead to follow Clausewitz's original dictum that "moral sensibilities have no place in war." Once war is set upon as a course of action, it is best to pursue the fight relentlessly and pitilessly, so that it may be brought quickly to a conclusion.

The second claim, regarding how we may have come over the past century or two to civilize and "tame" the worst excesses of war through law and heightened moral sensibilities, is *much* more dubious. Those idealistic and inspiring conventions regarding armed conflict that we summarized in the preceding chapter, adopted in meetings at The Hague and Geneva, were promulgated amid some of the most violent and destructive conflict ever inflicted by human beings on one another, and on such a massive scale as to defy imagination.

As this book is being finished, countries throughout the world are in the midst of commemorating the 100th anniversary of World War I, in which over 10 million combatants were killed and many more wounded, and the landscape ravaged with scars that remain to this day. The impact of that conflict is still deeply felt in small villages and towns throughout Europe and the United Kingdom, in which an entire generation, between

50 and 70 percent of each village's adult male population, was annihilated. And far from diminishing the impact of war on noncombatants, among the millions of casualties suffered in both wars, the percentage of noncombatant deaths to combatant deaths actually rose from World War I to World War II, from about 15 percent to something closer to 50 percent (and by some estimates, civilian noncombatant casualties constitute 90 percent of the total in wars fought at present).

The increase in the number of noncombatant casualties suffered directly as a result of World War II (as opposed to those civilian deaths attributed to disease and famine), in turn, was largely due to the pursuit of genocidal policies by the Axis powers, and by the responding policies of Allied forces to target German and Japanese cities with saturation bombing and the use of nuclear weapons, intended to force a total capitulation and surrender by the enemy. Those policies were deliberately and explicitly undertaken in disregard of the relatively new laws prohibiting the deliberate targeting of noncombatants. The late Robert McNamara, who served as secretary of defense during the Vietnam War, revealed in his memoirs toward the end of his life that US Air Force general Curtis LeMay (who personally ordered the firebombing of Tokyo during World War II), confided to his assistant secretary, McNamara, "We'd better damn well win this thing or we're both going to end up tried and executed as war criminals."[1]

Finally, lest we think nevertheless that, since Vietnam, or the Korean War, or the putative "end" of the Cold War (which, incidentally, is still very much alive and ongoing in the Pacific Rim), we have at last tamed war and civilized violence, we need only think of Rwanda, Bosnia, Kosovo, and the wars of epic duration in Iraq and Afghanistan.

Perhaps what we mean to claim, instead, is that it is not the *occurrence of war itself*, but the *behavior of warriors*, that has gradually become tamed and civilized, and subject to the rule of law. Technically speaking, that would be true, but only because the idea of actually writing down the rules of war is a fairly recent enterprise. Nothing in this account appears to offer hope or evidence either of increasingly widespread respect for the international rule of law outlawing and limiting the recourse to deadly force and armed conflict, or of the self-imposed temperance of warriors engaged in it. Instead, this description seems to verify the beliefs of skeptics and moral realists that in war, anything goes, and (as Cicero lamented), "the Law is silent." In any event, as we witness soldiers of the Islamic State slaughtering surrendering adversaries in Iraq and beheading hapless journalists in Syria and civilians in Libya, we have no reason to pride ourselves on being any less warlike or barbaric than those who lived in earlier centuries.

Is there any contrasting historical evidence, either of genuine regret over war's misery, or of a desire to guide or limit the violent and destructive behavior of combatants in the midst of war?

Actually, there is quite a bit of evidence that observers, participants (the warriors themselves), not to mention the victims of war in the past, protested against both the occurrence and the recourse to unrestrained and indiscriminate violence in the midst of war. This protest can be found in many cultures and historical epochs and is not simply an artifact of recent history. This protest is lodged by philosophers and theologians from many of the world's ancient and most enduring cultures and religions, together with poets and playwrights, both tragedians and comedians. Those currents of antiwar protest might be dismissed, of course, as the minority view of a given culture's *literati* and intellectual elites. But, once again, there is considerable evidence that these protests and suggestions met with popular approval, especially among the ordinary citizens who were otherwise called upon to bear the brunt of the costs of war in terms of their lives, personal wealth, and happiness.

    One of the most charming and amusing instances of this protest against unrestrained violence was written in the fifth century BCE, toward the conclusion of the Peloponnesian War, by the Greek comic playwright Aristophanes. The wives and lovers of the warriors in the play complain that women are tired of seeing their husbands march off to war to be slaughtered, only to suffer the vicissitudes of war at home as the enemy marauds through their cities, pillaging, raping, and slaughtering the remaining inhabitants. Men, their wives complain, seem to wish only two things: to fight, and to make love. Led by the play's heroine, Lysistrata, the wives organize a boycott (pun intended!). The men can't have it both ways, and if they won't give up warring and violence, then they'll have to do without the other of their central preoccupations!

Again, a single instance, let alone a comedy, doesn't prove much, other than that some people, even in the ancient world, did not accept that war was inevitable, and longed for some less destructive alternative. Another example, focusing upon restraint during combat itself, occurs in the Greek philosopher Plato's greatest work, *The Republic*. During a wide-ranging discussion of the ideal political organization of states and their conduct of policy (including the waging of war), Socrates invites the others taking part in the dialogue to reflect on, and question the wisdom and prudence of, some of the more excessive customary practices during war.

This philosophical discussion is especially poignant, inasmuch as Socrates himself had served as an Athenian soldier during the recently concluded Peloponnesian War, and it seems relatively straightforward an assumption that he, along with Plato's readers, would have had some of those experiences in mind.

Suppose, Socrates remarks, an army is obliged to put down a rebellion or treason in a formerly allied territory. Does it make any sense for the victorious army then to slaughter all the inhabitants and lay waste to the countryside (as was customarily done in such cases as punishment for the rebellion)? Wouldn't it make more sense merely to round up the revolutionaries or traitors, and put *them* to death, and leave the remaining (presumably guiltless) inhabitants of the city itself in peace? Wouldn't that be the more likely pathway to re-establish good and loyal political relationships, and ensure the future peace, security, and prosperity of the state?

The pupils are asked to consider other, more prudent departures from prevailing custom in war, such as learning to distinguish noncombatants from combatants, and refraining from vengefully or gratuitously injuring or killing the latter, or destroying their property. There are many good reasons for considering such policies, Socrates avers, but chief among them is the fact that wars eventually come to an end. The political conditions that then follow are more likely to be favorable to the victorious state if it has conducted itself with prudence and forbearance, and avoided engaging in slaughter, indiscriminate and disproportionate destruction, and the commission of senseless atrocities. (The religious literature of Judaism and Christianity, dating from about the same time, incidentally, records with approval the similarly enlightened policy of Persian emperors like Cyrus and Darius in this regard, as compared to their more vengeful and brutal Babylonian and Assyrian predecessors.)

The same goes with the treatment of enemy combatants who might be imprisoned and later pardoned, rather than enslaved or slaughtered. Especially when engaging enemies and attempting to defeat them in war, the army that is characterized by such prudent policies is more likely to achieve a speedy victory, since the opponents will not be led to drag out the fighting (presumably on the grounds that they have nothing further to lose by resisting their defeat and inevitable slaughter).

Here it seems worth emphasizing that these observations on the proper moral conduct of war are thus centrally featured among the teachings of the person who is himself universally recognized as the first teacher of the subject called "ethics." Clearly then, war and its conduct have from the beginning of human history and civilization, been central topics of moral reflection.

It likewise seems worth observing that, at another time in history, in an entirely different culture, and in a wholly disparate

region of the world, the great neo-Confucian military strategist Sun-Tzu offered similar military advice, for nearly identical reasons. In discussing effective military strategy, the Master
instructs his military pupils, in *The Art of War*, to fight only when
absolutely necessary, to avoid taking on causes or tactical objectives that are hopelessly out of reach or impossible to achieve,
and to use only as much manpower and materiel as is necessary
to achieve the military and political objectives at issue.

The advice from sages and moral philosophers in many distinct cultures seems to revolve around the baseline of "military
necessity": the prudent military commander (and, presumably
the statesmen who supervise them) do not engage in violence,
nor use deadly force frivolously. As Clausewitz, centuries later,
would likewise agree: military force is almost always used to
attain political objectives. Its use, therefore, should always be
governed strictly in accord with achieving those objectives.
Specifically, military necessity dictates discrimination, proportionality, and the economy of force: that is, don't attack targets
that are not absolutely central to the military objective, don't
use more force than necessary to subdue the military target,
and certainly do not gratuitously lay waste to the countryside
or kill those not directly implicated in the fighting. To do otherwise is to make wars ultimately much harder and costlier to
fight, and any hope for ensuring peace and political stability
more difficult to attain in the aftermath.

Are there other instances in the ancient world of such
discussions of what might be termed ethical issues,
or prudent professional military practice?

Frankly, such discussions are almost as ubiquitous as the
experience of war itself. Indeed, such discussions occur piece-
meal in almost every known culture, past and present, and
are as far from being merely a Western concept as the practice
of war itself. This could be explained by noting that the art
or practice of waging war constitutes a highly variable form

of what anthropologists sometimes term "cultural performance," and such performances are routinely accompanied
by equally unique forms of cultural discourse concerning the
circumstances under which the performance is to be staged,
as well as to what extent, and by whom, against whom, and
most importantly, for what ultimate purpose.

Arjuna and Krishna, for example, in the great Hindu literary classic the *Bhagavadgita*, debate the validity of Arjuna's
profound moral concern over having to fight and kill relatives
and innocents. Laws in ancient India clearly defined those
who were to be exempt from attack in the midst of war. The
"Blessed One" (Buddha) was himself of the Kshatriya ("warrior") class, and felt that the suffering wrought by perpetual
conflict could only be overcome by renouncing its underlying
causes in human desire and selfishness.

In China, Chairman Mao Zedong, in the modern era,
denounced the delicately nuanced views of the Confucian
strategist Sun-Tzu and thought Sun-Tzu's own limitations on
the practice of combat were "asinine." But then Mao himself
proceeded to proclaim his own "Eight Points for Attention"
governing the behavior of his insurgent forces in their conduct
of guerilla war in 1938, which followed closely the advice from
ancient sources concerning limiting violence and "winning
hearts and minds."

The Qur'an and its accompanying Hadith (commentary and
stories of the Prophet and his followers) declaim frequently
and at length upon when, how, and to what extent to make
war upon unbelievers, along with when, if ever, Muslims
should raise the sword against fellow Muslims.

The renowned political philosopher Michael Walzer writes,
"For as long as men and women have talked about war, they
have talked about it in terms of right and wrong. . . . Reiterated
over time," he observes, these "arguments and judgments
shape what I want to call *the moral reality of war*—that is, all
those experiences of which moral language is descriptive or
within which it is necessarily employed."[2]

Shannon E. French, a longtime professor at the US Naval Academy, wrote a remarkable book on the varied and intriguing cultural practices of warriors, *The Code of the Warrior* (2003), based upon materials from the class she taught for midshipmen every semester. It remains to this day the single most popular elective course ever offered at the Naval Academy. The book itself narrowly escaped being turned into a PBS miniseries, featuring the customs, habits, and ethics of warrior cultures ranging from Vikings to samurai to Native Americans, examining the moral codes and concepts of military professionalism attached to each.

One of French's favorite instances of what Walzer terms the moral reality of warfare occurs in the Greek poet Homer's account of the Trojan War in the *Iliad*: the desecration of Hector.

When reading the *Iliad* with her students, they noted that the work, supposedly composed by a Greek partisan, often portrayed Greek warriors like Achilles and Agamemnon in a poor light. Agamemnon was selfish, sly, and unscrupulous, and also not very bright. (He "had not the gift of number," as Socrates later ridiculed him—i.e., he didn't know how to count, and so was unable to keep track of the number of triremes in his fleet.) Achilles was vain, selfish, and spoiled.

It was the Trojans, defending their city, and especially the warrior Hector, who came across as the most noble and morally worthy characters. Hector is especially appealing as a reluctant warrior, called to be the loyal defender of his nation, who remains throughout the story a courageous and loving family man. When Professor French would ask her military students whom in the epic they themselves would most wish to be like, they would routinely answer: "Hector . . but a Hector who wins!"

Perhaps because of this admiration they, like most of Homer's listeners (and later, readers), took great exception to the disgraceful actions of the enraged Achilles. Having defeated and killed Hector in personal combat, Achilles dragged the victim's corpse behind his chariot three times around the city of Troy, to the horror of the citizens and, indeed, to the dismay and shame of his fellow Greek soldiers. Once again: "This sort of thing isn't done." It constituted dishonorable, shameful, and (dare we say) "unprofessional" behavior, notwithstanding the otherwise understandable rage felt by Achilles against an enemy who had earlier killed his closest friend.

The presentation of it as such (French would explain) helps demonstrate the existence, and almost universal awareness, of a "code of the warrior," according to which such behavior is prohibited as morally and professionally unacceptable. That prohibition, moreover, continues in force whether in ancient Greece, or medieval Japan, or contemporary Afghanistan, applying to Taliban insurgents who behead and parade the mutilated corpses of US Marines, as well as of Marines who urinate on the corpses of defeated Taliban insurgents. Both know that, whenever combatants do such monstrous things in anger and rage, they forfeit the right to call themselves members of the military profession. As to the complaint, often lodged by International Security Assistance Force (ISAF) coalition forces in Afghanistan, that the Taliban and al-Qaeda ignore contemporary laws of war and deliberately attack even their own fellow citizens, the reply from this perspective is that *it is precisely such morally reprehensible (and tactically gratuitous) behavior*, directed deliberately against their own citizens as matter of policy, that serves to identify them as criminals, thugs, and murderers, rather than legitimate combatants.

But aren't there other counterexamples from the same period, from which we see that the practice of warfare is an inescapable fact of life, and where the appeals to morality, in particular, are portrayed as wholly irrelevant to the declaration and conduct of war?

A critic who regarded my portrayal of the topic of ethics and warfare as one-sided would probably cite the historical account of *The Peloponnesian War*. This work was written by the Greek general Thucydides, in the aftermath of that war, at just about the same time as Plato's *Republic*. Thucydides is commonly regarded as the author of the first historical (as opposed to literary or mythological) account of war. He is at great pains both to document every phase and development in this long (26-year) war's history, and to attribute the motives for specific tactical decisions at each phase as based upon self-interest. Accordingly, this work has been frequently portrayed as the antithesis, the polar opposite, of a moral account of war, let alone of the conduct of warriors.

We have already encountered and commented several times on this perspective on war and international relations, which is widely believed, and which is known broadly as "realism." According to this view, there is finally *no such thing* as ethics or morality. At most, someone who is trying to uphold moral principles is merely revealed as a naive idealist, unaccustomed to the true ways of the world. More cynically, some realists believe that moral language itself is merely a sophisticated rhetorical tool for establishing good public relations, designed to win popular support for policies by portraying them as noble and honorable and just (and thereby disguising the politician's self-interested pursuits as something other than they really are).

In particular, realists hold that so-called moral concerns have no place and play no role in political relations generally, and certainly have no place in the pursuit of armed conflict. Once again, Clausewitz is often invoked, alongside Thucydides, along with the political philosophy of Thomas Hobbes, and many other sources for justifying this hard-nosed view of political relations. (The English realist philosopher Hobbes is famous for his depiction of human existence as, at bottom, "the war of all against all," and life itself as "nasty, brutish, and short"—"oh, and by the way, . . . have a nice day!")

In discussing this approach to military strategy, tactics, and international relations another accomplished scholar, Martin L. Cook (cited in the introduction), designed and taught an entire course on these topics for newly-promoted colonels at the U.S. Army War College, based exclusively on a close and careful reading of Thucydides's *Peloponnesian War*.[3] He noted the role this historical account of ancient warfare has come to play in teaching that the ruthless pursuit of national self-interest is, not merely the best, but *the only* reasonable policy alternative in the conduct of international affairs.

One significant episode during the Peloponnesian War is often cited as the perfect illustration of "realism" in this classic study. In this famous episode, the Athenian ambassadors meet with a council of citizens from the island of Melos, in order to negotiate their future relationship in the midst of war. The Melians argue that they have not taken sides in the wider conflict between Athens and the Spartan alliance and that, as a small and relatively powerless city, they pose no military threat to either side. They desire to remain neutral, and object when the Athenians demand that they either declare their allegiance to Athens or suffer siege and military conquest.

When the *Melians raise moral objections* to this ruthlessness, Thucydides portrays the Athenians as responding contemptuously to the concepts of justice and morality as beside the point. As the Athenians summarize it, in the real world the powerful do as they please, while the weak are forced to negotiate for the best bargain they can get. When, on moral principles, the Melians object to this political bullying, the Athenians vow that, should they refuse to join the Athenian alliance, their city will be destroyed and their citizens all put to death.

This is eventually what transpires, and virtually every political theorist since has regarded this episode as providing a harsh and irrefutable illustration that morality (justice, or fairness) plays no role in politics. Those like the hapless Melians who formulate policy and stake their claims on moral principles are destined to be swept aside by those who are sufficiently powerful and sufficiently ruthless to pursue their self-interests aggressively.

Cook (and also Michael Walzer) question this reading of the so-called Melian dialogue as erroneous and out of context.

Cook, in particular, invites his students and readers to consider the earlier portrayals in the book, of Athens, the democracy, the "city set upon a hill," the city of Pericles, espousing the highest possible moral and political ideals.

Indeed, earlier in Thucydides's account of the war, there occurs an episode eerily similar to the later Melian discussion, concerning what to do with a rebellious colony. Two eminent citizens of Athens rise to dispute the next steps. One espouses destroying the colony and executing its rebellious citizens to the last man, woman, and child, in order to set an example for others contemplating rebellion from the Athenian empire. He bases his views entirely, as he says, on "self-interest." The second citizen, however, argues for a very different view, likewise (he says) based purely upon self-interest. In that view, the Athenians should punish only those guilty of fomenting rebellion and leave the hapless citizens to return to their status as loyal subjects of the Athenian empire. That, he argues, will set an even better example, and so represents the more prudent and efficacious course of action. His argument carries the day, and the rebellious colonists are largely spared.

Fast-forward a few years later, to the encounter described in the Melian dialogue, where the opposite conclusion is reached and innocent cities and citizens slaughtered. The conclusion of readers of the whole work, Cook maintains, cannot simply be "too bad for the citizens of Melos, but that's the way things go!" Instead of this realist conclusion, most readers of the complete account of this war will properly wonder instead, "Wow! Is *this* what the 'city on a hill' has become?" In other words, their reaction will hardly be to affirm realism, but, like the Melians themselves, to react with righteous anger and outrage to the arrogant brutality of the Athenians as constituting a monstrous injustice, even while they marvel at the moral demise of Athenian culture itself.

The point is not, as realists would have it, that "whether just or not, great power triumphs over weakness inevitably," so much as a more familiar tragic refrain: "Pride goeth before the fall" (Proverbs 16:18).[4] For the story of Thucydides's great work is not how self-interest trumps morality, but how hubris leads the Athenians down a destructive path, until all their former allies are arrayed against them, and their destruction (and the consequent end of their empire) is all but inevitable. Michael Walzer observes that the very structure of Thucydides's work exhibits the pattern of a Greek tragedy, in which the audience already knows the ending, which is prefigured in the beginning, and exhibited as morally just in the deficient behavior of the tragic hero—in this case, the increasingly brutal, insolent, and self-regarding collective behavior of a once-great city-state.

Reflections on the moral reality of war, and on the moral challenges presented to its combatants, are thus not of recent making. Nor are such moral reflections on the behavior of men and nations at war simply a recent product of Western culture exclusively. Instead we observe that, throughout human history, for as long as there have been warriors engaged in war, they, and those that wrote, sang, performed, or taught about them, have opined on when if ever to fight, and on the better and worse ways of engaging in combat.

Notes

1. This story, related by McNamara, can be found in a documentary film, directed by Errol Morris, *The Fog of War: Eleven Lessons from the Life of Robert N. McNamara* (2003).
2. Walzer is, of course, the author of what is widely celebrated as the preeminent contribution to "just war discourse" in the 20th century, *Just and Unjust Wars* (New York: Basic Books, 1977), now in its fourth edition. The quotes above are from the opening chapter, "Against Realism," 1, 15; the citation of ancient Indian law concerning classes of noncombatants can be found in chapter three, "Rules of War," 43; and the description of Mao Zedong's doctrine of just war in chapter 14, "Winning and Fighting Well," 225–227.
3. Cook offers a full account of his approach to understanding and teaching this work to senior army officers in his book *The Moral*

Warrior (Albany: State University of New York Press, 2004), in the opening chapter, entitled, significantly, "On Becoming the World's Sole Remaining Superpower."

4. This insight from biblical literature mirrors the message regarding *hybris* in Greek tragedy, as signifying an excess of ambition or pride that ultimately causes the transgressor's ruin.

Further Reading

Classics on War and Ethics

All of the following are available in acceptable, searchable translations online.

Aristophanes. *Lysistrata.*

The Bhagavadgita.

Homer. *The Iliad.*

Plato. *The Republic.*

Sun-Tzu. *The Art of War.*

Modern Studies

Cook, Martin L. *The Moral Warrior.* Albany: State University of New York Press, 2004.

French, Shannon E. *The Code of the Warrior: Exploring Warrior Values, Past and Present.* Lanham, MD: Rowman & Littlefield, 2003.

Gray, J. Glenn. *The Warriors: Reflections on Men in Battle.* New York: Harcourt, 1959.

Kaplan, Robert N. *Warrior Politics: Why Leadership Demands a Pagan Ethos.* New York: Vintage Books, 2002.

Walzer, Michael N. *Just and Unjust Wars.* New York: Basic Books, 1977.

4

MILITARY ETHICS AND THE JUST WAR TRADITION

What is *the just war tradition?*

Several times in the opening chapters we made reference in passing to the "just war tradition," but, just like the concept of military ethics itself, this may be a phrase that is quite unfamiliar to a great many readers.

Put simply, the "just war tradition" is the name customarily given to debate and reflection carried out over many centuries, among a great many eminent figures in the Western literary and philosophical tradition more broadly, about the permissibility of using deadly force in international relations.

One theory about why this is such an important and long-standing discussion in Western culture, at least, is that Christianity was the dominant religion in that region—and Christian political doctrine is *essentially pacifist*, teaching that the use of force and violence is prohibited to believers as a method of conflict resolution. This presents political leaders in those regions of the world with a fundamental conflict or paradox not necessarily encountered in other parts of the world: namely, that the leaders and people residing in states composed largely of Christian believers are prohibited from using force to protect their borders, or secure the safety of their citizens from armed attack. But once again, with "congenial" neighbors such as Vlad the Impaler and Attila the Hun lurking on the borders of civilization, this proved to be a difficult assignment to fulfill!

Perhaps the most straightforward illustration of this long-standing discussion is found in a question, posed by the 13th-century Christian theologian St. Thomas Aquinas, whose name is closely associated with the origins of the just war tradition. At one point in his great work the *Summa Theologica*, Thomas poses this question: "Is it always sinful to wage war?"

Thomas is busy elaborating on "charity" and the duty of Christians to love one another. It is thus natural to wonder whether waging war is always a sin, since one would presume from this moral duty of charity that, in general and for the most part, waging war *is* indeed a sin (meaning that it is something that Christians ought not to do, nor to permit).

But the interesting wording of Thomas's question also seems to allow that, while it is *usually* morally wrong, there might be some occasions in which it is *not* morally wrong to wage war. What might those occasional exceptions to the normal moral prohibition against waging war be?

The answer Thomas gives to his own question seems to imply that it would be permissible (and for a Christian, forgivable or excusable) to wage war, when absolutely necessary, *if certain conditions are met*. Thomas specifically lists three important considerations that, while not exhaustive, would at least offer examples of situations in which an exception to the normal prohibition might be made. These three conditions have passed into history as the core of what has come to be called the just war tradition or (sometimes) just war theory (JWT).

Legitimate Authority

First, Thomas observes, not just any individual or group is authorized to declare war or call for armed uprising. The individual or group must be sufficiently representative of a nation or society, or hold some other symbolic and fully representative position as a sovereign of some sort. That person or group is then said to constitute a legitimate authority, or to exercise the sole legitimate authority to declare war on behalf of a society. This seems a bit unclear, and certainly not well or completely defined, but it does seem to suggest that a small armed group of insurgents or terrorists, or their leader, cannot lawfully or legitimately declare war on others, since they clearly do not meet this condition. They have no legitimate authority to speak for others. This was surely meant as an important limitation on the resort to war, since relatively few persons or groups would be found to possess the requisite authority to do so.

In medieval Europe, imposing this condition would have been important as an attempt to limit the violence of tribalism and regional "warlords" who did not speak for the entire population of a nation, limiting such authority to a recognized king, emperor, or perhaps even the pope. In our own time, armed conflict now arises more frequently from the activities of such individuals and groups than from the formal declaration of hostilities between sovereign nations.[1] Thomas's first condition seems to apply equally well to them: no matter what, or how legitimate, their grievances may be against larger society, these groups do not possess the moral or legal authority to declare war unilaterally on others.[2]

Just Cause

Second, when exercising the rightful authority to declare war, the king or emperor or other sovereign requires a *very compelling reason* for resorting to armed violence. This is known traditionally as having a "just cause" for war (or *casus belli*, in Latin).

Self-defense against armed attack by another group or nation is thought to be one such compelling reason to resort to war, and we find it enshrined to this day in international law: specifically, the UN Charter, Article 51, which states that nothing in the Charter shall interfere with a sovereign nation's "inherent right of self-defense." Self-defense is also a legitimate excuse for the use of lethal force by one individual against another. Indeed, the two cases of individual and national self-defense are thought to be analogous (although the analogy, under more careful examination, is not quite as close or obvious as it might at first seem).[3]

Additional reasons were originally considered by Thomas and other scholars to be just causes for declaring war, including rectifying injustice, punishing wrongdoing, and recovering stolen property. By and large such reasons have been subsequently thought insufficient by themselves as grounds for nations to declare war unilaterally. Nations that do so in any case are likely to be viewed just like individuals or groups who take the law into their own hands: namely, as vigilantes. Such complaints by one nation against another, we now believe, should be reconcilable instead through negotiation and diplomacy, or perhaps less severe forms of conflict, such as economic sanctions or boycotts.

On the other hand, attempting to control the recourse to war by limiting "just causes" only to self-defense against armed aggression can have the perverse effect of forcing nations with other legitimate and serious grievances to cast the pursuit of these as somehow constituting "self-defense."[4] Famously, or infamously (for example), Adolph Hitler cast his wars of aggression and territorial expansion as a defense of Germanic peoples and culture. However self-defense comes to be interpreted, though, it remains the case that the only just cause for war in the present era is thought to be the state's inherent right to defend itself against an armed attack (and perhaps also against a threatened and imminent armed attack).

Right Intention

Finally, Thomas demands that we identify the true underlying motivation and purpose for fighting the war. Does the declaring authority wish vengeance or retribution against a nation's enemies, or does the nation declaring war really seek to acquire wealth and territory, strike fear in the hearts of its adversaries, or otherwise achieve political aggrandizement in the eyes of other nations? These are not morally worthy goals to pursue, even if the authority is legitimate and the immediate, publicly stated cause for the war appears to be just. Only the desire to restore peace and establish justice under the rule of law constitute right intentions on the part of the declaring authority.

Together, according to the just war tradition, these three basic conditions—just cause, legitimate authority, and right intention—at very least must be satisfied before the declaration and subsequent waging of war can be morally justified. Otherwise, if these three conditions remain unsatisfied, then war itself remains "sinful" (i.e., morally prohibited), at least according to this influential and widely respected Christian theologian and philosopher.

Why would the topic of war be considered appropriate for a Christian theologian to discuss in the first place?

First, I am obliged to point out again that war and the morality of war and especially the ethical conduct of war, are not topics solely of interest to Christian theologians. Islamic theologians discuss these problems; Hindu philosophers examine them; Confucian and Greek philosophers and military strategists and historians are concerned with them. The topics of the morality of war and of the ethics of warriors are of widespread and general interest, and variations of the conditions that Thomas imposes upon Christians can also be found in the writings and moral teachings of many other religions and cultures throughout history.

What makes the topic of war of special interest to Christian thinkers in the just war tradition, as I mentioned above, however, is the straightforward but awkward fact that *Christians, as a matter of their moral beliefs, are committed to pacifism,* and to eschewing all resorts to violence and deadly force as means of resolving conflict among individuals and nations. Hence, war presents a peculiar and urgent (if not entirely unique) moral dilemma in the religious ethics of Christians, especially if they find themselves in positions of wielding legitimate political authority. As appointed leaders or statesmen, they have a duty to protect their nation and their fellow citizens from harm and the threat of harm. This public duty conflicts with their personal and collective religious duty to love one another, to espouse nonviolence in conflict resolution, and to respond with kindness when threatened or harmed. That is why Christian philosophers and theologians like St. Thomas were obliged to address this dilemma in extensive detail.

One solution to this dilemma is simply to recommend that persons with such religious convictions ought not to seek political office or responsibility, since they could not simultaneously fulfill their public and personal (religious) obligations. This, historically, was precisely the view of early Christians living in the Roman Empire. And some Christians, to this day, do believe (along with some Muslims, Hindus, and Buddhists) that the rough-and-tumble political world of conflict and violence is not the proper place to practice their spiritual faith or cultivate their religious duties. Others, however, fervently believe that they can do both, and indeed, if they are successful in adhering to their faith while exercising political office, they can help to bring an end to the perpetual occurrence of violence and war in human experience.[5]

As I mentioned earlier, these morally worthy aspirations and ideals have historically proven difficult to put into practice. From the earliest days of the Christian Church in the Roman Empire, citizens of a more practical persuasion were often extremely hostile toward Christians, believing Christians to be irresponsible, and sometimes even engaged in sedition and treason, for advocating pacifism. Even more problematically, following the conversion of the Roman emperor Constantine to Christianity in 311 CE, Christians suddenly found themselves in the extremely awkward political position of being more or less put in charge of a large empire. And that empire was undergoing rebellion in its own colonies, as well as suffering a succession of violent migrations of warlike peoples from north and east of the empire's borders. But how can a legitimate and responsible political establishment protect its citizens and maintain stability and control of its borders without at least sometimes resorting to military force?

This was the dilemma in which Christians found themselves and, technically, still face today. War is morally forbidden by their most sacred and fundamental religious teachings, and yet resort to some form of military force seems necessary, at least on occasion, in order to responsibly discharge the public duty to protect a nation and its citizens from enemies, and maintain the rule of law. Hence we find Christian theologians wrestling with this moral dilemma down through the centuries. The end results of those reflections (such as those of St. Thomas, cited above) give us a summary of the conditions that establish when, if ever, it would be permissible for Christians as soldiers, or a nation governed by Christian principles, to engage in warfare. This fundamental moral dilemma, the tension between two conflicting moral duties, and the resulting centuries of reflection upon that tension constitute the historical origins of what is commonly referred to today as the just war tradition.

What gives this tradition any moral authority, especially over non-Christians?

Despite its long history, something that is, finally, nothing more than an internal sectarian doctrinal debate of some sort would hold sway only over adherents of that particular faith. Such advice would have absolutely no authority over the behavior of individuals and societies who lie outside the boundaries of that faith. Put in this way, the just war tradition would be of little other than historical interest, in the same way we take interest in studying the teachings of other cultures and faiths to satisfy our curiosity about them, and perhaps learn something of value or historical interest.

This is why I have been at pains to remind readers that, despite this history, the issues at stake in the discussion of justifiable war and its conduct are not merely cultural artifacts or peculiarities of Christianity, or of Western culture. The same sorts of discussions are replicated in other cultures, so there is at least a commonality of interest about how to address the problem of war. And given the gravity of this question, central to the lives and welfare of entire civilizations, this fact of multicultural interest in the moral and political justification of war should hardly be surprising.

The entire attitude we bring to the examination of such matters, however, needs to be challenged. When it comes to matters of morality, in particular, we have a bad habit of trying to dismiss important human questions, and responses to them, as "merely matters of opinion." Thus, what Christians (or Muslims, or Buddhists, or Confucians) have to say about when to fight wars and how they should and should not be fought is merely "their shared opinion," and does not necessarily apply to us.

Socrates, on a rare walk outside the city of Athens with one of his young pupils (named Phaedrus), teased him about this strange attitude: "You young folks," he remarked (in effect), "are all concerned with knowing, not just what was said, but with who said it, when, and how it was said. *What difference does that make?* For my part, I am interested only in *what* was said, and *whether it is true or false.* As to who or where or when—I would gladly listen to the wind in the oak trees, if I thought it had something to teach me."

It seems odd that we adopt this casual and dismissive attitude toward moral questions concerning how we should treat one another and attempt to arrange our lives, but not to other areas of knowledge and belief. As an example of how strange this attitude is, consider everyone's "favorite" subject in high school: algebra. Algebra was developed primarily in Islamic culture, perhaps with resources and techniques learned from ancient India. Nevertheless, we no more dismiss algebra as merely "Arab mathematics" any more than we talk about "Christian physics" or "Roman Catholic analytic geometry" (Isaac Newton was a Protestant Christian, and the French mathematician and philosopher René Descartes, who literally invented analytic geometry, was a self-avowed, devout Roman Catholic). Instead, everyone, everywhere, now studies these subjects and avails themselves of their insights, notwithstanding their history and specific cultural origins.

"Ah! But those topics are scientific and mathematical," one might reply. "Our discussion regarding war is about law and morality, and these, by contrast, are not scientific or objective subjects." But we would be at pains to explain how killing one another and destroying one another's landscape and property are different. Certainly they are not any less factual than the solution of an algebraic equation, or knowledge of the speed of light in a vacuum. Simply asserting without proof that they are different, let alone that we should regard some historically created cultural artifacts (like algebra) as universally applicable, and others (like discussions of when and how to kill one another) as of limited cultural application, seems formally to beg the question—that is, to argue in a circle about the authority and applicability of moral knowledge and discourse, as compared to that of science and mathematics.[6]

But we make this mistake repeatedly, and at our great peril. In ethics, that is to say, we are prone to confuse the origins and subsequent history of an idea with the universality of its eventual application.

Christians, as a matter of faith-based principle, cannot tell Muslims or Jews what they *must* do, and vice versa. But they can wonder, and inquire, individually and in collaboration, about what they *should* do. And, like Socrates, they should be willing to listen to and consider whatever resources promise to enlighten them on these important matters. When they find themselves coming to similar conclusions, based upon similar reasoning (as we find in this case), that should count for something. Hence, the just war tradition is authoritative for all of us, regardless of race, color, religious creed, or national origin, only insofar as it provides teachings of universal applicability about when to fight wars and how to fight them. And this is exactly what that tradition aims to offer.

Isn't this talk of justified war merely a form of public relations, designed to win public support for morally and politically questionable decisions by political leaders?

Quite often one gets the impression that talk of justice in war, or the justification for going to war, is a kind of "sales pitch" designed to persuade a reluctant and skeptical public that they should support a proposal to go to war or to continue to endure the hardships of a war already in progress.

But once again, suppose we accept this very cynical portrayal of political leaders as clever, Machiavellian manipulators who mean to employ subtle rhetorical tricks to dupe us into supporting a war that has no justifiable cause, or serves no useful or significant purpose (other than, perhaps, resulting in some kind of personal gain for themselves and their immediate friends). Why should this ploy work? What makes us all, apparently, "suckers" for the attractiveness of moral arguments?

If our leaders wish to persuade us to fight in, and pay for, and suffer the risks and deprivations of war for their own personal gain—that is, if their real intention in declaring and waging war is narrow self-interest, as realists often claim—then their telling us the truth about that motivation is not itself very motivational. This is true even if we, with equal cynicism, believe that everyone in the world ultimately acts only in behalf of narrowly conceived individual interests. If we personally stand to gain nothing from the proposed war, we are unlikely to support it or to fight in it.

So, according to this cynical view, political leaders must instead learn how to appeal to our shared sense of justice and fairness, as well as to moral principles like the defense of human rights, in order to foster support for their war. These appeals to the morality and justice of our shared cause seem to have enormous positive appeal. Cynics might continue to argue that this appalling strategy finally works, because the average person is ignorant, gullible, and naive, and so open to manipulations through such "soft" appeals to our emotions and sentiments.

A less cynical observer, however, might think that such appeals address what President Abraham Lincoln (in his First Inaugural Address in 1864) eloquently termed "the Better Angels of Our Nature." That is, we are open to such appeals precisely because most ordinary people believe concepts like "morality" and "justice" are important, and that they have some authoritative claim on our choices and actions. In other words, we are subject to persuasion on moral grounds, because most of us, most of the time, are not skeptical or cynical regarding moral values and moral principles. It is only because most of us believe that ideals like justice and human rights are valid, important, and universally applicable that the manipulative ploy of the cynical statesman (if that is all it is) is finally able to succeed.

But if all this is so, then the proper response to discovering the cynic's deception is not to abandon our belief in the validity of moral principles, but to be rightly outraged by the attempt at deception. Deliberately and falsely appealing to such fundamental and widely shared values and principles as the justification for a war—if political leaders themselves really thought that, in point of fact, no such profound or universal principles are genuinely at stake—would constitute an extremely heinous and morally despicable action. And the moral wrong would be especially egregious if the genuine interests at stake that were leading to war were, instead, the most morally unworthy kind: for example, maintaining a privileged status quo, extending the reach of an empire, exercising arrogant or pointless political hegemony (as the Athenians proposed to do against the island of Melos), or enriching an economic elite at the expense of, and at grave risk of bodily harm to, the general public.

Outraged accusations of precisely this sort were made in the United States during and after the Vietnam War. The war, critics alleged, was brought on for cynical and narrowly self-serving reasons. It was not fought for the reasons widely proclaimed regarding the safety and welfare of the South Vietnamese people and the protection of their rights (and by extension, the rights of many other people) to live in freedom from communist tyranny. Military rank-and-file forces were thus led into an unjustifiable conflict, while their leaders refused to challenge the manipulative abuse of their troops and of the general public, who were led to support and to fight in the war in defense of what they presumed were important and legitimate political objectives.[7]

More recently, in Afghanistan, political elites on the Council on Foreign Relations argued that the US-led ISAF coalition could not afford to abandon the war, lest America's prestige, resolve, and image of superpower global hegemony fall into disrepute. I objected at the time, however, that such goals, and the preservation of America's political status in the wider world, were not at all what was originally proposed as the morally justified purpose of the war. If in fact considerations such as these were, and had been all along, the "real" purposes for a decade of sacrifice on the part of ISAF combatants from many nations, then those young people and their supportive citizens had been badly misled and cruelly deceived.

Our soldiers believed they were fighting a war of defense against unprovoked attacks by al-Qaeda terrorists and the Taliban who supported them, while coming to the rescue of ordinary Afghans who lived in fear of their own lives from such illicit forces. We might now come to admit, with sadness and regret, that we had failed or had achieved far less success in this mission than we had at first hoped. But were we now to transform the rationale for this war, it would be tantamount to admitting that we had lied to our military personnel and to the public all along, convincing them to risk their lives and personal welfare for decidedly unworthy purposes.[8]

Appeals to morality may sometimes disguise more cynical and unworthy motives. But when this is discovered, it does not constitute an argument against the importance of morality in making decisions about war. Rather it betrays the weak or duplicitous character of political leaders, who would dare to frivolously risk the lives of soldiers and citizens for decidedly unworthy or immoral purposes, and then try to trick them into believing otherwise. This sinister possibility should, in turn, foster the resolve of all of us, military and civilians, to become better informed, more responsible citizens, rather than giving up our most profound moral convictions.

Are there other historical figures besides St. Thomas who contributed to the development of this line of thought about war?

There are a large number of important and influential literary and philosophical figures in the history of Western cultural thought who have contributed to this discussion, which is partly why it has received such widespread attention. I have protested that the examination of the moral questions of declaring and waging war is not the exclusive purview either of Christians or of representatives of Western culture, inasmuch as this is a problem that affects everyone. Nevertheless, for the reasons cited earlier, Western, Christian contributors, and the extent of their written and public works on this topic, far outweigh those of any other culture or religious or philosophical tradition.

Unfortunately, this overwhelming prevalence of Christian and Western writers on this topic leads, in turn, to the frequent but mistaken assumption that this discussion is nothing but a preoccupation of Christians or of their legacy in Western culture generally. We have just subjected that unfortunate and mistaken classification of the just war tradition to cross-examination in the preceding question. But we should still pause to consider the positive side of that contribution, through the eyes of a few of its most prominent architects. These other important historical figures in the just war tradition were, by and large, citizens of nations and cultures in Western Europe after the fall of the Roman Empire, and were, for the most part, either Christians or inheritors of this Christian moral and theological legacy.

Thomas himself often mentions and cites the views of an important predecessor, St. Augustine of Hippo (fifth century CE), who is generally credited (along with Thomas) with being a founder of the just war tradition. In 410 CE, a coalition of rebellious colonists and northern invaders attacked and ravaged the city of Rome. While the empire in some form would linger on for a thousand years after that event, it is generally referred to historically as the "fall" or collapse of the Roman Empire (since it marked the beginning of the decline of imperial power in Western Europe). The sack of Rome, as it is known, was at least symbolic of the exhaustion of that political empire, from the ashes of which the individual nation-states of Western Europe would eventually emerge.

Blame for this political collapse and military defeat naturally fell on the shoulders of the Christians, who had come to political power and respectability barely a century before. By espousing pacifism, peace, and love of neighbor, they had (according to their critics in the old Roman aristocracy) betrayed the gods of their Roman forefathers, and weakened the moral fiber and the pagan warrior instinct that was the true legacy of Rome, thus leading to its inevitable downfall. In response, Augustine wrote a defense of Christian political ideals, *The City of God*, which attempted to explain and justify the role of faith in secular politics, including the reluctance of Christians to resort to the use deadly force, and their desire to promote peace.

This is a long and complex work, one of the great classical works of Western civilization. We need not dwell at length upon its more extended theological and philosophical argu-ments here. Suffice it to say that, in the course of sketching the larger portrait of political life within the "world of sinfulness and despair" in which we normally dwell, Augustine allows that even those committed to nonviolence and peace may need, on occasion, to take up the sword in order to defend the imperfect secular commonwealth (the "City of Man") and its citizens from even greater harm at the hands of evildoers.

The proper moral attitude toward war is thus one of regret and avoidance as contrary to the will of God, unless some great evil and profound suffering is threatened, sufficiently grave to overcome the moral requirement to live at peace. This is the just cause that we saw St. Thomas espouse above: resort to war can be justified only as a lesser evil, reluctantly under-taken in the face of a grave and serious threat that constitutes a greater evil. Christians are then permitted, Augustine argued, to assume the role of reluctant warriors, defending peace, the rule of law, and the safety and security of their fellow citizens. And, he added, because the resort to war is always a moral evil in itself, that resort to war should always be the last and final alternative to suffering the "greater evil" threatened (what we labeled in chapter 1 the principle of last resort).

With regard to the historical and cross-cultural features of this discussion, it bears mention that there was little that was genuinely original or specifically Christian in these observa-tions. They were derived from the writings of Augustine's own teacher, St. Ambrose, who gleaned them, in turn, from careful study of the great Roman orator (and pagan) Cicero.[9]

Augustine himself did introduce what, at the time, was an entirely new requirement regarding the attitude of the politi-cal leadership and its military forces toward war. This con-dition, which he first labeled "right intention," was imposed to prevent less honorable motives like bloodlust, vengeance, hatred—let alone the love of violence for its own sake—to play any role in the decision to go to war. Augustine was especially concerned that such "sinful and impure" motives not infect the hearts and souls of warriors themselves, who were already liable to grave moral injury through engaging in a bloody, miserable, and morally prohibited activity. The only morally proper motives for declaring war, or for fighting in it, were to defend or restore peace, establish justice and the rule of law, and protect the otherwise-defenseless citizens of the state from harm.

An often overlooked feature of these interesting views is that Augustine did not think that "self-defense" (in our ordinary understanding) was itself a morally justified cause for using deadly force, whether by individuals to defend themselves against attackers or by soldiers of the state engaged in waging defensive war. This may come as a surprise, but it is consistent with Augustine's foundation in fundamental Christian moral thought. One is not to be concerned with one's own welfare, and certainly not to the point of being willing to kill another person, even a wrongdoer, merely to save one's own life. In this sense, the underlying Christian moral commitment to nonviolence prevails unabashed and undimmed in Augustine's thought: on the individual level, we should continue to turn the other cheek, and to repay evil with good, even unto death.

Rather, it is *the intention of the warrior to defend*, not his or her own life, but *the lives of others*, that make resort to force morally permissible. It is this special and morally worthy *vocation of the warrior to serve others, protect others, and even sacrifice his or her life for the sake of preserving the lives of others* that constitutes the individual combatant's morally justified right intention for waging war, and thereby exempts him (or her) from blame in harming or killing others.

This seems an important insight, even if it is frequently overlooked or forgotten. It is not just in Christianity, but in virtually all cultures and religious traditions, that *the willingness to risk one's life and even sacrifice it for the sake of saving others* is considered the highest, noblest, most morally worthy intention upon which any individual can act.[10]

Why that should be so, almost without exception, among the human species is an interesting question that we cannot explore further here, but it is certainly worth observing that "self-sacrifice" is generally accorded a preeminent place of honor in the moral values of any society or culture. But it is most clearly in Augustine's thought that we see this *vocational objective* or *professional intention* singled out, both as morally worthy in itself, and as exonerating those who act in accord with it from moral or legal blame for the harm they inflict on the enemy.

This seems to constitute a very important and fundamental insight into a core value or defining principle of the profession of arms. "Killing people and breaking things" (as military personnel sometimes jokingly describe their vocational objective) is only permissible when doing so is *absolutely necessary*, and when it is undertaken *for the right reasons*. This distinguishes war itself from mass murder and mayhem, and separates a true warrior from a common murderer.

That permission, exemption, and moral distinction are lost, however, if the individual warrior forgets his unique moral and professional status, and fights for glory, or for material gain, or worse, out of the enjoyment of killing itself. Individuals engaged in such activities, even in the midst of an otherwise-justifiable war, have forfeited their moral exemption and subjected themselves to the risk of grave moral injury through their individual wrongdoing, even when they find themselves beyond the reach of the law.

Hence, Augustine's insight, widely shared by the sages and warriors of other cultures and religions as well, is important for a proper understanding of the role of the military and of military personnel individually. It becomes an important point of professional principle and professional pride for warriors themselves to discern that, at the heart of their practice is not death and destruction and the wreaking of havoc, vengeance, evil, and suffering. Rather, it is in defending their comrades and fellow citizens *against* such evils *already wrought by others* that gives this vocation or calling its moral justification. This, and this alone, constitutes (in Augustine's phrase) the right intention for resorting to force.

Are there still other figures, besides Augustine and Aquinas, whose teachings on justified war and its conduct are important for everyone to consider?

In 1519, in the midst of the Inquisition at home, and the con- quest of the New World abroad, a Dominican priest by the name of Francisco di Vitoria was invited by his fellow pro- fessors to deliver a series of concluding reflections on their semester's studies of St. Thomas Aquinas at what was then very likely the world's preeminent university, the University of Salamanca in Spain.

Vitoria responded with two public lectures, both of which surprised and startled his audience, and risked getting him into serious trouble with the Spanish authorities (not to men- tion the Spanish Inquisition). Their titles were, respectively, *De Indis*, and *De iuri belli*—"Concerning the Indians," and "Concerning the Laws of War." The first lecture denounced the Spanish military or "conquistadors" in the New World for their treatment of indigenous peoples (Amerindians) in Spain's wars of conquest. The harsh treatment of, enslavement of, and even the military operations themselves conducted by conquistadors against these people, Vitoria argued, were *not only morally unjust, but also illegal.*

This was an odd charge to make, especially since the "legiti- mate authorities," the Spanish monarchy, had licensed and approved of these activities. To explain these claims, the sec- ond lecture outlined, for the first time, a legal "code of the war- rior" that Vitoria alleged was being routinely violated by the Spanish military.

Vitoria was not a strict Christian pacifist. He did not deny that there were sometimes legitimate grievances on the part of the representatives of his government against native peoples for their "lack of hospitality and free passage," nor did he maintain that the use of Spanish military force in the New World was itself always inherently unjust. Indeed, he allowed that there are occasions, beyond self-defense, in which the use of military force would be justified, citing the passages of Thomas's *Summa Theologica* that we considered earlier, dealing with the punishment of "evildoers," recovery of stolen property, and punishment or rectification of injustice. Vitoria even approved in principle of the Spanish military intervening in local political affairs to remove indigenous rulers who were enslaving or murdering their own people or engaging in acts like cannibalism—what we would now term "humanitarian military intervention" for the purposes of regime change.

What concerned Vitoria was not the justice or legitimacy of the Spanish cause (namely, the pacification and Christianization of the population) but rather *the manner by which it was carried out*. Of particular concern, he noted, warriors in an otherwise just war are not permitted deliberately to target noncombatants, nor to attempt to win a military victory by decimating the enemy's nonmilitary population. Enemy combatants could, of course, be killed or taken prisoner during combat, but if the latter, then they must be treated with justice and respect, as they no longer represented a direct threat to the opposing military. These and similar provisions constitute the basis of what we now know as the law of armed conflict.

The idea of declaring such actions illegal was unusual, as there was at the time no overarching legal authority to which to appeal in adjudicating these claims. Vitoria appealed to what he termed *ius gentium*, the "customs and practices of civilized peoples." It was these, as well as the theological reflections of St. Thomas, that established the principles he advocated with the force of law, and which thereby constrained the behavior of combatants, even in wartime. *No one, he maintained, not even soldiers fighting during a war, is beyond the reach of this "natural" law.*

Vitoria's way of conceptualizing the moral duties incumbent on combatants during wartime helped inaugurate a revolutionary way of thinking.[11] In particular, his reflections suggest that otherwise-just wars may only be pursued by just (or "legal") means. This fundamental insight was taken up years later by another Spanish scholar, the Jesuit Francisco Suarez. Likewise examining St. Thomas's criteria of morally justified war, Suarez, on the basis of Vitoria's revolutionary lectures, argued that *right intention in waging a war meant that the militaries that would conduct the war, and the tactics they would employ, must intend from the outset to act in accord with the laws and customs of civilized peoples and nations.* That is to say, finally, that justified wars remain justified only insofar as they are carried out by justified means and practices. The conception of "right intention" in the declaration of war by politicians and statesmen is thus inextricably tied to the intentions and ultimately the conduct of their military forces when pursuing that conflict. Both must reflect the desire to restore peace and to abide by the moral dictates of law.

These insights came to fruition a century later in the work of the Dutch legal scholar Hugo Grotius in his work *De iuri belli et pace,* "Concerning the Laws of War and Peace" (1625). Written during the final throes of a century of wars of religious Reformation (and Counter-Reformation) in Europe, this great work is rightly taken by international lawyers and scholars to be one of the principal founding documents of modern international law. Grotius, a Protestant, agrees with the Catholic, Vitoria, that neither an individual's nor a society's religious beliefs constitute morally justified grounds for waging war against them. Hence, wars by Catholics against Protestants, or by Christian against Muslims, or against indigenous "pagans" and "barbarians" (or vice versa), when these are undertaken with the sole intention of forcible religious conversion, *cannot be morally justified.*

Instead, anticipating the forthcoming Peace of Westphalia that ended and outlawed such wars scarcely two decades later, Grotius conceived of nations as a kind of collective individual, with the rights of self-determination and freedom of choice.

Within their sovereign boundaries, nations are more or less free to believe and to act as they wish, so long as their behavior does not entail harm or the threat of harm to other nations. War is then justified only if a nation or people has a just cause or grievance against another, such as acts of economic or territorial aggression, armed attack, or infringement of free passage and trade on the high seas.

Sadly, apart from helping put an end to wars of religion in Europe, none of these protests and moral considerations had much impact on the behavior of heads of state or their military forces at the time. As Grotius complained in the preface to his work, war seems to be declared upon the slightest pretext, with no concern for moral or legal justification whatsoever.

The German Enlightenment philosopher Immanuel Kant, lamenting the continuing curse of seemingly endless wars fought on the flimsiest of moral pretexts, placed at least some of the blame on his philosophical and theological predecessors in the just war tradition itself. Far from helping to end, or even limit, war, he complained, these sorts of abstract considerations had merely provided political leaders with a tool for public relations in the international sphere, achieving little other than what Kant himself sarcastically dismissed as "providing comfort to war-mongers."

In response, in a series of widely read public essays and a short book entitled *Toward Perpetual Peace* (1795), Kant proposed a series of political and legal reforms that would make wars more difficult to pursue. The recommended reforms began with measures such as abolishing standing armies and avoiding engaging in arms races that would accrue enormous national debt through deficit spending on such items, and importantly, not imposing terms of peace upon a conquered enemy so ruinous as to become the cause of the next war. Subsequently, he proposed substantive new reforms, such as convening what he termed a "League of Nations" that would function as a kind of international parliament, hearing and attempting to resolve and adjudicate the legitimate grievances that nations had against each other, so as to obviate the need for resorting to war.

One of the most interesting of those many constructive and practical political and economic proposals for resolving the causes of armed conflict, however, was Kant's recommendations for winding up the wars that we do happen to fight. It matters *how such wars are ended*, he argued. Echoing the earlier desires of just war theorists for "right intention" in declaring and waging war, and even those early reflections of Socrates and his pupils for the stability of the peace that would follow, Kant recommended policies that would let conquered nations rebuild and restore their society along stable and morally just lines that would enable them, in the future, to live in peace with their neighbors. He likewise advocated policies for the victors that would (as Socrates, too, had recommended) bestow mercy and amnesty, and avoid imposing harsh financial reparations or punitive measures on the conquered, less the stringent terms of surrender and the reparations exacted from the vanquished provoke the kind of enduring bitterness and resentment, and desire for revenge, that would foment a future war.

Many historians today fault the Treaty of Versailles in 1918 that brought an end to World War I for imposing precisely the harsh, punitive conditions (including crippling financial reparations) upon Germany, all of which Kant had recommended *against*. These vengeful reparations are credited with having caused widespread economic suffering and political unrest that led to the rise of Adolph Hitler and the Nazis, and the onset of World War II scarcely two decades later. By contrast, historians credit the attempt by Woodrow Wilson after World War I to establish the League of Nations, and even more the US-led Marshall Plan following the conclusion of World War II, with ushering in an unprecedented era of peace among the nations of Europe—peoples that had been at war with one another ceaselessly on one pretext or another ever since the fall of the Roman Empire.

Kant, the critic of the just war tradition, thus inaugurated a third dimension of consideration, what we might term "justice after war," or (expressed in the Latin idioms of medieval law) *jus post bellum*. The considerations of Thomas and Augustine deal principally with when to declare war with justification and are known as *jus ad bellum*. The concerns of Vitoria and Suarez that connect with warrior ethics in the ancient pagan world, and continue directly into the law of armed conflict today, are usually termed "the just conduct of war," or *jus in bello*.

This book that you are presently reading, by contrast, is aimed primarily at the education and orientation of military personnel, as well as average citizens, about these various aspects of war and its proper conduct. These efforts constitute a fourth dimension of the just war tradition, termed "just preparedness for war," or *jus ante bellum*. Together, these four distinctive dimensions (*ante* and *ad bellum*, *in bello*, and *post bellum*) comprise the just war tradition.

How should we understand the relationship of this just war tradition to military professional ethics—especially when we recognize that not all combatants or military forces abide by these principles?

Sometimes people mistakenly infer that military ethics is simply identical to the discussions outlined above in the just war tradition. At other times, with somewhat more justification, people claim that the considerations encompassed in the justification of war (*jus ad bellum*) are the business of political leaders and statesmen, while the concerns encompassed in the just conduct of war and the law of armed conflict (*jus in bello*) constitute the primary focus and responsibility of the military profession and its ethics.

This is a very neat and traditional division of labor, but it cannot be right. First, as we will see in the remaining chapters of this book, "military ethics" involves a great deal more than the considerations included in the just war tradition, at least inasmuch as warriors are not always, or even usually, at war!

Second, many of the figures in the just war tradition include discussion of the responsibilities of individual warriors not to fight in unjust wars—leaving largely unaddressed just how the hapless individual soldier is supposed to determine which wars are just and which are unjust, let alone what exactly to do about this. And finally, what about the aftermath of war (*jus post bellum*)? And what about the proper preparation for declaring and fighting wars justly (*jus ante bellum*)? Rather clearly, military personnel are deeply engaged in that last project all the time, and they are often left to "clean up the mess" during the initial aftermath of war as well.

The neat and traditional division of labor does not even address these two enormous issues, both of which often fall to militaries to execute properly. Most of these important issues in military ethics have been largely neglected by scholars, academics, and even policymakers working on the just war tradition, because they themselves are neither practitioners nor familiar with the practices of military forces and personnel. Hence, in the remaining chapters of this book we will deal with these and other issues of military ethics that are related only tangentially to the traditional understanding of the just war tradition.

What are we to do when our enemies ignore or violate these just war principles?

We have purposely left the hardest question for last. What are military personnel and organizations to do when they find themselves in the midst of a conflict in which they are expected to comply with international law, and honor the moral values and traditions of professional military service, but encounter enemies and adversaries who have absolutely no regard for either?

This is probably the single most important question addressed in this book.

Much depends upon how military personnel themselves, as well as ordinary citizens, view these laws and moral values. If the values and principles are thought to be "dreamed up" by priests, theologians, and philosophers (as the just war tradition suggests)—and if the laws are thought in turn to have been conjured up by well-meaning lawyers in Geneva, none of whom know the least thing about what real combat is like, and none of whom have to shoulder the risks involved in attempting to comply with those laws (as international lawyers sometimes smugly and witlessly imply)—then it is likely that all other relevant stakeholders will view these historical constraints as reckless nonsense that is simply "getting our side killed" or "forcing us to fight with our hands tied behind our back." The attitude toward IHL and JWT will be one of contempt and disrespect.

Instead, however, if one comes to understand how these moral principles, core values, professional practices, and even legal constraints *arise from the practices of militaries themselves, and from their collective reflection on the ends they serve and the core values their shared practice embodies*, then the attitude is likely to be different. Military personnel will instead come to regard these laws and moral principles as embodying the very best about themselves and their profession. They will view these constraints as having been self-imposed voluntarily through their own desire to join, and belong to, the profession of arms. Their *adherence to these military virtues will not be forced upon them, but will manifest itself as what Clausewitz perceptively termed "professional pride."*

Soldiers, sailors, and Marines properly informed by pride in their profession will, in turn, no more be led to disobey or forsake their own core professional principles simply because their enemies and adversaries do, than would police be led to disobey the law because criminals do. Disobedience, disrespect, and utter disregard for the law is what defines criminals as criminals, who have set themselves against society and citizens, and is what distinguishes them from police and security forces, who uphold the law and defend citizens against them.

And likewise, combatants who disobey, disrespect, and utterly disregard the laws of armed conflict have thereby identified themselves as international criminals, thugs, and murderers. They are "unjustified combatants," not engaged in justified war, nor in justly wielding the sword in defense of others. They are criminals and murdering marauders, who have set themselves against civilized peoples and nations, and thereby distinguished themselves from the warriors and justified combatants who defend civilized peoples and nations from them.

St. Augustine had this pretty much dead to right: in the devastating and ambiguous moral wilderness we find ourselves inhabiting, there will always be those who choose to set themselves against others, against peace, justice, law, and order—choosing instead to inflict murder, mayhem, and misery upon helpless and vulnerable victims for their own, often incomprehensible, and always unjustifiable reasons. That is their choice, and the ensuing misery is their vocation.

The vocation of the military profession, by contrast, is to protect nations and peoples against such enemies, and *never knowingly or willingly to engage in such morally unjustified behavior themselves*. Their professional core values and ethical principles, some of which have come to be enshrined in law, are their reminder of who they are and the noble purpose they serve. These laws and principles, emerging from the just war tradition, are signposts of their own morality in this otherwise-featureless landscape, always guiding and encouraging them to adhere to the highest ideals of proper professional practice.

Notes

1. This may be because (as we will see below) the latter kind of war has been declared illegal under international law, save in cases of self-defense against aggression, or calls for collective security by coalitions of nations under the auspices of the United Nations Security Council.
2. It bears mention that an entirely equivalent limitation is imposed in both Sunni and Shiite Islam: in the former, only the caliph, the

recognized leader of the umma (the community of the faithful), is authorized to declare, let alone engage in anything other than wars of self-defense (i.e., "offensive jihad"). In both traditions, the requisite theological authority for offensive war against non-Muslims does not presently exist, and war against the faithful is strictly prohibited. The matter is even more complex in the case of Shiite Islam, since only Ali, the martyred Fourth Caliph and nephew of the Prophet, whose return or resurrection is awaited, possesses this authority. In effect, all wars save those of self-defense of the community of the faithful from armed aggression by infidels and unbelievers is prohibited, and the claims of any individual faction to exercise such authority on behalf of others is entirely without merit. See James Turner Johnson, *The Just War Tradition and the Restraint of War: A Moral and Historical Inquiry* (Princeton, NJ: Princeton University Press, 1981) and John Kelsay, *Arguing the Just War in Islam* (Cambridge, MA: Harvard University Press, 2007) for confirmation and more extensive treatment of these interesting issues of just war doctrine in Islam.

3. In a controversial and widely read study, for example, Oxford philosopher David Rodin examines the legal case for individual self-defense and finds it both quite limited in itself under many domestic legal regimes and, in any case, not at all comparable to the issues and interests at stake in international relations between states, to which (he argues) no compelling right of self-defense devolves. See David Rodin, *War and Self-Defense* (Oxford: Oxford University Press, 2002).

4. James Turner Johnson, *Sovereignty* (Washington, DC: Georgetown University Press, 2015).

5. See, for example, devout and principled Christian pacifists who decry this "realist" approach to justifiable war, and maintain a commitment to pacifism and non-violence in conflict resolution. E.g.: Stanley Hauerwas, *The Peaceable Kingdom: A Primer in Christian Ethics* (Notre Dame, IN: Notre Dame University Press, 1991), and *War and the American Difference: Theological Reflections on Violence and National Identity* (Ada, MI: Baker Academic, 2011); James E. Will, *A Christology of Peace* (Philadelphia, PA: Westminster John Knox Press, 1989), and *A Contemporary Theology for Ecumenical Peace* (London: Palgrave-Macmillan, 2014); John Howard Yoder, *The Politics of Jesus* (Grand Rapids, MI: Eerdmans, 1994); Glenn H. Stassen, *Just Peacemaking: Transforming Initiatives for Justice and Peace* (Philadelphia, PA: Westminster John Knox Press, 1992).

6. "Begging the question" does not mean neglecting or overlooking it altogether (as the phrase is often incorrectly used), but "arguing in a circle" by presupposing a specific answer when framing the question.

7. Such claims are made in works like US Army Brigadier General H. R. McMaster's book *Dereliction of Duty* (New York: Harper Perennial, 1998), and in the film documentary of Secretary of Defense Robert M. McNamara, *The Fog of War*.

8. George R. Lucas, "The Strategy of Graceful Decline," *Ethics and International Affairs* 25, no. 2 (Spring 2011): 133–142.

9. Cicero, in turn, was describing an ancient Roman custom of ensuring that the resort to war was always a last resort. The ancient custom, of which Cicero approved, was to warn the adversary in advance of Rome's grievances against it and offer it every opportunity short of armed conflict to resolve those grievances. This procedure, undertaken by the Roman high priests (the "Fetiales"), was repeated up to three times in an effort to avoid the necessity of war, and so avoid the risk of "offending the gods." If the adversary refused to negotiate, however, war would then be justly declared and fought. This condition is known in the just war tradition distinctively as "public declaration," but is in fact a procedure designed to fulfill another important condition, which we have identified earlier as the "principle of last resort." See the Cicero selections in Gregory M. Reichberg, Hendrik Syse, and Endre Begby, eds., *The Ethics of War: Classical and Contemporary Readings* (London: Blackwell, 2004).

10. It seems worth noting in passing that the "Blessed One" of Buddhism offered a similar caveat regarding self-defense as a justification for the use of force. Like Augustine, the Buddha taught that force may never be used for defense of the individual "self," since the self was unimportant and unworthy, something to be discarded or transcended. Rather *it is in defense of the lives of others* (presumably to permit them additional time to achieve Enlightenment and salvation on their own) that the committed Buddhist is entitled to take up arms. Likewise, in the bushido code of the samurai, self-defense as "self-preservation" has no place. The individual life of the warrior is of no importance to the warrior. Rather, it is placing his life at the service of the state and preserving the lives of comrades and fellow citizens that constitutes the warrior's highest calling. See Tyson B. Meadors, "Buddhist Perspectives on the Use of Force" (2007): http://isme.tamu.edu/ISME07/Meadors07.html.

11. For excerpts from Vitoria's own writings, see Francisco de Vitoria, *Political Writings*, ed. Anthony Pagden and Jeremy Lawrence (Cambridge: Cambridge University Press, 1991). A version of this story appears in Michael Walzer's essay (stemming in part from a lecture at the US Naval Academy in November 2002): "The Triumph of Just War Theory and the Dangers of Success," in *Empowering Our Military Conscience*, ed. Roger Wertheimer (London: Ashgate, 2010). My version, however, relies on an earlier article on Vitoria by Gregory M. Reichberg, in *The Classics of Western Philosophy*, ed. Jorge Gracia, Gregory M. Reichberg, and Bernard N. Schumacher (London: Blackwell, 2003), 197–203.

Further Reading

Bartholomeusz, Tessa J. *In Defense of Dharma: Just War Ideology in Buddhist Sri Lanka*. New York: Routledge, 2002.

Brough, Michael W., John W. Lango, and Harry van der Linden, eds. *Rethinking the Just War Tradition*. Albany: State University of New York Press, 2007.

Johnson, James Turner. *The Holy War Idea in Christian and Islamic Traditions*. State College: Penn State University Press, 1997.

Johnson, James Turner. *The Just War Tradition and the Restraint of War: A Moral and Historical Inquiry*. Princeton, NJ: Princeton University Press, 1981.

Kelsay, John. *Arguing the Just War in Islam*. Cambridge, MA: Harvard University Press, 2007.

Orend, Brian. *The Morality of War*. 2nd edition. Peterboro, Ontario: Broadview Press, 2013.

Reichberg, Gregory M., and Hendrik Syse, eds. *Religion, War and Ethics: A Sourcebook of Cultural Traditions*. Cambridge: Cambridge University Press, 2014.

Reichberg, Gregory M., Hendrik Syse, and Endre Begby, eds. *The Ethics of War: Classical and Contemporary Readings*. London: Blackwell, 2004.

Robinson, Paul L., ed. *Just War Theory in Comparative Perspective*. London: Ashgate, 2003.

Rodin, David. *War and Self-Defense*. Oxford: Oxford University Press, 2002.

Vitoria, Francisco de. *Political Writings*. Edited by Anthony Pagden and Jeremy Lawrence. Cambridge: Cambridge University Press, 1991.

5

MILITARY ETHICS APART FROM COMBAT

Does military ethics apply to matters other than declaring and waging war?

Military personnel are stationed in military posts and bases throughout their own countries and may be deployed on a continuing basis in other parts of the world. From there they participate in life-saving and natural disaster relief. Depending upon their nationality, they may be asked to fight piracy, provide border and immigration control, or (when legally permitted) to support domestic law enforcement and peacekeeping operations. Since the 1990s especially, the United Nations has increasingly called upon representatives from national military forces to assist in a variety of international law enforcement, peacekeeping, and stability operations, and especially to intervene in other sovereign nations to protect victims of violence and genocide.

Some military services used to refer to all of these various activities collectively as "military operations other than war" (MOOTW). But whether serving near home or deployed abroad, military personnel, both men and women, attempt to lead normal lives like anyone else. They serve as teachers, trainers, examiners, inspectors, musicians, office clerks, and supply personnel. They may supervise a base exchange (military department store) or commissary (military grocery store), coach the local soccer team, serve as elders in churches, synagogues, or mosques, and, in sum, live their lives as citizens, family members, parents with children, or as children with elderly parents who need care and support. And in all these activities, despite wearing uniforms to work, a good many of them will never fire a shot or participate directly in an armed conflict.

As such social beings, they will face a range of the same moral challenges and demands that all of us face. They will face "tests of character,"[1] as do we all, demanding that they strive to behave with integrity, tell the truth, resist corruption, refrain from lying, cheating, or stealing (or expressing excessive or uncritical loyalty toward those who do), remain faithful to spouses or significant others, care for their children (and perhaps their parents) with love and compassion, file honest and accurate income tax returns, and otherwise willingly comply with the law. They will be called upon to treat one another within their organization, as well as the members of the general public whom they serve (regardless of race, creed, or color), with dignity, integrity, and respect, and to avoid engaging in sexual opportunism or harassment in the workplace.

They will also face "moral dilemmas," as do we all, in which situations confront us with choices that are fraught with moral ambiguity and uncertainty, whether, and how much, to contribute in time or finances to assist the poor, homeless, or needy; whether or not to sanction the abortion of an unwanted or unexpected pregnancy; or whether to allow, or even assist, an elderly parent with a terminal illness to die with dignity. They will wrestle with how to cope with the bad or risky behavior of their children, or whether to "counsel" a colleague whom they suspect of engaging in imprudent, risky, or even illegal behavior in the workplace. They will struggle with decisions about what to do in response to suspected cases of inequality or unfairness, whether in hiring, promotion, compensation, or work assignments.

In publicly facing tests of character, or in wrestling with moral dilemmas, however, some members of military organizations may come to feel that the standards of moral evaluation applied to them specifically, on account of their uniform (so to speak), are different from, or more stringent than, those that would be applied to ordinary civilians. We will examine this question of whether military personnel are held to a higher moral standard in more detail below.

What are some examples of military operations or functions that are not war?

As we saw at the conclusion of the last chapter, military forces and personnel are frequently charged, or simply left, with the responsibility of restoring order and clearing up the chaos remaining in the wake of a war. This may include tasks like building schools and housing and repairing civil infrastructure (such as roads, sewers, water treatment plants, and electrical grids). These are extensive and expensive enterprises, and so military personnel will serve not only as civil engineers engaged in these activities themselves but also as program managers and procurement agents, contracting with and hiring local personnel, or bringing in outside contractors to assist with these projects, which will then be overseen by military supervisors and paid from funds they administer. The ethical challenges that arise here, especially amid the chaos and disorder and absence of rigorous accountability, transparency, and oversight, are predominantly tests of character: requiring each and every member of the military to avoid involvement in, or tolerance of, graft, corruption, bribery, or outright incompetence in the administration of these important tasks, while seeking always to remain in compliance with applicable laws and regulatory standards.

As we also saw, the military is perpetually engaged in preparing its members for engaging in war. They must recruit and train new personnel, both officers and enlisted, for example. Especially when recruiting new enlisted personnel, military recruiters may operate widely in far-flung regions of a country without immediate oversight or supervision. They may be required to meet recruiting quotas, which leads to the temptation to cajole, persuade, and even mislead interested civilians in enlisting in military service under false (or, at least, not altogether accurate) circumstances, or even result in the paying of illicit bonuses to leading members of a community (school guidance counselors, for example) to assist in enticing young people under their sway to enlist. In all these activities, temptations to bribery, corruption, misuse of funds, or disseminating false or misleading information to prospects must be resisted. While destructive wherever such abuses occur, these recruiting abuses are especially destructive to the formation of trained, professional military services in developing countries.[2]

Experienced military personnel are likewise expected to train or educate newly recruited personnel for military service. That training or education must be accurate, complete, fully competent, and strictly relevant to the proper performance of duties and discharge of military responsibilities. The training environment itself, however, presents supervisors with myriad opportunities and temptations to do otherwise: for example, to abuse their authority and trust by engaging in or tolerating hazing or bullying in the name of toughening up recruits, or by preying upon vulnerable recruits in other ways. Military forces and organizations, once the exclusive bastion of males, for example, are increasingly integrated across both gender and sexual orientation. Sexual harassment, predominantly (though not exclusively) of females by males, or of gay and lesbian service members by those disapproving or contemptuous of their orientations, are a frequent and vexing problem. Despite the historical tendency of military forces to be asked or ordered to serve in the vanguard of wider social programs to achieve equal opportunity and full integration, racism and sexism remain persistent and nagging problems. These difficulties, in turn, can be exacerbated by the propensities of the military's individual members, if left unchecked, to engage in alcohol or drug abuse.

A great many of these social problems, to be sure, are endemic to many other professions and organizations, as well as to the wider societies within which military personnel serve. That commonality does not exempt military organizations and their personnel from doing their utmost to combat such tendencies toward abuse of power and disrespect for one another, let alone engaging in outright illegal and immoral activities (rape, theft, drug abuse, or physical abuse or engaging in hateful actions directed at minorities). Military organizations, especially in countries like the United States and the People's Republic of China, are large, complex organizations providing employment to the widest conceivable diversity of personnel with a range of skills and educational backgrounds. It therefore constitutes an enormous challenge to ensure that all members of the profession are properly trained, well educated, and appropriately supervised in a manner that enables them to discharge their duties responsibly, and to avoid the myriad pitfalls of illegal and immoral behavior outlined above.

Are military personnel sometimes held to a higher moral standard than ordinary

That is a difficult question to answer, since it is often based upon individual impressions and anecdotes rather than empirical data. Certainly the complaint is often lodged by individuals in military services in many countries (e.g., the United States, Canada, Australia) that their behavior is more closely scrutinized in public, and that their mistakes or misdeeds are seized upon in the press and news media with much greater attention and severity of judgment than is usually applied to similar behavior by rank-and-file citizens generally.

But is this really true? And if true, is this fair?[3]

It is certainly true that misbehavior (like sexual dalliance or harassment) or illegal actions (like financial corruption) committed by high-ranking military officers are likely to attract a great deal of attention in the news media, and doubtless

reflect badly on their military organization. It is also undoubtedly true that widespread social ills like sexual harassment
and drug or alcohol abuse on the part of a sizable number of
the rank-and-file members of the military is likely to attract a
great deal of attention and reflect badly on the organization as
a whole. It is less clear that such behaviors attract any more
attention than they do when committed by prominent members of other professional organizations also in the public eye,
like the clergy or physicians—or, for that matter, public figures
like prominent politicians or film celebrities.

What is surely true is that rank-and-file members of the
public expect prominent senior figures (like politicians and
high-ranking military officers), as well as the members of
trusted professional organizations in general, to behave with
a degree of circumspection and moral rectitude that is in keeping with the high esteem and public trust otherwise accorded
them. The general public may, by contrast, be fascinated to the
point of sensationalism when Hollywood celebrities or sports
stars are caught behaving badly or breaking the law, but it is
probably not the case that they also expect such persons to
behave well in general, or are shocked, disappointed, or outraged when some of these people fail to do so. The general
public does seem to think, however, that its high-ranking public officials and the members of otherwise highly regarded and
trusted professions (like physicians, clergy, and members of
the military) ought to be expected to behave well. Certainly
such individuals should at least abide by the law, and therefore
members of society appear especially shocked, disappointed,
or outraged (depending upon the persons and the degree of
wrongdoing discovered) when these prominent officials and
professionals fail to do so.

In such cases, we can at least say that military personnel,
and especially high-ranking military personnel, are included
in a wider group of persons to whom especially strict standards of circumspect and upright public behavior are routinely
applied. The moral and legal standards to which such persons

are held are largely the same as those to which all of us are held. But the degree of public scrutiny applied and the level of compliance expected are especially high (and the public may sometimes seem to be less tolerant and forgiving as a result). Persons occupying these prominent roles may object or find this burden of public scrutiny sometimes hard to bear. But that does not mean that such scrutiny is unfair or somehow different from the expectations generally placed on people everywhere to do what is right and avoid egregious wrongdoing.

Hence, a high-ranking male officer who abandons his spouse and runs off to Buenos Aires with his female secretary and somehow manages to use funds from the Defense Travel System (DTS) to purchase airfare and lodging for this purpose, is likely to be viewed more harshly than the CEO of a local corporation who does exactly the same thing using company funds. Both have violated their respective organization's trust and broken the law with regard to financing their moral misadventures, but the military officer might be reasonably supposed to have known better and behaved better than the CEO on account of his professional experience and stature. Neither has behaved well, but the officer has likely brought dishonor and disgrace upon the uniform (and his fellow officers), while the CEO's behavior does not reflect strongly on other business personnel, perhaps not even those in his own corporation, in quite the same fashion. This (fellow officers might counsel their wayward peer) "goes with the uniform" and is a function of the esteem and stature otherwise accorded to the military, of a sort not usually enjoyed by members of the business community.

There are at least some situations, however, in which this so-called higher moral standard might seem unreasonable. The first would occur if members of the military are forced to operate under a strict regulatory standard that includes strictures and prohibitions that are irrelevant to the performance of their duties. In the United States, for example, the Uniform Code of Military Justice (a body of legal regulations legislated by Congress to govern the behavior of US military personnel) includes a provision that prohibits an officer from "committing adultery." Adultery itself—that is, the betrayal of trust, and the breaking of vows and promises of fidelity made to a spouse in marriage—is morally wrong for anyone who engages in it, not just military officers. But it is not illegal and is a moral wrong that is quite often committed by a great many people for all kinds of personal reasons—some of which may, on occasion, constitute grounds for excuse or exemption from, or forgiveness for, the moral error.

On its face, this may seem to constitute both a higher moral standard and one that is unfair or unreasonably applied exclusively to military personnel. Some members of the military themselves nonetheless think this stricture reasonable. "If someone willingly betrays the trust of his (or her) spouse," they ask, "how can he think he can earn and maintain the trust of subordinates and the public?" But many others think this particular prohibition inappropriate as codified in law and regard it as a quaint anachronism that is likely to be repealed to accord with general social practice and acceptance.

A second example is likely both more serious and even more unfair. This has to do with the occurrence of widespread ills that affect organizations and organizational behavior. Human beings are far from morally perfect, and many often engage in behavior that is egregiously wrong or morally outrageous, even in instances where it is not strictly illegal. Two of the most prevalent of these organizational plagues are sexual harassment and alcohol abuse. When these practices are found to occur in military organizations, they are accorded harsh judgment by the public and by high-ranking public officials who rightly think they have no place in military organizations. But such behaviors have no place in *any* organization, civilian or military. Is it fair to hold military personnel and organizations not just to a standard of zero *tolerance*, but to a standard of zero *occurrence*, of such widespread and unfortunate behavior, when other organizations are not held to quite so strict a standard?

Probably not. But that will all depend upon the leadership and the organizational climate tolerated, or even inculcated, regarding these behaviors within specific military organizations.

If, on one hand, the leaders set and enforce a stringent standard of zero tolerance and likewise *set a good example* for subordinates through their own behavior, without hypocrisy or excuse—and if everything within reason is done within the organization to deter such behaviors and to punish them when they occur—then it is probably unreasonable to hold those organizations any more accountable for the occasional and inevitable failures than we would the leadership and members of any other large and complex organization.

If, on the other hand, senior leaders themselves are found to engage in the predatory and abusive behavior in question; or to tolerate such behavior by select, favored members of their organization; or to enforce the regulations and punish the violations arbitrarily or inconsistently; or to fail to take every reasonable measure to educate the organization and its members about the nontoleration of such behaviors—then it would be quite appropriate to hold the organization and its leadership to strict account.

But which is it, finally? That is an empirical question, and one about which it is often difficult to obtain reliable data. The behavior of senior leadership and the policies put in place (and the efforts at education toward avoidance) may all be externally evaluated upon occasion to determine whether good-faith efforts are indeed being made. Another test, less frequently applied, is "benchmarking" the behavior of the military organization to that of other organizations of similar composition: large businesses, or college students and athletes, or incidence of occurrence of the undesirable behavior among the general population. Picking the benchmark or comparable peer group is itself a challenge.

But suppose that we attempt to do so and employ several such benchmarks. If we find that the incidence of, say, reported sexual harassment is much higher in the military than in the benchmarks, we would be correct to demand a serious realign-ment and rectification of the organization's tolerance for this behavior.

If, however (as is often alleged), the percentage of incidents among (for example) a random control group of one million military personnel is lower than among one million college students, or one million college athletes of similar age—or if the percentage of incidents among the military control group is found to be considerably less than is found among busi-nesses collectively employing one million people, or than that recorded among a random selection of one million mem-bers of the general public—then it is probably unreasonable and unfair to hold the military organization more strictly to account than these other groups.

In these instances, the military organization might be found to be functioning reasonably well, even if not perfectly. If the military organization and its members are nonetheless criticized by senior leadership or the general public for the incidents that do nonetheless occur, that might constitute an example of a higher standard, or a double standard, unfairly and unreasonably applied (often with seriously demoralizing results for the members of the military organization).

Political leaders and the general public do not always do an adequate job of making and applying such reasonable dis-tinctions, sometimes leading military personnel to think they are being unfairly held to a higher moral standard than is appropriate.

One final example will likely exhaust this complex and sensitive topic. That is the question of whether the moral and legal standards, of whatever degree of severity, apply only when on duty or when acting in an official capacity, or whether they should apply (as military personnel themselves say) 24/7—meaning all the time.

If morality and the law apply 24/7 to military personnel, but not to others, then this, too, would constitute a higher moral standard, unreasonably and unfairly applied. And some members of the military profession do worry, or object, that they are held to a higher standard in this respect. But this, too, will be difficult to ascertain with reliability.

Military leaders may be apt to enjoin subordinates under their command to remember that the moral and legal standards by which they are judged apply 24/7, and not just when they are in uniform or on duty. That seems reasonable and also prudent advice, since, indeed, moral and legal standards and expectations apply also to police, clergy, politicians, lawyers, and even ordinary members of the public all around the clock. It is not clear that military personnel, when off duty or out of uniform, should be expected to behave any better than off-duty police, or clergy in plain garb at home, or anyone else for that matter. All who are members of respected professions that serve the public and enjoy its trust should never forget who they are, even when they are off duty and out of uniform. All such persons, and not just military personnel exclusively, are required to recognize that their individual behavior always will reflect well or poorly upon their peers in their profession, as well as upon themselves, and so at all times strive to behave with dignity, integrity, and moral rectitude. (And so, too, for that matter, should all of the rest of us, even if we sometimes fail to maintain this standard.)

Do members of the military have a special moral obligation to dissent and to refrain from fighting in unjust wars?

This is a moral dilemma peculiar to the military profession. Often labeled the problem of selective conscientious objection, it goes to the heart of individual professional autonomy and freedom of judgment, which are thought to be the hallmark of any profession. Just as doctors may refuse to employ their skills to operate on patients or engage in medical research whose moral probity is in question, so we might think that soldiers should not be compelled against their judgment to fight in wars that they deem unjust or illegal. Individual members of any profession are thought to exercise a degree of autonomy, and, in particular, to refuse to engage in activities that they believe, with good reasons, might constitute professional malfeasance.

That much has occasionally been affirmed by the major figures in the just war tradition, whom we discussed in the previous chapter. Both Aquinas and Vitoria (among many others) emphatically held that individual soldiers should not fight for an unjust cause. But the affirmation of this right, or this duty, has been vague and imprecise, largely out of sympathy for the plight of the individual soldier whose ability to ascertain the justice of a war in question, let alone to act upon that judgment, seems to be seriously circumscribed. Until recently, for example, it was deemed permissible for military leaders to order individuals who objected to fighting in a particular conflict to be put to death as deserters, traitors, or cowards. Selective conscientious objectors, even at present, are still likely to face court-martial and, if convicted, imprisonment or other punishment for refusing to fight, even on grounds of deeply held principle.

Selective conscientious objection at the individual level may therefore seem an implausible moral burden to impose. And yet, in the past, we have imposed this duty and punished at least some combatants, and morally shamed many others, for having willingly or complicitly participated in wars that they should reasonably have known were unjust. The victorious allies in World War II held Japanese and German soldiers respectively accountable for such knowledge and punished at least a few. Critics of the Vietnam War held American soldiers liable for having fought in an unjust war, and at least some of those soldiers then or subsequently came to agree. So how is an individual combatant, especially if conscripted, expected to know for a fact that a given war is unjust (on his or her own side, at least)? And what is the person to do in response to such convictions?

International law is notoriously equivocal and tolerant on this point. Individual soldiers under the law of armed conflict are *not* held legally liable for the moral justification (or lack thereof) for their nation's wars. They are held strictly liable only for their own individual conduct during a war. This principle, enshrined in law and identified explicitly in the "war convention" of the eminent contemporary just war theorist Michael Walzer (mentioned several times in earlier chapters), is known as the "moral equality of combatants."

Yet if soldiers are expected to suspend their individual moral judgment and simply to fight in the wars they are ordered to fight for their nation, they are collectively behaving as what Col. Don Snider, a highly regarded professor at the US Military Academy (West Point), poignantly calls "an obedient bureaucracy," rather than as members of a profession. Indeed, it seems difficult to have it both ways. If military service is a profession, and if its individual members constitute something more than merely an obedient bureaucracy in blind service to the state, then they incur some responsibility as individuals for ascertaining whether they are being ordered to engage in professional malfeasance. They should refuse to fight in conflicts that lack a just cause, or are disproportionately destructive in light of their political objective, or that fail to fulfill some of the other requirements of morally justified war.

Admittedly, this places a severe burden upon them as individuals. This requires, at minimum, that they be individually acquainted with, and themselves believe in the validity of their professional principles and core values of professional practice as enshrined in the just war tradition. It also means that their supervisors, both senior officers and enlisted, and the civilian authorities that may ultimately wield authority over them, be willing to grant them a certain degree of latitude in law and regulation in order to formulate a professional judgment, and to act in accordance with their final determination.

Traditionalists, however, maintain that such measures would result in an unworkable absurdity. If (they argue) each soldier has a right to veto his or her nation's decision to wage war, then no wars would ever be fought, whether just or unjust, and military organizations themselves would quickly degenerate into anarchy and self-serving, self-preserving disobedience.

As a matter of organizational psychology, however, this conclusion is open to dispute. It takes extraordinary courage and conviction for an individual to speak up and challenge the conviction of a large organization, even when the person is not immediately subject to severe punishment for doing so. And even if the individual musters this courage and objects, he or she is unlikely to gain the assent of the remaining members of the group, unless the objector's moral unease is widely shared, and the evidence against the justice of the cause seems almost overwhelming.

In point of fact, modern military organizations have seemed remarkably resilient to tolerating dissent in a host of far less grave circumstances: accommodating needs of spouses (including those also serving in the military) and their families, for example; dealing with preferences for, or objections to, specific service assignments and deployments; and many other routine matters that have not caused the organization itself to collapse into anarchy. In light of these experiences, it does not seem impossible to conceive of military organizations coming to respect, and even to require the exercise of, responsible professional judgment on the part of their individual members in this core professional matter, even as they now do routinely with matters of far less consequence.

What responsibility do military personnel have to offer professional advice to the leaders of their own governments regarding the moral justification (or lack thereof) for using military force in international relations?

This, too, is a vexed question of professional ethics, and, like the preceding question, requires individuals (this time senior, experienced military officers) to balance duty to the profession with the prospect of exceeding their rightful authority, or seeming to be insubordinate or self-serving. Once again, however, if the military is to be (as Col. Snider forcefully puts it) a true profession rather than merely an obedient bureaucracy, the duty to offer military advice to civilian political leaders that is both technically and morally competent, and in accord with the best practices of the profession, is one that must be firmly and forcefully shouldered, even if that advice should prove to be unwelcome.

On this topic, one of the most priceless observations is that of the Spanish Dominican priest and professor Francisco di Vitoria, mentioned in the last chapter. On this topic, and with respect to decisions by the sovereign as the "legitimate authority" to declare war, Vitoria cautions that, on occasion, "the King may be mistaken, and might fall into error. He needs our advice!" And indeed (just to offer the conclusion of that interesting historical case from the last chapter), Vitoria himself fell ill and died of natural causes while making his way to Madrid at the request of King Phillip the Second of Spain, who had summoned Vitoria, with the utmost respect, in order to hear more of that courageous and thoughtful scholar's advice on the proper conduct of Spain's military campaigns in the New World.

More recently, by contrast, senior military leaders like US Army Brigadier General H. R. McMaster were seriously critical of their predecessors' collective failures in this regard during the Vietnam War. McMaster termed it a grave "dereliction of duty" for those earlier senior officers not to stand up to Secretary of Defense Robert McNamara, both to oppose his war policy and to object to the failure to report its disappointing results accurately to the American public.

Even more recently, during the controversial "war of preemptive self-defense" ordered by President George W. Bush in Iraq in 2003, a significant number of retired senior military officers united to protest both the conduct of that war and the accuracy with which it was being portrayed to the American public by Secretary of Defense Donald W. Rumsfeld. Although the propriety and professionalism of this "Revolt of the Generals"[4] was heatedly disputed by other active-duty and retired military personnel, it did have the effect of altering the conduct of the war, resulting in the retirement of Secretary Rumsfeld and the promotion of one of the dissenting active-duty officers (General David H. Petraeus), who commanded that campaign with much greater success than had his predecessors.

The duty to offer sound professional advice, even disappointing or unwelcome advice, is thus an important moral responsibility within the profession of arms. This duty, principally borne by the most senior military personnel, reflects back upon a disturbing feature of the previous question pertaining to dissent, obedience, and selective conscientious objection to particular wars that are suspected of being unjust. The duty of all military professionals not to fight in unjust wars is (at least in the abstract or hypothetical case) an important component of military ethics and professional autonomy. But it is a very odd profession indeed that would place so momentous a responsibility solely on the shoulders of its least-experienced, most junior members. Yet that is often what outside critics of the military, advocating for this professional responsibility, seem to be recommending.[5] This represents a ludicrously inverted sense of professional moral responsibility.

Instead, it is the senior military leaders that must be educated, experienced, and competently prepared to offer this, the most important of "military advice"—to be willing, as Vitoria put it, to help their civilian leaders avoid making terrible moral (as well as political) mistakes. And they must likewise be willing figuratively to "fall on their swords," if necessary, in order to protect the most vulnerable junior members of their profession (to whom they themselves must listen carefully and respectfully), in order to protect their profession's future leaders from being forced to commit professional malfeasance by fighting in wars of questionable moral justification.

It is perhaps in this vital area of *jus ante bellum*—the preparation of military personnel to fight only in just wars, and to fight them justly—that all of us who are collectively engaged in the preparation, education, and leadership development of both present and future military personnel have most frequently and seriously failed.

Notes

1. In Stephen Coleman, *Military Ethics* (Oxford: Oxford University Press, 2012) we find a useful distinction in ethics between "test of character" and genuine "moral dilemmas." A test of character arises in circumstances in which the morally right choice is readily apparent, and the wrong things to avoid are clear, but the individuals confronting those choices are faced with a kind of "test" of their moral courage and resilience: are they willing to do what is right (despite the costs or difficulties) or avoid the temptations to do what is clearly wrong (despite the obvious temptations and immediate rewards of doing so)? A "moral dilemma," by contrast, arises when an individual or group faces a decision in which clear awareness of right and wrong themselves are very confusing, despite the good character and best intentions of those individuals to adhere to what is morally right or legally required.

2. Alain Fogue-Tedom of the University of Yaoundé (Cameron) offers a dramatic and thoroughly depressing account of the impact of corrupt recruiting practices, in particular, which persistently undermine the capabilities and professional demeanor of African national defense forces at present in many of the developing nations of that continent, urgently in need of well-trained and highly committed military professionals to aid their transition to full participatory democracy. See "Effective Democratization and the Development of Moral Competencies in the Armed Forces of African States," in *The Routledge Handbook of Military Ethics*, ed. George Lucas (New York: Routledge, 2015), 113–122.

3. See the essay on this topic of the "higher military standard" by US Air Force Major J. Carl Ficarrotta, in *Kantian Thinking about Military Ethics* (London: Ashgate, 2010).

4. See the essays by Major General Paul D. Eaton (whose letter of protest to the *New York Times* in March 2006 inaugurated this "revolt") and

former dean of the Army War College Col. Jeffrey D. McCausland, on the "revolt of the generals" and the duties to offer reliable military advice, in *The Routledge Handbook of Military Ethics*, ed. George Lucas (London: Routledge, 2015), 220–227, and 228–234, respectively.

5. Jeff McMahan, "Can Soldiers Be Expected to Know Whether Their War Is Just?" in *Routledge Handbook of Ethics and War*, ed. Fritz Allhoff, Nick Evans, and Adam Henschke (New York: Routledge, 2013), chap. 1. For a rejoinder to this line of thought, see George Lucas, "Advice and Dissent: The Uniform Perspective," *Journal of Military Ethics* 8, no. 2 (2009): 141–161.

Further Reading

Carrick, Don, James Connelly, and Paul Robinson, eds. *Ethics Education for Irregular Warfare*. London: Ashgate, 2009.

Coleman, Stephen. *Military Ethics*. Oxford: Oxford University Press, 2012.

Cook, Martin L. *Issues in Military Ethics*. Albany: State University of New York Press, 2013.

Ellner, Andrea, Paul Robinson, and David Whetham, eds. *When Soldiers Say No: Selective Conscientious Objection in the Modern Military*. London: Ashgate, 2014.

Fogue-Tedom, Alain. "Effective Democratization and the Development of Moral Competencies in the Armed Forces of African States." In *The Routledge Handbook of Military Ethics*, edited by George Lucas, 113–122. New York: Routledge, 2015.

Gross, Michael L., and Don Carrick, eds. *Military Medical Ethics for the 21st Century*. London: Ashgate, 2013.

Latiff, Robert. "Ethical Issues in Defense Systems Acquisitions," In *The Routledge Handbook of Military Ethics*, edited by George Lucas, 209–219. New York: Routledge, 2015.

McMahan, Jeff. "Can Soldiers Be Expected to Know Whether Their War Is Just?" In *Routledge Handbook of Ethics and War: Just War Theory in the Twenty-First Century*, edited by Fritz Allhoff, Nicolas G. Evans, and Adam Henschke, 13–22. New York: Routledge, 2013.

McMahan, Jeff. "What Makes an Act of War Disproportionate?" Annual Stutt Lecture in Ethics, US Naval Academy, Annapolis, MD, 2008: http://www.usna.edu/Ethics/_files/documents/McMahan.pdf.

McCausland, Jeff. "The Revolt of the Generals." In *Routledge Handbook of Military Ethics*, edited by George Lucas, 220–227. New York: Routledge, 2015.

Robinson, Paul, Nigel de Lee, and Don Carrick, eds. *Ethics Education in the Military*. London: Ashgate, 2008.

Snider, Don M., ed. *Forging the Warrior's Character*. 2nd edition. New York: McGraw-Hill, 2008.

Snider, Don M., ed. *The Future of the Army Profession*. 2nd edition. New York: McGraw-Hill, 2005.

Snider, Don M., and Suzanne Nielsen, eds. *American Civil-Military Relations: The Soldier and the State in the New Era*. Baltimore, MD: Johns Hopkins University Press, 2009.

Wertheimer, Roger. *Empowering Our Military Conscience: Transforming Just War Theory and Military Moral Education*. London: Ashgate, 2010.

Wolfendale, Jessica, and Paolo Tripodi, eds. *New Wars and New Soldiers: Military Ethics in the Contemporary World*. London: Ashgate, 2012.

Part 2

ETHICAL CHALLENGES FACING
THE MILITARY PROFESSION

6

THE ETHICS OF DEFENSE AND PRIVATE SECURITY CONTRACTING

What is "defense and security contracting"?

This simple phrase refers to an enormous diversity of private commercial enterprises that support military operations. They can be either combat-related or not. Typically, national defense departments have hired private firms to do work in three broad areas: (1) weapons and engineering; (2) logistical support and the operation of facilities; and (3) armed protection for specific individuals or events, also known as security contracting.

For the first area, think of the companies whose names are commonly associated with defense contracting: Lockheed-Martin, Northrup Grumman, BAE Systems, Thales, Airbus Defense & Space Industries, General Dynamics, Raytheon, and a host of other firms. These companies specialize in weapons, military transportation equipment, and systems engineering. You could find the wide range of products of such companies displayed in *Jane's Defence Weekly* and its companion publications on military hardware. These companies have been contracted by the military to help conceive, design, manufacture, test, and ultimately deploy advanced aircraft (like the F-22, the F-35 Defense Strike Fighter, the Typhoon, or the MV-22 Osprey personnel transport vehicle) and weapons systems (like Tomahawk Cruise and Hellfire missiles, or the Patriot antimissile defense system). They also contract to build tanks, armored vehicles, helicopters, littoral combat ships, and a variety of conventional and nuclear-powered submarines and aircraft carriers.

Other large multinational corporations provide support in the second area, "logistical support" (such as food services at temporary posts) and facilities (such as refueling stations) for land and maritime military forces deployed throughout the world. Companies like Halliburton and KBR (Kellogg, Root & Brown) maintain enormous naval seaports, with ship supply and refueling stations, but they are also contracted to build and maintain airfields and army posts. Such companies are commonly used for a wide variety of civil engineering projects and logistical services ranging from barracks, showers, and latrines to food services and dining facilities. Many of these kinds of projects, institutions, or services were once handled directly by military services and personnel directly, a topic to which we will turn in a moment.

Finally, there is a third type of military contracting, known as armed security contracting. Private companies— Blackwater Worldwide was for a time the most well-known example—provide armed security guards for logistical supply convoys transporting food, fuel, and other essential supplies to military forces who are forward-deployed to outposts in disputed territories or zones of active combat. Private security contractors like DynCorp and Triple Canopy provide police services for military posts, and provide training for local police and military personnel who will serve in routine domestic and international security operations for their own country upon conclusion of an ongoing armed conflict. Often such services involve activities normally expected of military personnel themselves and, indeed, have been thought more properly to constitute the primary responsibilities of uniformed national militaries, rather than of employees in the private sector.

Defense and security contracting bring with them a host of ethical issues. Engineers working for private defense firms that have designed and built a new weapons system for the military may find themselves deployed by their company to the front lines of combat, in order to assist military personnel at war in learning to use, maintain, and sometimes even re-engineer the new system to adapt to local needs. In those support roles, whether aware of this or not, they become, for legal purposes, hostile combatants rather than immune civilian personnel. Private security guards for a logistical convoy may be attacked by insurgents and quickly find themselves pinned down and embroiled in a firefight that looks for all the world exactly like a conventional military altercation with the enemy.

Another kind of ethical question arises because most private-sector security employees were formerly uniformed, active-duty military personnel. This means they gained their own experience, training, and expertise while serving in their country's military service, and then either retired or separated from that service in order to assume similar duties with private firms at much higher rates of compensation.

Yet another ethical controversy erupted recently when the US Army, urgently in need of greater cultural knowledge and expertise in the midst of complex military counterinsurgency operations in Iraq and Afghanistan, proposed to hire civilian academic experts in these subjects, give them some military training at Ft. Leavenworth, and deploy them to advise and assist Brigade Combat and Reconstruction Teams fighting in those two theaters of war as part of a controversial program known as the "Human Terrain System."[1] Interestingly, the *American* academics were actually recruited, trained, and then initially deployed and paid as private security contractors in the employ of a *British*-based defense contractor, BAE Systems.

In general, the wide range of contracted support enterprises presents military personnel and public policy officials with a never-ending sequence of moral quandaries. There can be serious conflicts of interest between personal and corporate gain on one hand, and the interests of the public and the welfare of its fighting forces on the other. The garden variety temptations to graft and corruption are magnified by the sheer complexity of many of these contracting arrangements, as well as by the vast sums of money involved. Navigating the maze of moral dilemmas and tests of character can pose tremendous moral challenges for individuals caught up in this process, as well as for corporations, government agencies, and branches of military service.

Is there a difference between defense contracting and "private military contracting"?

The differences are not well defined and are seldom carefully discussed.[2] Traditionally, "defense contracting" referred to large domestic corporations or state-owned enterprises that engaged in systems engineering and weapons development. These enterprises date back to the period of Galileo (who initially designed and manufactured his telescopes primarily for the use of the Venetian Navy in its ongoing sea conflicts with the Turkish Navy, rather than for the purpose of scientific astronomy per se), and even further, to the skilled shipwrights and shipyards operated by kings and governments, at least as far back in history as the manufacture of the magnificent triremes in ancient Athens.

It was the enormous growth in the size, cost, and political influence of these corporate interests during the two world wars of the 20th century, however, against which the US president, General Dwight D. Eisenhower (formerly the supreme commander of Allied forces in Europe during World War II) warned the American public in his farewell address upon leaving public office in January 1961.

The political dynamics that had come to alarm Eisenhower were these. Large industrial firms donate substantial sums to political candidates in democratic elections; the jobs provided and the wealth generated in local districts constitute powerful incentives for those political figures, in turn, to prioritize the interests of their constituents in the award of lucrative contracts, often ahead of the genuine needs of military services for equipment. This can make it difficult for the nation to provide adequately and wisely for defense, especially since this puts defense in competition with other urgent national needs like roads and schools.

Not infrequently, in addition, senior military officers involved in the acquisitions of military weapons systems have, upon retiring from active duty, gone to work in these firms. In the private sector, the value of their engineering expertise in designing and operating these systems is matched only by the power of their influence within the military itself (an inevitable effect of having a network of friends and associates still on active duty). It was this behemoth, and its outsized political and economic power, that Eisenhower first labeled the "military–industrial complex." The private corporations subsumed within this complex are what are customarily meant today by "defense industries."[3]

The term "private military contracting" is more conventionally applied to the third area, the remaining phenomenon described above. These are distinct from large weapons and military systems procurement. PMCs are generally companies that provide more immediate logistical and security needs in support of deployed military forces in the midst of an armed conflict. While one can argue that nations and militaries have availed themselves of this kind of private service from the time of Miles Standish and John Smith (both of whom were armed private security contractors),[4] the enormous growth in this kind of contracting, leading to the conundrums described above, began to occur only during and after the so-called first Gulf War of 1991, involving the effort by a US-led United Nations coalition force to repel an invasion of the nation of Kuwait by Iraq, then under the leadership of Saddam Hussein.

Needs for logistical support expand abruptly in wartime. This can present tremendous business opportunities in the private sector. In the early 1990s, companies that had previously specialized in large, nonmilitary logistical tasks and construction projects (like KBR and Halliburton) as well as established defense contractors (like British Aerospace and General Dynamics) amended their conventional business models from the exclusive pursuit of large, expensive government contracts to bidding on a range of smaller but more reliable and ongoing ventures. The web pages of large defense contractors now offer links to the new range of services which they may be counted upon to provide.

These opportunities also led to the founding of brand-new private corporate firms specifically addressed to these needs, who also began competing for newly available federal work. The best known of these are the new security firms, with names like the aforementioned Blackwater (since reorganized under different names), Triple Canopy, Aegis, and Dyncorp International. One of the first of these private security contractors was a South African firm with the innocuous name Executive Solutions, staffed by former South African defense force personnel from the apartheid era. It was employed in the early 1990s by the nation of Liberia to assist with national security and the protection of vital oil fields during an onset of civil war in the early 1990s. Attention was first drawn to the exponential growth of such firms, and to the numerous moral and legal anomalies to which they led, by Brookings Institution senior fellow Peter W. Singer in his book *Corporate Warriors* (2002).

Why does any military service need defense contractors? Can't military personnel themselves already do all the things that they are now hiring contractors to undertake?

Contractors present an interesting solution to a very difficult problem. Without doubt, military personnel can do, and in the past have done, the things that we now pay contractors to do. But there are some good reasons why we would not want them to continue doing so. The main reasons are cost and efficiency. In some cases, however, there is an unexpectedly urgent, but temporary, need for the acquisition of specialized subject-matter expertise that military personnel don't have and cannot quickly acquire otherwise.

In the past, soldiers (especially newly enlisted) might be assigned to perform menial tasks like KP duty, peeling potatoes, washing dishes, and mopping the floors in the mess hall. Or, as punishment for minor infractions, soldiers might be assigned to "police up" (i.e., clean and straighten up) barracks, bathroom latrines, or the parade or training grounds. Between these tasks and routine military drills, a conscript might complete his or her two years of military service without ever serving in an armed conflict. Thereafter, the conscript or recruit, having completed their term of military service, would be entitled to a fairly generous list of veteran's benefits, including university tuition assistance and perhaps healthcare at military hospitals. Re-enlistment, even with the same list of menial duties, might qualify them to receive additional benefits, including a pension at retirement if they had served a sufficient number of years. And in the meantime, if they were duly enlisted for a specified term of service and had performed satisfactorily, they were entitled to keep their positions even if (during a peacetime "drawdown" of troop strength) there was little in the way of specialized military work for them to do.

This is an expensive and extremely inflexible pattern of manpower use, with some additional disadvantages attendant upon trying to perform all manner of tasks using the military personnel one has at hand. The results can be comical. Readers of American print media, and film and television fans from many other countries, might recall cartoonist Mort Walker's comic strip *Beetle Bailey* (c. 1950–present), or films and television shows about military service like *Sergeant Bilko*. These amusing portrayals of comic military characters actually reveal the underlying structural problems with these earlier customs.

As his name suggests, for example, Bilko, a fictional US Army sergeant in charge of an army post motor pool, was a cigar-smoking, card-playing, whiskey-drinking rascal with a slightly seedy moral reputation. He was unreliable, lazy, and invariably engaged in schemes, scams, and financial cons, avoiding work at all costs, running an inefficient transportation system, and occasionally stealing spare tires, fuel, or mechanical parts to sell on the black market. Meanwhile, Beetle and his friends Zero, Killer, and the slightly pudgy and bespectacled Plato would be assigned to KP with Cookie, the burly, unshaven mess-hall cook, preparing meals of somewhat questionable gustatory provenance for the remaining hapless camp members, or else assigned by Sarge to perform some of the other menial chores (like latrine duty) described above.

While entertaining and perhaps reminiscent of the lighter side of the *esprit de corps* among military personnel from a bygone era, we now question the efficacy of this arrangement. To be blunt, we cannot afford Sergeant Bilko in the motor pool: we need more technically proficient and reliable mechanical service and transportation for our modern militaries than he and his cronies could ever provide. And Beetle, Zero, and Sarge should be out fighting the Taliban, not clowning around on some backwater stateside army post with worn-out, befuddled, and incompetent old "General Halftrack." Finally, when discussing the pros and cons of private military contracting with a wide range of military personnel newly returned from deployment, I often ask them in the same spirit if we *really* want Cookie back in the mess hall brewing up creamed dried beef on toast. The universal and unequivocal answer is no.

Today's logistical contractors do a vastly better job of supplying and caring for combat troops than did the real counterparts of these comic characters. The food is much better, for one thing, and if an "army travels on its stomach," as the old saying goes, today's army can travel a lot further, for a lot longer, than could past army personnel dependent upon their own soldiers to undertake these tasks. Most importantly, reliance on logistical contracting frees up additional military personnel to engage in their primary professional activity: training, preparing for, and fighting in their nation's wars.

Advocates of the private contracting system claim that this entire arrangement is both more efficient and less costly ("faster, better, cheaper" is their motto) than the system of internal military self-reliance that it replaces. It reduces the number of active-duty personnel needed to maintain combat readiness, for one thing. Amortized over what would have been the entire range of Bilko's, Sarge's, and Beetle's anticipated active-duty careers and subsequent retirement, this can amount to considerable savings. Private firms claim to be more flexible, and more able to respond quickly to changing circumstances, than the personnel in military organizations. Mobilizing personnel from peacetime to full combat readiness for war can take a national military several months, even years, while a private firm can hire (or fire) personnel quickly and deploy them where needed with remarkable rapidity.

Some of that flexibility stems from the ability of private firms to staff combat-theater operations with members of the local population, who are often desperately in need of work to survive the vagaries of a war-torn economy. This has the added advantage of giving the local economy a much-needed lift. Contractor personnel can also include "TCNs": "third country nationals" from relatively poor economies (e.g., the Philippines), from which workers with specifically needed skills who are eager for these lucrative jobs can quickly be recruited.

And finally, when the war is over, this entire process can be quickly reversed. Unlike postwar demobilization (which likewise takes national militaries months or years to achieve) the private firms can offer a final paycheck with severance pay, then decamp, and ship everyone and everything home. This can be done at a fraction of the military's cost, and with no residual, long-term employment or financial obligations due its private employees.

If this all works so well, what is the problem with increasing reliance on military contracting?

Contracting and outsourcing components of the wartime workload presents formidable administrative challenges, as well as ethical problems of transparency, accountability, oversight, and adequate control. Contractors themselves are "anomalous" personnel in the battle space, largely ungoverned (and largely unprotected) by either domestic or international law. This is problematic for all forms of contracting, but especially, as we shall see, for *armed private security contractors.*

From a strictly moral standpoint, we might immediately flag the issue of fair and equitable treatment of contract employees themselves. The final sentences from the preceding answer, in particular, ought to raise moral concerns. For example, even if well-paid while working under hazardous combat conditions, are the locals and TCNs being exploited as an expendable and inexpensive source of "sweatshop" labor? They receive no benefits, like healthcare or insurance, so what happens to them or to their families if they are gravely injured or killed on the job? Here we might be faced with the same ethical concerns that plague outsourcing and reliance on inexpensive labor sources in other industries, like textiles and manufacturing. Are the cost savings realized through exploitative labor practices—carried out among desperate and vulnerable populations, for whom any bargain, no matter how unsatisfactory or unfair, is likely better than none—*morally justifiable* from the standpoint of justice, fairness, and basic human rights?

Second, logistical contracting presents some ethical challenges in common with defense contracting back home. Just as with the procurement of new weapons systems, logistical contracting requires the military to first identify tasks, systems, supplies, and services that are required, then put these contracts out for bid. This publicizes the opportunity for competitive bidding among rival firms, before a contract for logistical services is awarded to any one of them. Keeping this whole process fair and equitable is as fraught with difficulty as any other mode of acquisitions or procurement. Military personnel have to be devoted to awarding, and then managing the contractors. Subsequent oversight and accountability for contract performance also falls upon the military.

Especially in midst of an armed conflict, it can be hard for even the most diligent military personnel to control the contracting process. The confusion, chaos, and enormous sums of money involved mean proliferating opportunities for fraud and corruption. Opportunities abound as well for innocent mistakes that lead to serious problems. At one point, midway through the controversial war in Iraq, there were some 1,800 private contracts awarded in one critical sector alone, overseen by a total of two military personnel who had been pressed into emergency service without prior training or experience as acquisitions and program management specialists.[5] This undermanning raises serious questions about whether such contracts could possibly be fairly bid out or adequately monitored for proper performance.

Finally, readers should note that I have limited my description of the procedural and ethical challenges, and putative benefits that might accrue from private contracting, to those stemming from increased "outsourcing" of *logistical* tasks by the military. We have not yet discussed private military or *armed security contracting* in detail. APSCs, as they are sometimes called, present a special range of moral and legal conundrums. We take these up at the conclusion of this chapter.

But first we should take note of some numbers. During the 2003–2010 Iraq war, at the height of personnel deployment in that region, there were roughly 160,000 military personnel, outnumbered by more than 210,000 private contractors. Almost all of these contractors were on the logistical side; only about 10,000–12,000 (around 5 percent) of these personnel were armed private security contractors, performing "inherently military" and security duties. Notably, that 5 percent minority accounts for a disproportionate majority of moral and legal dilemmas encountered in private contracting.

So there were more private contractors than military personnel. One might wonder, as did the newly incoming secretary of defense, Dr. Robert Gates, in 2006: "Who are all these people, and how did things get to this point?"[6] The answer is that this outsized reliance on private military contracting was driven mainly by fiscal expediency in the moment, rather than by any preconceived strategic plan. For reasons of cost, efficiency, and real-time response and flexibility, it proved easiest to outsource certain specific needs encountered while ramping up the fighting force to engage in the Iraq war. Outsourcing provided contractors with employment opportunities. As a result of these opportunities, the combat theater and "staging areas" were overwhelmed by eager personnel looking for jobs and profit. One disgusted former Navy SEAL and military journalist described Kuwait City, a staging area for entry into Iraq, as having quickly come to resemble the famous bar scene from the movie *Star Wars*, with all sorts of odd and fearsome characters sporting firearms, tattoos, and earrings wandering around looking for employment.[7]

As noted earlier, this becomes a perilous ethical proving ground. Against the chaotic backdrop of the "bar scene" in Kuwait, real personnel have to try to negotiate and solve pressing logistical and security problems on a rapid, real-time basis. Imagine the opportunities for cronyism, favoritism, bribery, graft, corruption, greed, and straightforward waste, fraud, incompetence, or abuse of public resources! Allegations swirled during this period (and have ever since) in both the Iraq and Afghan war theaters, suggesting that massive amounts of public funds were diverted, misappropriated, misspent, wasted, or simply embezzled. By most reckoning, there has never been adequate oversight or full accountability for these funds. As a general rule of thumb, the entire situation of private contracting (logistical as well as security) raises questions concerning adequate strategic planning and tactical oversight.

Aren't armed private security contractors simply mercenaries?

To their collective consternation, this is often what armed security contractors are labeled. This is problematic, not the least because serving as a mercenary is technically illegal under international law. According to the United Nations General Assembly Resolution 44/34 (December 4, 1989; as revised and ratified on October 20, 2001), technically known as the International Convention against the Recruitment, Use, Financing and Training of Mercenaries,[8] members and signatory states "are not to recruit, use, finance or train mercenaries," who in turn are defined (originally in Article 47 of Protocol Additions to the Geneva Conventions of August 12, 1949) as persons hired to provide security or to engage in warfare who are not citizens of the state at war, nor under the control of, nor sent in an official capacity as representative of another state, but are privately engaged in conflict strictly for personal financial gain.

Do armed private security contractors qualify as mercenaries under these definitions? That is a complicated matter, but the answer is probably not, despite the general public's tendency to label them, and to regard them, as such.

Some firms will argue, for example, that their employees are not engaged in acts of war on behalf of another nation in which they are not citizens, but are usually working (albeit indirectly) for their own governments. They are engaged in recognized interstate conflict, and are often providing security for personnel (like State Department or Foreign Office employees), or else guarding unarmed convoys of vital supplies transiting insecure areas. Other APSC firms will claim that their employees are engaged in peacekeeping, law enforcement, and simple training of local citizens for assuming security responsibilities themselves. And in all cases, whatever the motive of individuals joining the company, the company itself is engaged in supplying armed force for specific contracted purposes, under the auspices (and with at least the tacit approval) of both the host government and the company's domestic home government. In such an environment, these companies are fully subject to the laws and regulations of their home government.

Arguments about status, oversight, and legal jurisdiction go to the heart of the moral concerns about mercenaries and soldiers of fortune and the attempts to outlaw them. There is fundamental moral conflict of interest in serving as a mercenary. Wars, and the killing and destruction that they cause, are thought to be morally wrong, and so should be avoided insofar as possible. But the mercenary makes his or her living by fighting, and so, simply from interests of livelihood, must be committed at some level to desiring, rather than abhorring, war. In sum, the mercenary does not seem to fit Augustine's portrait of the morally justified combatant who engages in war reluctantly, or with regret.

The reputedly ruthless, "realist" Italian political philosopher Niccolò Machiavelli complained vociferously about this underlying conflict of interest and vigorously protested the widespread reliance of Italian city-states on mercenaries during his lifetime. Motivated by financial gain, he grumbled, mercenaries serve the best paymaster, rather than any discernable political purpose. They are prone to quit, to run from the conflict, or even to switch sides if the financial incentives change, or if the conflict itself becomes too risky in light of their compensation. Accordingly, Machiavelli argued, mercenaries are unprincipled and wholly unreliable. They interfere with, rather than advance, the goal of wielding political power and control with ruthless efficiency. Instead, they tend to promote chaos and political instability through the misalignment of their personal motives with the overarching political goals of state leaders. Although Machiavelli is portrayed as eschewing ethics in politics, one is hard-pressed to find a more telling moral critique of the practice of using mercenaries than his.

The question remains, does any of this fairly characterize the behavior of today's modern armed private security contractor or firm? Once again, most individuals and corporate representatives insist the answer is no. Their employees are highly trained professionals, often, indeed almost exclusively, recruited from the ranks of (former) active duty members of the military profession. Their professional values carry over into private practice in just the manner in which we would expect the professional values of public health officials to carry over with them when they subsequently engage in private healthcare practice. Habits and ideals of the profession of arms are not so easily laid aside—assuming they were present initially and properly inculcated.

But this confident assertion of professional continuity and reliability truly raises the question of whether professional values, grounded in public service and sacrifice, *can* carry over so easily into a corporate, for profit environment. And we should also be a bit uneasy about *what values* are, in fact, inculcated to carry over into that environment. This book is testimony to the fact that professional ethics in a military context remains vexed, contested, and not well understood by the public. If we take the problem of uncertainty and disagreement over professional ethics and military virtues out of its public context and place it instead in the private sector, we generate even more difficulties. For example, is it professional proficiency or core military virtues, like courage, that one requires in the private sector? Can these Clausewitzian military virtues survive intact in a corporate environment?

And what becomes of what Vice Admiral James Stockdale once described as the core military virtues of service, obedience, and sacrifice? In a famous essay written shortly after the conclusion of the Vietnam War, Stockdale argued that the virtues of military practice simply do not accord well with those of business and commerce.[9] They are different and fundamentally incompatible. Stockdale's devastating critique of the corporate-management philosophy of the Robert McNamara era might apply equally well to that of subsequent armed private military contracting.

Finally, the questions of the contextual compatibility and transference of "professional military virtues" into the private sector may be unrelated to the personal motivations of a great many individuals who go into this field. The designation of "mercenary" suggests their motives are all about wealth and financial gain. What we know about actual PMCs, however, belies this tidy, psychological reduction. Pulitzer Prize–winning journalist Steven Fainaru carefully followed the lives and deaths of four young former military enlisted personnel who subsequently joined a poorly organized and inadequately resourced private security firm in Iraq.[10] Very soon thereafter, all four were kidnapped and finally executed by al-Qaeda insurgents. Their remains were returned to their grieving families without the military honors that normally accompany active military personnel killed in action. In essence, their prior military service and their very lives (their families felt) were simply swept aside and forgotten.

And for what? Fainaru's interviews with the families and his acquaintance with the victims persuaded him that they were animated not so much by the prospect of financial gain as by psychological damage and moral injury sustained during active duty combat. Service in the Iraq war had transformed all four into "adrenaline junkies," unable to readjust after deployment to the normalcy of civilian life. They proved to be vulnerable to the seduction of employers who offered combat-area jobs (as well as being tempted by the good pay).

If it is the case (as old automobile bumper stickers from the Vietnam era used to warn) that "war is not good for children and other living things," it is likewise not good for combatants. Former Naval Academy colleagues and philosophers Shannon French and Nancy Sherman write movingly about the impact of these recent wars on returning wounded warriors. French focuses upon the historical and cultural rituals of "cleansing" and reintegration of warriors into their respective societies following the experience of combat, while Sherman compassionately analyzes numerous contemporary instances of the

impact of incomplete or inadequate reintegration for those trying to attempt it.[11]

Both sets of discussions bear poignantly on the problem that
Fainaru's profoundly troubling book highlights. It is not only
the increasingly recognized problem of post-traumatic stress
disorder (PTSD) and "warrior's heart," but also the addictive excitement and heightened sensitivity that participation
in combat produces that damage the normal coping capacities
of human beings exposed to it.[12] The very existence of armed
private security corporations provides, not simply alternative employment for returning veterans, but the temptation
through the prospect of lucrative financial gain for some to
re-engage in the most addictive and harmful (and dangerous)
elements of their former profession. It would be more salutary
for them instead to begin the difficult task of moving beyond
their wartime experiences toward successful reintegration into
civilian society following their military service.

What Is the principal ethical difficulty with employing private military security contractors?

Apart from the subtle psychological effects alluded to above,
perhaps the clearest example of the moral and legal problems
that can be occasioned through private security contracting
is the so-called Nisour Square massacre of September 2007.
There are many accounts of the details and circumstances,[13]
but a useful summary of the event that emphasizes its morally
salient features is a case study, "War Is Big Business," written
shortly after the event by military students, some of whom had
witnessed the event, as a class project in military ethics at the
Naval Postgraduate School.[14] In brief compass: armed guards
employed by the firm Blackwater Worldwide, while providing
transportation security for US State Department personnel on
official duty, opened fire on Iraqi citizens in Baghdad's Nisour
Square, for reasons that are still contested. Fourteen Iraqi civilians were killed and several others wounded in the gunfire.

All the local citizens who witnessed the tragedy claimed that only the Blackwater guards were armed and that no imminent threat was in evidence (a matter that the guards themselves disputed).

Because they were employees of an American-based firm legitimately employed for security purposes by a US government agency, the existing "Status of Forces" (SOF) agreement exempted the guards from prosecution under local domestic law. As civilians, however, they were not (at that time) subject to the provisions of the Uniform Code of Military Justice (under the UCMJ, military service personnel involved in such an incident would have been court-martialed, imprisoned, and tried by a military court). Four years after the incident, following several unsuccessful attempts to prosecute the case on the basis of investigation by US and Iraqi authorities, five of the Blackwater security guards were finally charged by a US grand jury with voluntary manslaughter and reckless discharge of a firearm. They were subsequently tried in a Utah court under the terms of the Military Extraterritorial Jurisdiction Act (MEJA). All were initially acquitted on the grounds of insufficient evidence. Further legal actions stemming from this case, ongoing at the time of this writing, eventually resulted in the convictions of four of the former Blackwater guards on murder and manslaughter charges.[15] Those convictions are currently under appeal.

The case perfectly illustrated what, at the time, were the legal perplexities of private military security contracting. Companies and their employees fell neatly between the seams of overlapping legal regimes, accountable to no one for their actions. The international law of armed conflict had no jurisdiction over noncombatants, who in any case were not engaged in a military conflict. Immune from local law by otherwise routine interstate agreements, the contractors were finally tried under a very tenuous extension of jurisdiction for MEJA, which was designed to hold civilians accountable in US courts for behavior abroad (such as child molestation) that would constitute an actionable offense under US domestic law. The length of time and ultimate geographical distances involved in pursuing the case made custody of evidence and securing the testimony of eyewitnesses difficult to ensure.

Morally speaking, most eyewitnesses and commentators felt that the behavior of the guards in these circumstances was reckless and negligent, and that they should have been held accountable and somehow punished for the deaths of the Iraqi civilians. The CEO of Blackwater, Eric Prince (who was himself a former US Navy SEAL), vigorously defended the integrity of his company and the behavior of the guards themselves. The guards, in turn, steadfastly maintained that they had believed themselves to be under attack from insurgents hidden in the crowd.

The case brought to the fore numerous earlier charges that employees of Blackwater routinely behaved with a kind of ruthless arrogance in the Iraqi theater. Blackwater employees were accused of frightening and angering local citizens, who simply viewed them as "Americans" or American soldiers, and did not differentiate their behavior from that of active duty military personnel. The problem highlighted the difficulties of having private security contractors operating in a war zone, hearkening back to the abduction and murder of four contractors early in the war, whose bodies, burned and mutilated, were hung from a bridge leading into the hotbed Sunni-insurgent city of Fallujah. That horrifying incident subsequently triggered one of the most violent and bloody battles of the war.

All of these issues of law, jurisdiction, and policy regarding private contracting are obviously complex and important. Some, like matters of legal jurisdiction and accountability, have subsequently been addressed. The UCMJ was amended to cover the activities of military security contractors under US employ and to permit local police to investigate crimes by contractors that occur within their precincts. Blackwater itself was

disbanded and its operations reorganized under other separate corporate names to provide security training, but would
never again (its founder vowed) engage in direct, military-like
operations of its own within a zone of combat.

One matter remains outstanding. Mr. Prince rightly claimed,
in defense of his company, that they had performed with enormous success and effectiveness in Iraq. Their job was principally to provide security to US State Department personnel.
For the duration of their contract, Prince observed, not one single State Department employee had had so much as a hair on
his or her head disturbed. Judged purely from a business perspective, this security detail was a highly successful operation,
when viewed from the standpoint of the satisfied client and
"customers." But the wider political price paid for this success
had been the defamation of American service personnel, who
were wrongly associated with the contractors' aggressive and
hostile behaviors. This, in turn, led to the further alienation of
a terrified local populace. But winning the hearts and minds
of that population had constituted the principal objective of
the Iraq war. In effect, Blackwater's very corporate success
threatened to undermine, and very possibly did undermine,
whatever moral authority and legitimacy remained for the
war itself. This aspect of the use of private contractors remains
unresolved. In fact, it has scarcely been addressed.

*Is there, nonetheless, a legitimate role for armed private
security contractors to play in armed conflict?*

Well-trained and professional military personnel in the employ
of private firms can (and almost certainly will) continue to
provide certain services that were once the domain of military
police (MPs) and Marine guards. Private security contractors may undertake "guard duty," and conduct routine police
patrols, on established and secure military posts and domestic or ally-based military installations. A consensus emerged
after the Blackwater incident that armed private contractors

ought never be deployed "outside the wire," that is, in areas of dispute and active armed conflict. Those areas, by law and by tradition, should be solely the province of professional, active-duty military personnel subject to full accountability under national and international law. This leaves unaddressed the question of how to provide security for logistical supply convoys operating in such areas. That relatively limited task can probably be returned to military control without proving to be an unsustainable burden on manpower requirements. These are among the policy and professional questions remaining to be ironed out.

Humanitarian operations are another arena where private security contractors might play a legitimate role. Foreign affairs expert Max Boot of the US Council on Foreign Relations first suggested that nations—and the United Nations—fund and hire private firms to undertake humanitarian military operations. Humanitarian military interventions (to which we will turn specifically in the next chapter) are operations that are designed to protect victims of social unrest, insurgency, or ethnically inspired, genocidal violence.[16] As members of the United Nations agonized over how best to cope with the civil unrest and ethnic violence in southern and western Sudan in 2006, Boot argued that a small force of Blackwater security guards could have brought matters to a quick and satisfactory resolution, at a fraction of the cost of deploying reluctant national militaries.

While this suggestion was quickly overshadowed (and seemingly discredited) by the Nisour Square incident, there is some anecdotal and conceptual evidence that some variation of this proposal just might work. Conceptually, humanitarian interventions are situations where the "vector" of corporate responsibility to protect the client aligns perfectly with the interests of the population at large, inasmuch as the potential victims of genocide are, in this instance, the "clients" of the private security firm. In the Iraq war scenarios, protecting the client was achieved in utter disregard for the welfare of the general population. In the case of humanitarian intervention, by contrast, the welfare of the general population, and their protection from harm by marauders bent on genocide, would constitute precisely the "corporate mission" for which success would be financially rewarded.[17]

It is the plight of nations and peoples like this, wracked by civil war and ethnic strife, to which we now turn. In all other contexts, the perils of outsourcing inherently military operations to private contractors should provoke concern and cautious oversight. If the military is a profession, characterized by the professional military virtues of honor, obedience, courage, public service, and sacrifice (as Vice Admiral Stockdale asserted), then it seems hard to understand how a corporate or business model could replace it. The military, as a profession, is characterized principally by public service. For businesses, the public interest is of principal concern only inasmuch as it affects profit and personal gain, which come first.

There is much of value that is at stake in this newly emergent challenge to ethics and the military profession. One can find similar arguments in cost-cutting proposals for replacing professionals like local police and firefighters with private contractors. These proposals could work and might even save (or at least appear to save) scarce public funds. Perhaps, in the aftermath of a global financial crisis and dwindling public resources in many nations, this is all we can afford.

But one might reasonably wonder whether such private contractors would do what professional first responders have done. Would private contractors have unflinchingly pushed themselves up the stairs of the World Trade Center to rescue victims of 9/11? Could we simply pay contractors to perform the heroic feats that life-saving and security-providing professionals accomplish in the spirit of public service? Something important is in danger of being lost if we assume that a personal commitment to selfless public service is merely another commodity for hire. This concluding observation is not intended to settle the question, but precisely the opposite: to raise it as an example of the profound challenges to military and professional ethics that will emerge in the remaining chapters of this book.

Notes

1. See George Lucas, *Anthropologists in Arms: The Ethics of Military Anthropology* (Lanham, MD: AltaMira Press, 2009).
2. A glance at the extant literature shows that, apart from commentaries on General (President) Eisenhower's phrase "military-industrial complex," there are no formal histories of the origins and growth of defense contracting. Most mentions of this phrase are instead faintly polemical, as referring to an incipient evil or malevolent force, rather than objective studies of the historical rise of these firms. Most of the academic and historical attention has gone instead to the relatively recent phenomenon of private military contracting. But see http://www.militaryindustrialcomplex.com/what-is-the-military-industrial-complex.asp for an account of the former.
3. An excellent if sobering account of the myriad moral dilemmas and serious tests of character that arise in defense weapons systems and procurement in such firms can be found in the analysis of this complex labyrinth by one of the United States' most senior and experienced defense industry military liaisons, Major General Robert Latiff, US Air Force (retired): "Ethical Issues in Defense Systems Acquisitions," in *The Routledge Handbook of Military Ethics*, ed. George Lucas (New York: Routledge, 2015), 209–219.
4. See Sarah Percy, *Mercenaries. The History of a Norm in International Relations* (Oxford: Oxford University Press, 2007). I do not include some of the most famous of the Spanish conquistadors two centuries earlier only because a majority if not all of these famous military explorers were technically on "active duty" directly in the service of the King, as opposed to "retired" from active duty and/or private employed, as were both Smith and Standish.
5. See the account in Jeffrey D. McCausland, *Developing Strategic Leaders for the 21st Century* (Carlisle, PA: Strategic Studies Institute Press, 2008): http://www.au.af.mil/au/awc/awcgate/ssi/devel_strat_ldrs.pdf.
6. Anecdotal at the time; recorded subsequently in his memoirs: Robert M. Gates, *Duty: Memoirs of a Secretary at War* (New York: Alfred A. Knopf, 2014).

7. Dick Couch, *The Sheriff of Ramadi* (Annapolis, MD: Naval Institute Press, 2008).
8. http://legal.un.org/avl/ha/icruftm/icruftm.html.
9. James Stockdale, "Military Ethics Is Not at Home with Business Values," in *A Vietnam Experience: Ten Years of Reflection* (Stanford, CA: Hoover Institution Press, 1984), 110–112.
10. Steven Fainaru, *Big Boy Rules: America's Mercenaries Fighting in Iraq* (Philadelphia, PA: DaCapo Press, 2008).
11. Shannon E. French, *Code of the Warrior* (Lanham, MD: Rowman & Littlefield, 2004); Nancy Sherman, *Stoic Warriors* (Cambridge: Cambridge University Press, 2005). Sherman, who turned to these topics in earnest after serving two years as a guest professor at the US Naval Academy in 1997–1999, has since written two additional books on these tragic and complex issues: *The Untold War: Inside the Hearts, Minds, and Souls of Our Soldiers* (New York: Norton, 2011) and *Afterwar: Healing the Moral Wounds of Our Soldiers* (New York: Oxford University Press, 2015).
12. John Glenn Gray likewise described this strange affection for the heightened sensibilities of combat involvement in his study of returning World War II warriors in his famous book *The Warriors* (New York: Harper & Row, 1954). Jonathan Shay touches on this phenomenon in passing in his analysis of PTSD in his likewise-famed work, *Achilles in Vietnam: Combat Trauma and the Undoing of Character* (New York: Atheneum, 1994).
13. E.g., a subsequent Reuters account of the event and subsequent trials: http://www.reuters.com/article/2013/10/17/us-usa-crime-blackwater-idUSBRE99G1A320131017. See also coverage in the *Washington Post*: http://www.washingtonpost.com/world/national-security/new-charges-brought-against-former-blackwater-guards-in-baghdad-shooting/2013/10/17/9307b562-3759-11e3-8a0e-4e2cf80831fc_story.html.
14. LT Matt Courtney, LT Sean Maloney, LCDR William Pugh, and LCDR Andrew J. McFarland, USN, and Mr. Joseph Prisella, DOD/USN (Patuxent River Naval Air Station, MD), "War Is Big Business," in *Case Studies in Ethics for Military Leaders*, ed. George Lucas and W. Rick Rubel, 3rd ed. (New York: Pearson Publishers, 2010): pp. 53–56.
15. See Spencer S. Hsu, Victoria St. Martin, and Keith L. Alexander, "Four Blackwater Guards Found Guilty in 2007 Iraq Shootings of 31 Unarmed Civilians," *The Washington Post* (14 October, 2014): https://www.washingtonpost.com/world/national-security/

verdict-expected-in-blackwater-shooting-case/2014/10/22/5a48825
8-59fc-11e4-bd61-346aee66ba29_story.html.

16. Max Boot, "Send in the Mercenaries: Darfur Needs Someone to Stop the Bloodshed, Not More Empty UN Promises!" Council on Foreign Relations, http://www.cfr.org/publication/10798/send_in_the_ mercenaries.html; "Accept the Blackwater Mercenaries!" http://www. cfr.org/security-contractors/accept-blackwater-mercenaries/p14359; see also James Pattison, "The Principled Case for Employing Private Military and Security Companies in Humanitarian Interventions and Peacekeeping Operations," January 29, 2010. Available at SSRN: http://ssrn.com/abstract=1544463.

17. The anecdotal, historical evidence comes from the performance on such a mission by one of the first distinct private security firms, South African–based Executive Solutions. Composed of former South African security forces disbanded by President Nelson Mandela during the dismantling of apartheid in South Africa itself, the company was subsequently hired by the government of Angola to provide security and stability in the aftermath of a hotly contested election (whose results an insurgent group, UNITA, refused to accept). The firm quickly re-established law and order, trained the local militia, defeated UNITA, protected the population, and guarded Angola's civil infrastructure (including its valuable oil fields) from insurgent attacks. In the initial confusion regarding the use of "mercenaries" by the Angolan government, however, these efforts were denounced and the company forced to withdraw. Civil unrest quickly resumed thereafter. Perhaps, in hindsight, this was a moralistic or legalistic rush to judgment, based upon an underlying conceptual confusion and moral uncertainty about the mercenary problem, rather than a wise and prudent policy decision for the people of Angola.

Further Reading

Baker, Dean-Peter. *Just Warriors, Inc.: The Ethics of Privatized Force.* London: Continuum, 2011.

Fainaru, Steve. *Big Boy Rules: America's Mercenaries Fighting in Iraq.* Philadelphia, PA: DaCapo, 2008.

Pattison, James. *The Morality of Private War: The Challenge of Private Military and Security Companies.* Oxford: Oxford University Press, 2014.

Percy, Sarah. *Mercenaries: The History of a Norm in International Relations.* Oxford: Oxford University Press, 2007.

Scahill, Jeremy. *Blackwater: The Rise of the World's Most Powerful Mercenary Army.* New York: Nation Books, 2007.

Singer, P. W. *Corporate Warriors: The Rise of the Privatized Military Industry.* Rev. edition. Ithaca, NY: Cornell University Press, 2008.

Tagarev, Todor, ed. *Building Integrity and Reducing Corruption in Defence: A Compendium of Best Practices.* Geneva: NATO/Geneva Center for the Democratic Control of Armed Forces, 2010.

7

MILITARY INTERVENTIONS FOR HUMANITARIAN RELIEF

What is "humanitarian military intervention"?

Humanitarian interventions (HI) are among the list of military operations other than war, discussed briefly in chapter 5. As the name implies, the goal here is strictly to provide assistance to victims of natural tragedy or political crisis, quite devoid (presumably) of any political interests or payback. Civilian populations are sometimes the direct target of hostilities intended either to drive them out from some geographical area or to exterminate them entirely ("ethnic cleansing"). In such circumstances, when it appears highly likely that destruction, immiseration, and widespread death are imminent, these vulnerable victims may need protection.

Armed interventions to prevent such atrocities are carried out by the military forces of nations that are sufficiently concerned to order their troops to intervene. Humanitarian crises in which military interventions were called for have occurred during the past two decades in Rwanda, in the Darfur region of Sudan, in Syria, as well as in Somalia, provinces of the former Yugoslavia (Bosnia, Croatia, Kosovo), Haiti, and Libya. In some cases, these calls met with responses that were moderately successful (Bosnia, Croatia, Haiti), while in other instances the calls largely went unmet (Sudan, Rwanda, Syria) or ultimately failed (Somalia, Libya).

Military interventions undertaken allegedly for humanitarian purposes have taken place for centuries.[1] Often, however, observers harbored suspicions that the intervening military forces were using humanitarian concerns to disguise the hidden political objectives of the intervening state. Often in past centuries, the intervening state actually wanted to take advantage of the ensuing chaos to establish control of, or subsequently lay claim to, territory or resources encompassed within the zone of impending humanitarian tragedy. Because of this, humanitarian intervention has traditionally been viewed with suspicion in classical and contemporary just war theory and international law, where such activities are thought to disguise self-interested motives and threaten the territorial integrity of otherwise sovereign nation-states.[2]

Humanitarian military intervention, on whatever motive or pretext, does assuredly threaten the centuries-old Westphalian model of state relations (as outlined in chapters 2 and 4), in that it necessarily involves a violation of sovereignty by the intervening nation or nations. Such interventions are not deemed hostile acts of armed aggression, however, since they are (purportedly) carried out for humanitarian motives, rather than as a direct expression of the political interests of the intervening state. But this account is question-begging, if it is simultaneously alleged that ulterior (and less morally worthy) state interests constitute the real, underlying motivations for such interventions.

To escape this circularity, let's put the question this way: if it is really the case that no vital state interests are at stake, why (if ever) would one nation risk its own military forces to intervene in the affairs of another? Presumably, under such conditions, a state would do so only if

(1) Compelled by treaty;
(2) Asked (or ordered?) to do so by some wider international coalition of states, morally concerned to prevent a humanitarian disaster; or finally

(3) The leaders and population of the intervening state were sufficiently concerned with the impending moral tragedy (e.g., massacre or genocide) so as to willingly take upon themselves *the moral duty* to intervene with their own military forces in order to prevent the threatened tragedy from occurring.

Cases of (1) are almost nonexistent. Treaty obligations seldom directly address the internal affairs of their signatories, let alone authorize, or require, external intervention by one signatory in the internal affairs of another. Furthermore, what occasions HI is almost always a function of internal "state failure" or political collapse. Thus, the state named in any relevant treaty would be an evanescent entity rather than the actual party to the pact. This would nullify any treaty's contractual force.

Cases of (2) and (3), however, do occur. The defining motives for (2) and (3) also pose a formidable challenge to realist-based theories that prevail in the academic discussions of international relations. Remember that "realists" deny the validity of any motives other than self-interest as the ground of state policy. From that perspective, all HI that does not involve disguised (though ultimately discernable) self-interests of the intervening states must necessarily represent confused and incoherent (and therefore unwise) state policy.

Such criticisms could very well prove valid in some instances. However, this position is caught in the vicious circularity mentioned earlier. We cannot argue that authentic (i.e., non-self-interested) interventions never take place by assuming what we are trying to prove (i.e., that states only act on self-interest). If history offers examples of humanitarian interventions where no ulterior motive can be found, we settle nothing by dismissing these as "mistakes" after having stipulated that states only act out of self-interest.

Conceptually, as well as politically and practically, humanitarian interventions are therefore deeply problematic for the international community. When one state intervenes in a humanitarian crisis in another state, it threatens the underlying international order based on state sovereignty. Judged according to prevailing realist doctrine, humanitarian intervention is either suspect or unwise and therefore must be avoided. Yet such judgments seem tangential to brute facts when large numbers of people are suffering. There have been helpless victims for whom nothing less than military intervention will suffice. Abstract theoretical objections from the field of international relations are beside the point.

In reality, the motives for humanitarian military intervention are often mixed. A threatened genocide or destructive civil war in one nation may provoke acute concerns among others, both for purely humanitarian reasons and because of larger geopolitical consequences. One country might want to intervene in a crisis within its neighbor's border because it hopes to rescue people from atrocities, but at the same time because it fears the political and economic instability that will follow from large numbers of refugees trying to flee the massacre.

India, for example, sent its military forces to intervene in an ongoing massacre in what was East Pakistan in 1971, in order to stop the persecution and slaughter of native Bengalis by the military leadership of West Pakistan. The Indian government defended its decision based on the moral abhorrence of the atrocities being committed, and their moral outrage at West Pakistan was widely shared within the larger international community. But India was also compelled to intervene militarily in order to stem the wave of some 10 million Bengali refugees who fled across the border into India, generating an enormous economic and humanitarian burden.

A similar set of mixed circumstances in 1978 prompted Tanzania's president at the time, Julius Nyerere, to send his military forces into neighboring Uganda. Nyerere was thwarting an attempted attack on Tanzania by Ugandan troops, but he also meant to put a stop to the persecution,

oppression, and murder of Ugandan citizens under the reckless and ruthless internal policies of the infamous Ugandan
dictator, Idi Amin.

*It would seem that any war that is not strictly defensive could
be construed as a humanitarian intervention. Would Vietnam
count? Would World War II count?*

Legitimate and urgent HIs certainly qualify as morally justifiable examples of nondefensive use of military force. In some
cases, the need can be so obvious, urgent, and morally compelling as to obscure the fact that, without UN Security Council
authorization, such interventions would be classified as illegal
(no matter how well intended they might be).

Vietnam has long been portrayed by supporters as an
example of such a situation. The justification for US military
intervention, without UN authorization, was allegedly to
prevent a bloodbath in the south. This was the predicted outcome if Viet Cong insurgents (with military assistance from
North Vietnam) otherwise succeeded in overthrowing South
Vietnam's government and establishing a communist regime
in its stead.

While the resulting eight-year war was itself something
of a bloodbath, the eventual triumph of North Vietnam and
subsequent reunification of the country under communist rule
did not produce the anticipated and threatened massacre of
political adversaries. A flood of political refugees, to be sure,
steadily emigrated from the new nation during the ensuing
decade. But ironically, it was the communist rule of neighboring Cambodia under the Pol Pot regime that subsequently
produced the kind of massive "killing fields" that would constitute a case for humanitarian intervention. And, even more
ironically, it was the newly united nation of Vietnam that
finally carried out the intervention (once again for allegedly
humanitarian motives, but almost certainly also to stem the
flood of Cambodian refugees).

World War II, in hindsight, put an end to perhaps the most shocking and extensive genocide known in history, the Holocaust. But it would be somewhat hypocritical, as well as historically counterfactual, to label that war a humanitarian intervention. European nations were conquered by the Germans, leaving their resistance forces to join with Great Britain to fight what was almost certainly a war of straightforward self-defense in response to German aggression. The United States was petitioned frequently to help put a stop to the Holocaust prior to its decision to enter the war on the Allied side, but refrained from doing so. The final decision by the United States to join the allied coalition was driven by a number of other political factors, including the Japanese attack on Pearl Harbor (December 7, 1941) and cannot realistically be described, let alone credited, as having been carried out for humanitarian motives. The lesson taken by its victors and survivors from the Holocaust was, rather, that humanitarian considerations alone seldom motivate other nations to come to one's aid. This is a point Michael Walzer initially made with perceptible resentment in the initial edition of his great work (1977).

It could be tempting to go back and revise military history to lessen the moral burden or ambiguity of nations and governments that have gone to war (or failed to do so when asked for aid), by reclassifying many past wars, like the US war in Vietnam, as humanitarian interventions. It seems unlikely that much of genuine value or historical accuracy would result from this. Instead, perhaps it would be better to realize from these instances just how confusing and mixed the motives for waging war can be, and how difficult it might be at the time to discern morally legitimate motives (such as humanitarian concern for the welfare of victims of genocide) from those responding to what the 19th-century English philosopher John Stuart Mill eloquently condemned as "morally shabby" motives (i.e., interventions grounded only in the narrowest conception of national self-interest).[3]

Calls for humanitarian intervention appear in the news regularly nowadays. Why has humanitarian intervention come to play such a dominant role in recent international relations?

Despite its long history as a secondary purpose for the use of military force, HI came to play an increasingly dominant role in international relations, ironically, after the end of the Cold War and the fall of the Berlin Wall in Western Europe in 1989. Symbolically, this termination of superpower rivalry was supposed to lead, at long last, to a period of unprecedented peace and prosperity throughout the world (although no one seems to have informed the nations of the Pacific Rim of this expectation).

Instead, the withdrawal of political control in many parts of the globe unleashed pent-up animosities that burst forth into some of the cruelest ethnic violence witnessed since the Holocaust itself. Whole populations were subject to attack, as in Rwanda and Bosnia, solely on the basis of their race, culture, or religious beliefs. These conflicts were exacerbated by state failure or state collapse, as when Somalia found itself unable in 1992 to control the rival warlords who vied for supremacy within a virtually nonexistent framework of national order.[4]

The rise of intrastate conflicts and ethnic violence inevitably follows closely behind the decline of quasi-imperial national power, according to one grand theory. A similar rise in the incidence of vicious and incessant regional conflicts attended the fall of the Roman Empire in Western Europe. The withdrawal of any authority, no matter how legitimate or morally illegitimate it may be, opens the opportunity for aggrieved populations to exact vengeance on their closest neighbors. The present tragedy in Syria is unfolding in this manner. But why is this?

Sometimes, as in present-day Syria, fierce political rivals have only been united in chafing against the yoke of authoritarian leadership. Sometimes that leadership has actively suppressed factional violence (as the communist dictator, Tito, did so successfully throughout the Yugoslav federation during his lifetime). When the authority weakens (or, when the strong leader dies), those suppressed grievances resurface. Political philosophers like Plato had opined that "the state is man writ large," while the German philosopher Hegel had, in effect, replied that the state is, somewhat more romantically, "the family writ large." What is revealed when authoritarian power relinquishes central control over many of these states, however, is that many of these "individuals" are pathological or that their "families" are discovered to be severely dysfunctional.

According to widely discussed theories about imperial decline, the decay of any strong international system of order (such as the superpower nuclear rivalry of the Cold War era) unleashes chaos and confusion, rather than leading to peace and harmony. This theory is often raised in connection with what appears to be the waning of unilateral US "hegemony" in the present decade, as prognosticators try to anticipate the eventual outcome of this political transformation.[5] With the breakup of the former Soviet Union, unquestionably, came the opportunity for long-repressed aspirations and hostilities among former Soviet states, especially in Central Asia. These former "socialist republics" not only declared their independence from the Russian Federation but also began to target one another over offenses of religion or former religious persecution. At the same time, extremist religious and ethnic groups now had the chance to spread that same poisonous ideology throughout the world.

Whatever their exact cause, there is no doubt that a rash of humanitarian crises and disasters followed the putative end of the Cold War and dominated the decade just prior to the onset of the "global war on terror" following 9/11. Humanitarian disasters, ranging from Darfur (Sudan) to Libya and Syria, continue to plague the international community at this writing. It is helpful to divide the occurrence, and the understanding, of these tragedies into three broad epochs or "waves" of crisis and concern.

The *first wave* of HI, prior to 1990, was marked by the pre-dominance of strategic and defensive wars, the infrequent occurrence of HI, the prevalence of self-interested motives, and (hence) skepticism about any "humanitarian" justifications for armed conflict. During the *second wave* at the end of the last century, however, legitimate humanitarian interventions (or crises that called for them) became more frequent. This era began with the US military intervention in Somalia. At that historical moment, following the presumed end of the Cold War, both the need for, and conventional uses of, national military forces seemed to have ended. World leaders called for a drawdown of conventional armies, as well as for the disbanding of old, Cold War military alliances like NATO. But what transpired instead was that those alliances and their military forces found themselves quickly caught up in the new cycle of regional and ethnic violence.

In the *third and present wave*, the incidence of these humanitarian crises have abated somewhat, and concern regarding them has been somewhat eclipsed by increased concern over terrorism. At the same time, however, this third period has given rise to a worldwide movement to improve international understanding and to carve out procedures for responding to humanitarian crises when they do arise. This new movement is known as "the responsibility to protect."[6]

Who is responsible for intervening when a humanitarian crisis threatens?

In the 1990s, it was widely but mistakenly assumed that the United Nations Genocide Convention of 1948 contained explicit provisions obligating states to use military force, if necessary, to prevent acts of genocide. The Convention actually contained no such provisions. It did not even specify a procedure for defining genocide, let alone a way to allocate responsibility for putting a stop to it. Instead, that Convention obligated signatory states to refrain from acts of genocide themselves and to refuse political sanctuary to fugitives (such as former Nazi leaders) who might seek asylum in their countries. Signatory states agreed instead to identify and extradite such perpetrators of genocide for criminal prosecution.

As valuable and as historically significant as this Genocide Convention was in responding to the unimaginable horrors of the World War II Holocaust, its provisions proved utterly irrelevant in attempting to put a halt to the wave of humanitarian crises that ensued during the 1990s and beyond. Responsibility or authority (permission) to intervene militarily devolved, accordingly, either to

(1) Nations or coalitions whose own political interests seemed somehow threatened; or to
(2) Those with some historical attachment or connection to the nation or region in question (e.g., as a result of former colonial ties).

In the absence of either kind of connection, the task was left to those nations whose own leaders or citizens evinced sufficient moral concern for the welfare of victims to be willing, in effect, to volunteer to undertake the requisite humanitarian mission.

Thus, even though humanitarian operations were undertaken, they were haphazard. Some good was done: the United States and allies "stepped up" during a politically induced famine in Somalia in 1992; a few countries were able to "provide comfort" in Haiti in 1994; an Australian-led coalition helped stem ethnic violence in East Timor in 1999. But these responses were ad hoc and somewhat arbitrary, and proved inadequate for addressing all the crises that ensued during, and after, that troubled decade. A UN-led peacekeeping force, for example, failed miserably on multiple occasions to end a Serbian-backed policy of "ethnic cleansing" in Bosnia and Herzegovina and was finally supplanted by a more organized, well-led, and properly resourced coalition of forces from NATO nations.

Meanwhile, in the spring of 1994, the nation of Rwanda experienced what was undoubtedly the worst single case of genocide since the Holocaust. Mobs of angry, marauding ethnic Hutus (who comprised the large majority of Rwanda's population) exacted terrible revenge for decades of what they believed was political exclusion that had contributed to their abject poverty. The mobs, armed largely with machetes rather than firearms, beset members of the ethnic Tutsi minority (and anyone else who attempted to support or protect them), massacring nearly one million people in a period of only 100 days. This occurred despite the presence of a small international peacekeeping force that had been sent by the United Nations specifically to deter this terrible tragedy.

This small and wholly inadequate UN force was commanded by an able and committed Canadian Defense Force general, but staffed largely with a small contingent of 2,000 largely untrained and seriously underequipped troops. Its abject failure to protect Rwanda citizens from attack prompted agonized soul searching on the part of international diplomats and senior UN officials, many of whom were blamed (or blamed themselves) for this tragic failure. Their subsequent recognition of the procedural inadequacies of existing legislation and institutions to cope with the new forms of humanitarian crises led to the movement cited above: "the responsibility to protect." This new international effort was dedicated to ensuring that such tragic occurrences would never again go unchallenged.

What is the "responsibility to protect"?

The "responsibility to protect" (R2P, or RtoP) is the name for the formal institutional response during the third and present wave of concern to avoid or prevent humanitarian crises of the sort that ravaged Rwanda (and that threatened more recently to ravage the populations of the Darfur region in Sudan).

Specifically, R2P refers to a body of proposals and recommended institutional arrangements adopted by the United

Nations in 2005. It was the product of sustained diplomatic pressure brought to bear initially in 2001 by an ad hoc international coalition of concerned diplomats, led by the former Australian ambassador-at-large Gareth Evans. Begun as an assembly of "eminent persons" meeting under the auspices of the Canadian government in Canada, Evans and members of the "Crisis Group" (composed of former UN staffers headquartered in Brussels, Belgium) began to draft legislation that would clarify the responsibility of UN member nations to act more decisively to intervene when there was compelling evidence that a humanitarian crisis was either pending or already in progress. After several revisions and much discussion, the revised document was adopted unanimously at the 2005 World Summit of the United Nations.[7]

This body of legislation and procedural recommendations represents an advance over the disorganized situation during the second wave of HI. It clarifies when and how the international community should convene, recognize, and assign responsibility for military intervention when diplomacy and sanctions have failed to avert the crisis. It also attempts to clarify the nature and scope of that military intervention, how it should be managed, and most importantly, how it should be understood.

In particular, the legislation attempts to do what the UN Genocide Convention of 1948 clearly did not: to establish armed intervention, when it appears absolutely necessary, as a *duty of the international community* as a whole, rather than as an option for which permission may be granted. The rhetoric of the document emphasizes the moral duty of bystander nations to come to the aid of vulnerable victims of violence, rather than to stand by helplessly as witnesses to the tragedy.

The document's rhetoric, however, remains highly state-centric in its conception. It does not, in other words, resolve the fundamental tension between state sovereignty and this new duty to override it. R2P calls for overriding national sovereignty whenever this seems necessary for the protection of basic human rights. The concept of state sovereignty, however, has been paramount and sacrosanct in international relations ever since the Treaty of Westphalia in 1648, in which (as we saw) this compromise had itself been formulated precisely in order to put an end to centuries of relentless religious warfare in Europe. Countries are understood to have the right to do as they see fit within their own borders.

How, then, can other countries be said to have a duty that violates such sovereignty? One answer is to portray state sovereignty as a *right* that comes with attendant *duties*. If a nation-state is not fulfilling its duties to its own people, its right to sovereignty is compromised. That seems eminently reasonable, but what exactly are a nation's duties to its people?

The R2P document attempts to define the duties that accompany the right of sovereignty, but it equivocates on the pivotal issue. It does not revoke the political right (in the name of sovereignty) to do "unlimited wrong" within the borders of one's sovereign territory (such as occurred in Uganda, and in Sudan prior to its partitioning). And it fails to clarify exactly how other sovereign nations and their citizens are supposed to act in specific instances to protect the individual rights of their neighbors who are themselves the *victims* of these political atrocities carried out under the cloak of sovereignty. Thus, the document unfortunately preserves, rather than addresses, the underlying tensions that give rise to many of these humanitarian disasters.

Those underlying tensions stem, in turn, from a profound but stubbornly unacknowledged flaw in the entire foundation of international law itself. Unlike domestic law, international law attempts to define the basic rights of *two* fundamentally distinct and unlike entities, whose interests (especially during a humanitarian crisis) are at odds with one another: ordinary ("biological") *individuals,* on the one hand, and *nation-states* on the other, each of which is itself treated like an "individual" under the law.

Some bodies of international law address the basic human rights of individuals, while others stress the rights of states.

In many cases, owing to the primacy of state sovereignty, the rights of states invariably trump individual human rights, even the rights of their own citizens. Meanwhile, bodies of legislation addressed directly toward the welfare of "real" individuals (such as the 1948 UN Declaration of Human Rights, and subsequent international human rights law emanating from the International Committee of the Red Cross, for example) are often at odds with the authority of formal international treaties and their conceptions of the rights of states.

R2P was drafted entirely by diplomats and politicians with, at best, one foot in each camp (so to speak). The drafters tried to have it both ways: preserving the underlying priority of state sovereignty at the same time they endorsed individual rights. The drafters remained wedded to the underlying Westphalian paradigm of international relations and exhibited a vested interest in protecting the existing status of states, especially with respect to state sovereignty. No dissenting voices, nor advocates of other conceptual approaches toward international law itself, were invited or permitted to contribute. And this remains a deep, nearly fatal flaw with this entire movement. These flaws were glaringly evident in disastrous attempts to invoke and apply R2P during the Arab Spring uprisings in 2011, particularly in Libya. They have also proven utterly ineffective in addressing the ongoing humanitarian crisis stemming from the current civil war in Syria that began in 2013.

From the perspective of the topic of this book, finally, R2P suffers from its complete and utter lack of representation of the points of view, and of the previous experiences, of military personnel (past and present). Military personnel from many nations were the "first responders" during the humanitarian crises of the second wave. Their experiences and their reflection on how to improve (or to understand the inherent limitations of) *military* interventions carried out for humanitarian purposes[8] are noticeably absent in this legislation.

Can we justifiably require members of a nation's self-defense force to serve in HI?

Here is yet another glaring problem, not even addressed in R2P legislation, but one of the enduring perplexities of the second wave of HI.

Martin L. Cook, a military ethicist now at the US Naval War College (Newport, RI), captured the dilemma perfectly in a widely read lecture and subsequent published essay for military audiences in the immediate aftermath of the second wave. The title of the presentation was "Why Serve the State?"[9] In proposing to examine "the moral foundations of military service," Cook's article outlined an equally fundamental tension in the understanding of military service that we have likewise wrestled with in this book.

Are military personnel merely servants of their respective nations, called upon precisely to defend it and its interests as ordered? If so, it does not seem any part of that arrangement (nor of the implied contract tacit within it, between military service personnel and their state) that they should be obliged to serve or protect other, nonaligned or foreign states and their populations, especially when this may involve the loss of their own lives.

This problem was inherent in the ambivalent attitude of the 90–100 Belgian soldiers deployed as part of Canadian Defense Force General Romeo Dallaire's UNAMIR military contingent in Rwanda.[10] It was evident in the final unwillingness of "DutchBat," the battalion of 173 Dutch soldiers deployed to defend Srebrenica from the Serbian army in 1995, to intervene to save thousands of Muslim men and boys in the city from eventual slaughter at the hands of the Serbs.[11] It has even led on a few occasions to the refusal of individuals from national militaries to accept delegation to serve in UN military missions, even under threat of court-martial and imprisonment.[12] The reasons cited by dissidents and critics of HI are never individual cowardice, but matters of basic principle concerning the fundamental meaning of "national self-defense" as the basis for military service. It is extremely unclear in this customary understanding of military service whether states that recruit, equip, and train military forces ostensibly for the stated purpose of providing for their nation's self-defense have *any right whatsoever* to compel their individual military service personnel to serve in international peacekeeping and stability operations (as HI is now often termed) unless that individual explicitly volunteers to do so.

On the other hand, Cook notices that the military profession also encompasses a more universal, non-state-centered conception of selfless service and sacrifice: not for the sake of "nations" per se, but *in defense of the basic human rights of their individual citizens*. This constitutes, he argues, the most valid, and also the most inspiring, moral justification for military service, as it likewise does for the profession of arms itself. This alternative understanding of military service makes sense of, and justifies, humanitarian interventions, but does so at the expense of unwavering respect for the sovereignty of the state, which no longer exercises sole compulsory authority over even its own military personnel (the second, aforementioned tension implicit in HI, but left unaddressed in the R2P legislation).

Individual military service in the midst of a humanitarian crisis constitutes a very noble and morally worthy calling. It expresses the moral ideals we found at the heart of justifications for use of deadly force for any purpose whatever, by the likes of St. Augustine and the Buddha. The defense of others (*not* of oneself), even to the point of self-sacrifice (as we discovered in chapter 4), is universally recognized as the most morally praiseworthy of individual acts in any and every culture and religion. *Military personnel called to this service, however, operate under a moral mandate that is no longer the exclusive province of their own state.* There have been specific cases, such as that of US Army Captain Lawrence Rockwood in Haiti in 1994 that revealed the depth of the underlying unresolved paradoxes of military service, obedience to orders, and loyalty to the larger mission in the midst of a humanitarian crisis.[13]

In sum, the intermittent but urgent need for humanitarian military interventions threatens to erode the concept of national sovereignty. Humanitarian interventions also problematize the reigning state-centric conceptual and political foundations underlying current international law itself. Meanwhile, military service during such an intervention goes to the heart of the terms of the implied or implicit contract between soldiers and the state, as Cook observes, and continues to pose a profound challenge to a full and complete understanding of the demands of professional ethics inherent in military service itself.

Might we avoid these problems by instead hiring and paying armed private security contractors to undertake these missions, rather than continuing to rely on national military forces?

As discussed in the previous chapter, humanitarian missions might constitute an acceptable use of private security firms, as well as offering a practical solution to some of the problems that have plagued prior humanitarian military interventions. As we noted in the previous chapter, moreover, some have proposed this as an ethically sound use of private security contractors, while the CEOs of private security firms themselves have expressed willingness, even eagerness, to take over such missions if invited to do so.

Others, however, who remain uneasy with the basic idea of armed private military contractors (like former chairman of the US Joint Chiefs of Staff, Army General Robert Shelton), have proposed an alternative solution. General Shelton, testifying before the US Congress near the end of his term in the late 1990s, was asked to address the problems encountered when undertaking humanitarian military missions. He proposed the creation of a special international force, composed entirely of volunteers drawn from participating national militaries. Unlike the current "blue helmet" UN forces, however, such volunteers might perhaps be placed directly under UN command, with the General Assembly or perhaps the Security

Council directly delegated and authorized to carry out international humanitarian military interventions, rather than merely attempting to build consensus and willingness among their current member states to pledge their national forces for this purpose.

Both of these proposed solutions are viable alternatives to our current policies. But both entail difficulties, and both come with a price. Defenders of the traditional Westphalian conception of national sovereignty (including the governments of many of the most powerful nations on earth at present) are not eager to delegate even more authority to, let alone provide a distinct, dedicated military force exclusively for the use of, the United Nations. They view this, even more than the occasional HI tasks themselves, as a genuine threat to the bedrock conception of state sovereignty. Apparently, the collective political will simply does not exist, nor does it seem likely to exist in the near future, to support General Shelton's proposal.

This returns us to the prospect of private contractors undertaking these missions. From a practical standpoint, contractors might prove highly effective, less expensive, and even more enthusiastic in the pursuit of these duties than have the members of some national militaries. If this alternative would enable the international community to respond more quickly and effectively to emergent humanitarian crises, and thereby save lives, then perhaps it is worth a try (provided funding can be found for the experiment). What effect such measures might eventually have on the formation of a cross-cultural, international professional military ethic, however, is a topic we will postpone for the final chapter.

Notes

1. Brendan Simms and D. J. B. Trimm, eds., *Humanitarian Intervention: A History* (Cambridge: Cambridge University Press, 2013). The editor's introduction provides a useful synopsis of this history, while the concluding chapter by Matthew Jamieson, "Humanitarian Intervention since 1990 and 'Liberal Interventionism,'" outlines the contrast in

motivations between the liberal interventionism of the 1990s and the earlier, far more self-interested and cynical episodes of this history. See also George Lucas, "Revisiting Humanitarian Intervention: A 25-Year Retrospective," in *The Ethics of Armed Humanitarian Military Intervention*, ed. Don Scheid (Cambridge: Cambridge University Press, 2014), 26–45.

2. E.g., as in Michael Walzer's initial treatment of this topic in *Just and Unjust Wars* in 1977. By the time of the publication of the third edition of this important work (2000), however, Walzer's views on HI had changed dramatically in the aftermath of the experiences of the preceding decade.

3. This is Mill's phrase denouncing decisions to refrain from military interventions where humanitarian disasters loom, simply because no immediate national self-interests are thereby implicated. He makes the comment in an essay written in 1859: "A Few Words on Non-intervention," the same year in which he published his great work *On Liberty*.

4. The military rivalries helped exacerbate a terrible drought and famine, making it impossible for relief workers and supplies to reach the famine victims. A US-led military intervention followed, initially to provide security and safe passage for famine relief workers.

5. This "decline literature," including a recent focus on the implications of a decline in US strategic power abroad, is a perennial topic. A classic treatment in terms of the significance of power in international relations generally is John J. Mearsheimer's *The Tragedy of Great Power Politics* (New York: Norton, 2001). See also Robert J. Lieber, *Power and Willpower in the American Future: Why the United States Is Not Destined to Decline* (Cambridge: Cambridge University Press, 2012); Michael Cox, "Is the United State in Decline—Again?" *International Affairs* 83, no. 4 (2007): 643–653; and Niall Ferguson, *Civilization: The West and the Rest* (New York: Penguin, 2011).

6. See George Lucas, "From *jus ad bellum* to *jus ad pacem*," in *Ethics and Foreign Intervention*, ed. Don Scheid & Deen K. Chatterjee (New York: Cambridge University Press, 2003), 83–92.

7. See http://www.responsibilitytoprotect.org/.

8. E.g., General Romeo Dallaire in Rwanda: http://www.pbs.org/wgbh/pages/frontline/shows/ghosts/interviews/dallaire.html. See also the observations and advice of US General Anthony C. Zinni (USMC, retired) regarding the intervention and lessons learned in Ethiopia, in George Lucas, *Perspectives on Humanitarian Intervention* (Berkeley: Berkeley Public Policy Press, 2001).

9. See chapters "Why Serve the State?" and on the Kosovo intervention, in Martin L. Cook, *The Moral Warrior* (Albany: State University of New York Press, 2004), 39–54, and 135–149, respectively.

10. UNAMIR is the acronym for United Nations Assistance Mission for Rwanda. See the case of Belgian captain Luc Lamaire at the Don Bosco school compound, "Intervention in Rwanda," in *Case Studies in Military Ethics*, ed. George Lucas and W. Rick Rubel, 3rd ed. (New York: Pearson Publishers, 2009), 59–62.

11. Paolo Tripodi, "Massacre in Srebrenica," in Lucas and Rubel, *Case Studies in Military Ethics*, 63–68.

12. http://articles.baltimoresun.com/1995-10-13/news/ 1995286005_1_soldier-newt-gingrich-phil-gramm.

13. See the case study "Acting on Conscience: Captain Lawrence Rockwood in Haiti," by Stephen Wrage, in Lucas and Rubel, *Case Studies in Military Ethics*, 69–74.

Further Reading

Bellamy, Alex, *The Responsibility to Protect.* Cambridge: Polity Press, 2009.

Dallaire, Romeo. *Shake Hands with the Devil: The Failure of Humanity in Rwanda.* New York: Carroll & Graf, 2003.

Hoffman, Stanley. *The Ethics and Politics of Humanitarian Intervention.* Notre Dame, IN: Notre Dame University Press, 1996.

Lucas, George. *Perspectives on Humanitarian Intervention.* Berkeley, CA: Berkeley Public Policy Press, 2001.

Pattison, James. *Humanitarian Intervention and the Responsibility to Protect.* Oxford: Oxford University Press, 2010.

Scheid, Don, ed. *The Ethics of Armed Humanitarian Military Intervention.* Cambridge: Cambridge University Press, 2014.

Scheid, Don, and Deen K. Chatterjee, eds. *Ethics and Foreign Intervention.* New York: Cambridge University Press, 2003.

Teson, Fernando. *Humanitarian Intervention: An Inquiry into Law and Morality.* New York: Transnational Publishers, 1997.

8

MILITARY ETHICS AND UNMANNED SYSTEMS

What are "unmanned systems"?

This is the generic term coined by engineers for remotely piloted or remotely operated devices such as robots or drones. Unmanned systems include those that are programmed to operate by themselves (automatic and autonomous systems), as well as those that are operated by remote control. Unmanned systems have many current uses, from housecleaning to bomb disposal. Potential applications range from emergency medical evacuation to elder care.

These systems can operate with greater effectiveness, and with ever less supervision, than previously imagined. And their capacity to do all this grows exponentially each day, in accordance with a principle known as Moore's Law. Named after its original formulator, Dr. Gordon E. Moore, cofounder of semiconductor silicon chip manufacturer Intel Corporation, this law initially referred specifically to the number of miniaturized transistors that could be manufactured on a single silicon wafer of a fixed size. That number, Moore noted, was doubling every two years. Since these "wafers," or transistor- and circuit-board-containing chips, in turn, constitute the fundamental engine of computing power, Moore's Law came to refer to the technological gains obtainable through the increased power and capability of the silicon processors themselves.

We now say that the pace of technological change *itself* is subject to Moore's Law, and that our technological abilities, or "technological reach" *itself*, doubles about every two years. Indeed, that rate of change has now been estimated to double more like every 12–18 months, rather than every two years! Nowhere is this rapid, exponential pace of change more evident than in robotics and in the military applications of advances in unmanned systems technology.

"Military robotics" refers specifically to the use of unmanned systems for military purposes. Those purposes and uses are as numerous and as diverse as in the civilian sector, and often (as with most technologies) lead to unanticipated spin-offs or applications in the civilian sector. At present, robots can find and dismantle improvised explosive devices (IEDs) or climb deep into the caves of Tora Bora in search of terrorists and enemy insurgents. They can fly reconnaissance missions of long duration, and, if armed, can attack and destroy targets when those targets are finally discovered, positively identified, and cleared for attack by their human operators, perhaps from thousands of miles away.

As many as are the current uses of robots in the military and on the field of battle, many more are envisioned or actually under development for use in the near future. Robots are used as armed sentries at contested borders in Israel and in the demilitarized zone between North and South Korea. Robotic helicopter "Fire Scouts" may soon swarm autonomously (i.e., without direct or continuous human oversight) around an aircraft carrier nearing a port call, providing security against a surprise terrorist attack. "Scan Eagles," launched from a small catapult (located either on land or on a ship) provide accurate, long-endurance area surveillance. Unmanned submarines (UUVs) now patrol the sea on intelligence, surveillance, and reconnaissance (ISR) missions and, in principle, could one day be armed as "attack subs." Battlefield extraction-assist robots (BEARs)[1] may soon be able to roam the battlefield, gently gathering wounded combatants and returning them to military

hospitals for care. Robotic convoys, rather than private contractors, may soon ferry the important logistical supplies
described in chapter 6 to military outposts in contested zones
of conflict, without further need for either private armed security guards *or* Marines.

The myriad and rapidly expanding use of robots and
unmanned systems for military purposes was the topic of a
major, bestselling work by Brookings Institution senior fellow
Peter W. Singer in 2009. The ethical and legal issues surrounding their increased use, and their incorporation of ever-greater
degrees of autonomy, was discussed in a lengthy report for
the Office of Naval Research by renowned roboticist George
Bekey, collaborating with two philosophers at the California
Polytechnic University who have since done pioneering work
on the ethical implications of military robotics, Patrick Lin and
Keith Abney.[2]

What are the ethical issues involving military uses of robotics?

Apart from one glaring exception—to which we will turn
in a moment—the military uses of unmanned systems
raise few new ethical or legal issues. Nor do they pose any
deeply troubling problems for the military profession or
for ethical behavior on the part of military personnel. This
is because, at present, engineers are mainly designing systems to assume activities formerly performed by military
personnel themselves, and which will operate under direct
and immediate human supervision. New ethical issues will
arise if our technological aspirations go much beyond the
current capabilities and applications of unmanned systems
in combat.

What capabilities and applications are these? Experts
joke that we want robots for any activity that is "dull, dirty,
and dangerous." Hunting for, and disarming, IEDs (or other
forms of enemy sabotage) is one activity that perfectly fits
this description. Using a robot, under control of a human at

a remote distance, to carry out this critical, but obviously dull and dirty (and certainly dangerous), chore violates no laws and poses no great ethical dilemmas or professional conundrums. It has the moral benefit of helping reduce the risk of cruel and dangerous harm to human combatants, who could be killed or wounded by such devices. And if the robot is destroyed, assuming a replacement can be afforded, there is little else at stake. Unlike the imaginary "robots" (androids) in the film fantasy *Star Wars*, these machines have no self-interests and do not care whether they are damaged or destroyed (let alone "melted down").

Another category of dull, dirty, but also potentially dangerous activity is ISR: intelligence, surveillance, and reconnaissance. Most of the "search, detect, and report" missions vital to security and the pursuit of war objectives are time-consuming and, 90 percent of the time, fruitless. An unmanned system with sensors capable of discriminate detection and what, in the military, is called "target recognition" capacity can perform these chores much more effectively than can humans, who might become bored or have their attention diverted momentarily and miss some important detail. ISR is currently the predominant use for unmanned systems on land, beneath the sea, and in the air. Once again, this military use of robotics raises no new or compelling moral or legal issues in itself. The ethical issues are the same as those that are always encountered when humans engage in military activities.

We come now to the glaring exception: the use of armed ISR aerial systems, like the Predator and Reaper air platforms, not just for surveillance and reconnaissance, but also for target identification and destruction. This usage of remotely piloted aerial systems for hunting down and killing enemy insurgents in Afghanistan, Pakistan, and occasionally also in other parts of the Middle East (e.g., in Yemen) is deeply controversial and raises a host of legal and moral issues to which we should now turn.

What moral or legal problems are likely to arise from using unmanned aerial systems (drones) to attack and kill enemy combatants?

The problems are not exactly due to the fact that the systems are *unmanned*. The underlying ethical and legal problem with the current use of "drones" is that these missions involve the selective, "targeted killing" of adversaries. Now if the targets are legitimate enemy combatants (or, as known terrorists were formerly labeled, "unlawful" combatants), operating within an internationally defined zone of combat, then the use of drones is not especially problematic. To attack and kill regular combatants with drones is no more or less problematic, from either a legal or professional ethics standpoint, than doing the same with ground troops or piloted aircraft.

Suppose an air force pilot, Captain Smith, can, with moral justification and legal clearance, fly a *manned* mission in an F-16 to drop a bomb on the house of an enemy Taliban insurgent across the valley who is known to be engaged in hostilities against ISAF forces. If this can be done without serious reservation, then the same mission can be legally performed by Captain Smith even if he is now sitting at a Predator control station somewhere in Nevada. A legally permissible and morally justified combat mission does not suddenly become illegal or immoral simply because the pilot has been removed from the cockpit of the attacking aircraft.

In both cases, the mission described is already subject to a clearly defined set of legal constraints, which in turn are drawn directly from fundamental moral principles contained within the *jus in bello* ("just conduct of war") professional traditions of armed conflict that we examined in the first four chapters of this book. As codified in the international law of armed conflict (LOAC), these principles demand that the attack be carried out in an identified zone of combat by bona fide personnel of recognized national military forces legally engaged in that conflict. The attack on the house, whether carried out by a piloted fighter jet or a remotely piloted drone, must meet the criterion of military necessity: that is, the destruction of the home and the killing or wounding of its owner must fulfill an important military objective (e.g., thwarting his plans to lead an armed attack the next morning against a village protected by ISAF forces).

Furthermore, if the attack mission is launched against one significant individual in one home, then there is no need to send an entire squadron of F-16s to bomb the entire village: that would represent a disproportionate (unreasonably excessive) and also an indiscriminate use of force—one that would illegally subject nearby villagers and their property to risk of severe harm, and which is therefore prohibited.

Exactly the same legal and moral constraints apply to drones. Providing that the conditions described above are fully met, the attack, whether carried out by a piloted F-16 or a remotely piloted aircraft, is acceptable as an act of war, from both a legal and a moral standpoint. Proponents of drone warfare and advocates of the greater use of unmanned systems in war argue in fact that the use of the drone is morally superior to the use of the F-16 for two reasons. First, and most obviously, the use of the drone removes all risk of harm to the pilot involved in the mission. All things considered, that seems a good thing, and not a bad or morally objectionable thing in itself.[3]

Second, proponents of unmanned systems argue that the two important constraints imposed to protect innocent third parties and their property from harm (i.e., the principles of *proportionality* and *discrimination*) are more easily and completely satisfied using unmanned or remotely piloted systems. This is because the human pilot has a relatively short time to fly his or her mission, identify the target, drop the ordinance, and return to base before running out of fuel (or being shot down). This increases the pressure to carry out the mission quickly and thereby increases the chance for error.

The fuel-efficient and largely riskless drone, by contrast, can afford to linger over the target. It can take the time to ensure that the enemy combatant is at home and wait until his neighbors, who may have happened unexpectedly to drop by for tea, can leave. Thus, the drone can be superior in terms of discrimination and proportionality. There is considerable evidence that drone strikes have in fact been more selective than pilots in aircraft could be. There is also established policy that *requires* that such discriminate practices be utilized in the drone case. Accordingly, there is a moral case to be made in favor of the use of drones in such circumstances, and certainly no law prohibiting their use.

Have such arguments convinced concerned critics that drones are nothing to worry about?

Not really! Critics of drone warfare, for one thing, simply deny that these discriminate practices occur and claim instead that (in the words of one persistent protest group in the United States) "when drones fly, civilians die."

If that were so—that is, if drones could be shown to be haphazard in their targeting and to cause more civilian collateral deaths and harm than conventional justified attacks then their use would need to be discontinued and possibly even outlawed, as inflicting what international law identifies as "superfluous injury or unnecessary suffering."

It is part of the ongoing public controversy over the use of remotely piloted systems by the United States in Afghanistan that opposing sides draw diametrically opposed conclusions and cite different bodies of evidence to support their positions. It seems highly unlikely on the basis of any current, decisive evidence that remotely piloted systems would, in fact, be outlawed or denounced as somehow constituting weapons (such as poisonous gas or hollow bullets) that do cause such "superfluous injury or unnecessary suffering." In most instances, it is certainly far from clear that their use involves more risk of civilian casualties than conventional tactics.

The balance of evidence seems to suggest, in fact, given a choice between the two modes of attack—conventionally piloted versus remotely piloted—drones are better. Fewer civilians are killed or wounded inadvertently in drone attacks than in conventional attacks (although many civilians have, undoubtedly and regrettably, been killed or wounded in *both* kinds of attacks).

But there is another, much more plausible moral objection to drones: *they enable the undertaking of combat missions that would be too risky*—or simply not feasible—for manned aircraft. In that sense, drones use might produce an overall increase in the total number of civilian collateral deaths, injury, and damage from a purely statistical standpoint. But this is due, not to something nefarious about the technology, but the greater number of military missions flown against legitimate enemy targets than would otherwise be possible. But even this concern does not top the list of legal and moral objections to the use of drones.

The principal remaining moral and legal objections have centered on the undertaking, by remotely piloted systems, of "targeted killings" of adversaries. These targeted killings have even taken place across the sovereign borders of countries, like Pakistan or Yemen, with which we are not technically at war. Because these missions are undertaken outside defined and recognized zones of conflict, moreover, military personnel cannot legally engage in them, and so civilian intelligence and covert operatives must carry them out instead.

To be sure: civilian "clandestine services" personnel, engaged in covert actions in other countries, have engaged in the "targeted killing" (i.e., extrajudicial execution or assassination) of adversaries and enemies for centuries, employing more conventional means. We might therefore ask whether we are now objecting to the *policy of targeted killing* itself, or to the *use of drones* (military hardware) by civilian operatives, in order to carry out these covert missions.

In the case of the United States (which happens to be the country most engaged in drone missions at present), there are domestic laws prohibiting the undertaking of military missions by civilians. There are laws, likewise, prohibiting the military from undertaking missions that are not directed against legally defined and morally justified military targets. The advent of the so-called war on terror over the past decade has seriously blurred these distinctions and exacerbated the moral concern attached to them.

"Spy versus spy" assassinations have always seemed morally murky at best and are activities largely ungoverned by international law. Under virtually any domestic legal regime in which such killings or attempted killings occur, moreover, they are strictly illegal. International law prohibits the deliberate attempts to assassinate state leaders; permitting such attacks, it is reasoned, would increase instability and magnify the risk of war. Similar policies have been adopted within domestic legal jurisdictions of many nations, prohibiting their intelligence agents from deliberately assassinating representatives, even of avowed enemy governments. But such prudent restraints have fallen on hard times in the aftermath of 9/11.

What seems to disturb the wider international public the most about targeted killings is something else entirely. It is the public image that such killings project that seems somehow morally objectionable. That is to say, the use of remotely piloted systems to hunt down and kill suspected criminals and adversaries in every conceivable corner of the globe portrays an image that is distasteful or hubristic. These killings seem to portray the actions of a dominant and arrogant world military power, engaging with impunity in the pursuit and destruction of its enemies anywhere in the world, without regard for others, using a technology that (and please forgive the allusion) reminds them of the Death Star from *Star Wars*, now operated at the behest of an evil empire. This vast technological superiority and its reach, including the removal of any risk of harm to the military or civilian pursuers, seems grotesquely unfair, persecutory, oppressive, abusive, and therefore morally repugnant.

*Is it unfair for one side in a military conflict to possess
the seemingly vast and asymmetrical technological advantages
over its enemies and adversaries that military robotics
provides?*

What is beyond doubt is that the possession and use of this sophisticated technology presents its users with an enormous public relations problem. That is, even if they use this technology properly and judiciously, while carefully obeying all applicable laws and moral considerations, they may yet still be perceived as engaged in the waging of a kind of war that appears tyrannical, ruthless, and monstrously unfair.

There is little use in arguing about such public perceptions: they are what they are. The entire matter is more fruitfully portrayed as a conflict between legitimate military (tactical) objectives, and larger (strategic) political objectives. If the military objective is to defeat the enemy soundly, then to restore peace and order, and if new technologies like robotics assist (as they most always do) in this endeavor, then it makes sense to use those new technologies. But if warfare's larger, strategic purpose is the pursuit of political objectives by other means, and if the successful pursuit of tactical military objectives is vastly outweighed by their negative strategic political effects, we should change tactics. Even if the political fallout comes from confused and misinformed public opinion, it could be argued that the political or strategic price outweighs the tactical military gain achieved through the use of such technologies. If that is the case, we would be wise to desist.

This appears to be what has transpired in the case of drones and targeted killings. Even if these are carried out with the utmost care and caution, scrupulously adhering to existing law, and are undertaken only against fully justified targets (according to both law and morality), the impression of killing with impunity, or killing mercilessly by remote control, will persist. And this negative impression constitutes an unmitigated strategic disaster for the nation or coalition pursuing an otherwise-justified tactical military policy by this means. Especially when it appears that most of the truly high-value military targets in the war on terror have largely been destroyed, it might be well for those possessing and using this sophisticated military technology to rethink the political costs of now *discontinuing* their use, at least for the moment.

In other respects, the "fairness" question in combat more generally, I strongly suspect, is something that is badly muddled in the public eye. In sports competitions, for example, fans in the public often root for the underdog and come to resent the perennial power of one or two large, dominant, well-staffed, and lavishly resourced sports teams.

But war is not a sport, despite the terrible analogies often drawn between the two human activities. We don't usually fault domestic police for using superior technology to gain an advantage against ruthless criminals from whom they are trying to shield the public. Nor do we doubt that legitimate and proper law enforcement (as opposed to reckless abuse of police power) should be undertaken at the least possible risk to the individual policemen and law enforcement officials themselves. Law-abiding citizens would gladly see their security enhanced, and the risk to legitimate law enforcement officials undertaking this task on their behalf reduced, if they could manage to do so.

As Bradley J. Strawser has maintained (see note 3, above), that is exactly, and only, what military robotics has thus far done for the military. Warfare has always relied upon asymmetry and superiority of some sort, whether technological, tactical, or strategic. The stunning German blitzkrieg of World War II was not "unfair." Rather, it represented admirable technology and remarkably superior tactics employed in the service of wholly illegal and decidedly immoral ends. Had the same German military forces been used instead to repel an invasion of the European continent by hordes of murderous aliens, thereby protecting the Germans themselves and their European neighbors from harm at the hands of these deadly invaders, then their technology and tactics would have been celebrated rather than condemned.

Let me emphasize again that war is not analogous in the least to a sports competition. It must not be thought of as, say, an elaborate version of a medieval jousting match. Instead, war is finally about the *moral justification* (even more than the technical adherence to legality) of tactical military objectives and strategic political ends. War's purpose, and its justification, finally, have little to do intrinsically with which side in the conflict possesses (as one invariably does) better technology than the other! We desire that the morally justified and legally compliant side in a conflict prevail over the side that is bereft of moral legitimacy or legal justification for its war-making. If the morally justified side can prevail through the use of superior technology, then that is a good thing, or at least a relief, and certainly *not* a situation of unfairness.

Shouldn't we worry, though, about attempts to develop a killer robot that is fully autonomous and lethally armed?

That is another matter altogether, and a very serious one. Autonomous functioning in robotics has long been a goal for artificial intelligence research. Sometimes that goal has seemed to go hand in hand with the uses of armed unmanned platforms. When we move past the current debate about drones and targeted killings, the remaining, substantial moral and legal question is, what happens if we "marry" the two capabilities? What happens if we succeed in creating an unmanned system that is independently mobile, does not require continuous human oversight, can operate fully on its own to develop and change its tactical objectives, and can make targeting decisions and carry them out (i.e., "kill people and break things," entirely on its own recognizance) without any executive oversight or supervision?

That is a very difficult and disquieting scenario. And some elements of it are not that far from being attainable. But other important capabilities necessary to build and operate a safe and reliable autonomous system that is fully armed are not even close to realization. Still, the ethical question is this: Should we continue to attempt to pursue such a technological objective?

A case can be made that we should. And that case is made by a very eminent, thoughtful, and morally concerned roboticist at Georgia Tech University, Dr. Ronald C. Arkin. In sum, Arkin's argument is that such robots would be more safe and reliable, and even more compliant with the laws of armed conflict, than would their human counterparts. (In that very limited and legalistic sense of ethics as full and faithful legal compliance, Arkin describes his robots as ultimately being more ethical than humans in combat.)

This is so, Arkin claims, because robots have no fear or anger, and they have no interests or concern with their own self-preservation when they are put at risk (apart perhaps from being programmed for prudent avoidance of unnecessary harm). Lethally armed, autonomous combat robots, faced with exactly the same situation as confronted the human members of SEAL Team 10 in our opening chapter, for example, would not even be led to consider the choices that faced the human warriors. Once the robots recognized that the three goatherds were noncombatants, they would leave them alone and go on about their ISR mission, until they succeeded, or until they were apprehended and perhaps destroyed. It would not matter to them.

Still (as I like to say, with apologies to my Hollywood alter ego), if we imagine this as R2D2 and C3PO, fully weaponized and roaming the hills of southern Afghanistan entirely on their own, we get an eerie picture. It is a horrifying scenario if those robots make decisions on their own to kill or attack human beings. One is more likely led to think of the horror movie *The Terminator* rather than of the lovable fictional characters from the first *Star Wars* movie. That does not seem, for a great many people, to constitute a desirable goal toward which to aspire.

Objections to continued pursuit of lethally armed autonomous operation as a research engineering goal have been
lodged by many critics. Most prominent among them are computer scientist Noel Sharkey at the University of Sheffield in the
United Kingdom and a prominent ethicist at Yale University,
Wendell Wallach. Sharkey has been a leading critic of the mistaken assumptions and misleading interpretations made by
his colleagues regarding machine behavior. "Moral reasoning"
is not even a plausible category, he maintains, with which to
describe the likely prospects for the behavior and governance
of unmanned systems.

This is because, by design, robots lack the requisite features
of consciousness, intentionality, concern, and care that serve
to motivate human behavior. They can operate in all relevant
respects without these sometimes annoying capacities, and
there is no need to imagine otherwise—let alone to mislead the
public by speaking of designing "moral machines" or "ethical
robots." People are easily confused and misled (including the
staffs of military and scientific funding agencies) by the abuse
of metaphorical language that is simply inaccurate. The public
has been confounded by wildly fanciful predictions (and time-
lines about when such goals would be reached). In truth, moral
machines and ethical robots are not, by definition, achievable.

Robots that are autonomous in the machine sense (but not
in the human, moral sense), however, are quite achievable.
And so Wallach has proposed to ban any attempt to equip
unmanned autonomous systems with the ability to use lethal
force. Such an attempt, he argues, would constitute reckless,
perhaps even criminally negligent, scientific research, as would
designing and building new weapons of indiscriminate, mass
destruction. And like such weapons that currently exist and
are banned from all use in any circumstances, lethally armed,
fully autonomous robots should be legally classified among
the means of waging war that are *mala in se*, which is Latin
legal terminology for weapons (like poison gas and hollow
bullets) and means of warfare (like rape) that are, inherently,
"wrong in themselves."

Such a designation might serve to direct proper research in more fruitful and acceptable directions. Greater degrees of machine autonomy would be sought for robots, like BEAR, that have a range of tasks to perform, but that are not designed to harm anyone. Unmanned systems that are lethally armed, however, would remain under human supervision and "meaningful human control" as, at best, semiautonomous.

The larger issues are still being discussed and debated. For the present, military researches and funders have adopted policies surprisingly close to those of the critics. The US Department of Defense, for example, stated flatly (in a recent directive on unmanned systems and future technological development) that full autonomy would *not* be sought or provided for any proposed unmanned system that would also be lethally armed.[4] The latter must remain fully under human supervision and control, at least for the present, with a human being held finally accountable in every case for decisions to target and shoot.

R2D2 and C3PO can rest easy, for the moment at least. they are not about to get drafted, let alone court-martialed and melted down for engagin in war crimes!

What moral challenges, finally, does the advent of military robotics present for ethics in the military profession?

Once more, robots in their present status as dull, dirty, and dangerous task-performers within the overall force mix of human combatants present very little in the way of moral dilemmas or professional challenges. That will remain the case, as long as robots, even when more fully autonomous in operation than at present, remain a part of the overall force mix, and remain (especially if equipped with lethal armament) firmly under meaningful human operational control.

But ultimately, robots present the same range of challenges, surprisingly, as do military contractors on the human side. That is because if robots (like private contractors) can one day do everything (and not just assist in doing some things) that military personnel can do—and if robots (like private contractors) can be said to do it better, faster, and cheaper than military personnel—then what becomes of the notion of a true profession of arms?

On the other hand, if inherently military functions remain the province of professionals, in part because of what Clausewitz termed (in the opening quotation in this book) their "professional pride" and "military virtues" (including the ethics of professional practice that we have labored to examine in this book), then there must still be some things that only military personnel can properly be trusted to do. And in that case, not only does the military profession itself remain intact, but it remains a domain of trusted, specialist activities that robots (like private contractors) must never be allowed do, because they could not conceivably undertake those inherently military functions.

This is called the problem of "professional jurisdiction," and it shows up in other professions as well, like medicine, and can precipitate some ferocious debates. That is because members of the profession may not recognize that "times have changed" and technology has improved to the point that their individual skills are no long so specialized or urgently required. They can, effectively, be replaced by machines (or elements of their practice can be outsourced to the private sector at lower cost and greater efficiency).

But the practitioners of the threatened profession may still rightly sense that *not all* that they do can be adequately outsourced or mechanized, perhaps because those are the activities that involve intimate personal and moral relationships among and between human beings, and such relationships cannot be simulated. Or perhaps there are inherent moral limitations on special activities that must be attained through a kind of practical reasoning that, unlike strict legal compliance, is "fuzzy" and ambiguous, and can't really be programmed reliably. If so, it behooves the members of the profession to recognize and clarify exactly what those activities are and why they need to remain solely within the profession's jurisdiction.

Finally, to summarize this line of thought and its importance for the military: suppose that the range of activities in question is not just inherently military but also inherently moral activities. That is, the core activities and jurisdiction of the profession do not simply include ethics but are founded upon, and in every respect embody, ethical values and principles. Machines, as Noel Sharkey rightly points out, can't "do ethics" or "be ethical" (let alone be "more ethical" than humans). They can only be safe, reliable, and legally compliant. Morality is much more than compliance with the law, while moral relationships like trust, or like Stockdale's "obedience, service and sacrifice" cannot exist apart from beings who "care about these things, for whom such things matter importantly, and figure essentially into their regard for themselves—and just as importantly, in their regard for others.

In the first half of this book, we examined historical evidence and cases, as well as famous selections from history and literature, supporting the notion that the military not only was a profession (with traditions, customs, specialized language and vital skills), but that, at its core, it was also founded upon moral values and important ethical considerations. St. Thomas placed his discussion of the sinfulness of war, and of conditions defining rare exceptions when it was not sinful, squarely within a discourse on "charity"—that is, on the Christian idea of love. Augustine defended the notion that the "right mindfulness" or right intentions of the warrior must be *to engage in armed conflict reluctantly*, and only for the purpose of defending or restoring peace and justice. Socrates and Sun-Tzu seemed to regard war as an art as much as a science, or at least as entailing considerations that involved prudence, judgment, experience, and wisdom, of the sort that cannot be simply boiled down to a few bullets on a wallet card or a legal checklist—let alone to a flow chart for a computer program.

If all the foregoing is true, then the bearing of arms in defense of the state and one's fellow citizens (and now, perhaps, in behalf of vulnerable victims of cruelty and violence everywhere), is a *special calling*, infused with moral values, and requiring ethical judgment and discernment. As such, it cannot simply be programmed into a machine, any more than it can be outsourced to someone who simply "loves combat" (or is instead tragically addicted to it) the way others love extreme sports, or who does this merely for personal and financial gain.

War-fighting, and preparing for it, just doesn't work like that, somehow. There is something about what we ask the warrior, the armed combatant, to do that cannot be mechanized, could never be routinized, and must not ever be thoughtlessly or unmindfully performed. Accordingly, it cannot be modeled by computer algorithms any more than it can be subordinated to the accountant's green eyeshade or managerial proclivities.

That activity is not "killing people and breaking things" on command, until another command is received to stop. Robots can certainly do that. (So, for that matter, can private security contractors, if they work solely for pay and serve at the command of their client.) Ironically, if the common misperceptions of military personnel and combat were accurate, we could easily replace professional military personnel with robots and contractors, and be done with it.

Instead, we have discovered that, at bottom, the core professional mission of the warrior is being prepared to kill, to employ deadly force when and if necessary, *in order to protect the lives and welfare of others*. It is being prepared to use force, and only as much force as the situation requires, not for the purpose of killing in itself, but for the purpose of protecting others from being killed or injured, that forms the moral essence of the military profession.

This professional mission includes repelling and, if necessary, destroying those who *do* act with the deliberate intentions of killing and of wreaking terror, exacting vengeance, or engaging in murder and mayhem for pleasure, power, or personal gain. Undertaking such missions for the sake of others is therefore satisfying, when they are successful, as well as morally commendable. And when last I checked, apart from the robot Bender on *Futurama* (relaxing with a beer and a cigar), real robots, unlike us "fleshbags," can't experience satisfaction in a morally worthy job that is well done.

This all requires that citizens be able to entrust their military personnel with the sole custody of deadly force. This also requires that military personnel themselves have a proper and complete, and not a mistaken or misguided, sense of who they are and what is expected of them. This all requires that they exhibit (at all times, and not simply when on duty) proper professional decorum and morally upright behavior. And especially, as Augustine noted, this requires that they remain right-minded about, and exhibit and act only on, the right intentions that reflect the moral foundations of the military profession.

But all this is precisely why the present debate about robots and the earlier debate about private contractors are so important. Those debates, and the threats those institutions and technologies pose in a confused and troubling way to the future of the military profession, *force members of that profession and of the public whom they serve to reflect on, and come to a more complete and accurate understanding of, the moral foundations of their practice.* These are things that military personnel and members of the general public—indeed, everyone—urgently need to know.

Notes

1. Under development with assistance from the Defense Advanced Research Projects Agency (DARPA), whose funding and support have encouraged a wide range of such futuristic and promising projects. In this case, see http://www.vecna.com/research.
2. P. W. Singer, *Wired for War: The Robotic Revolution and Conflict in the Twenty-First Century* (New York: Penguin, 2009); see Patrick Lin, George Bekey, and Keith Abney, "Autonomous Military

Robotics: Risk, Ethics, and Design," report prepared for the U.S. Navy Office of Naval Research: http://ethics.calpoly.edu/ONR_report.pdf.

3. Indeed, a colleague at the Naval Postgraduate School, Bradley Strawser, has labeled this the "principle of unnecessary risk," suggesting that we owe it to our war-fighters, otherwise engaged in legally permissible and morally justified armed conflict, to do all we can to ameliorate the risk of harm that might befall them in carrying out their mission. See Bradley J. Strawser, "Moral Predators," in "New Warriors/New Weapons: Ethics & Emerging Military Technologies," ed. George R. Lucas, *Journal of Military Ethics* 9, no 4 (2010): 357–383.

4. Department of Defense Directive 3000.09, "Autonomy in Weapons Systems," 13 (November 21, 2012): http://www.dtic.mil/whs/directives/corres/pdf/300009p.pdf.

Further Reading

Arkin, Ronald C. "The Case for Ethical Autonomy in Unmanned Systems." *Journal of Military Ethics* 9, no. 4 (December 2010): 347–356.

Arkin, Ronald C. *Governing Lethal Behavior in Autonomous Robots*. Boca Raton, FL: Chapman & Hall / Taylor & Francis Group, 2009.

Arkin, Ronald C., Patrick Ulam, and Alan R. Wagner. "Moral Decision Making in Autonomous Systems: Enforcement, Moral Emotions, Dignity, Trust, and Deception." *Proceedings of the IEEE* 100, no. 3 (March 2012): 571–589.

Guiora, Amos and Jason Shelton. "Drones and Targeted Killings: Facing the Challenges of Unlimited Executive Power." In *The Routledge Handbook of Military Ethics*, edited by George Lucas, 368–379. London: Routledge, 2015.

Human Rights Watch. "Losing Humanity: The Case against Killer Robots." 2012: http://www.hrw.org/sites/default/files/reports/arms1112ForUpload_0.pdf.

International Committee for Robot Arms Control. "Berlin Statement." 2010: http://icrac.net/who/.

Krishnan, Arman. *Killer Robots: Legality and Ethicality of Autonomous Weapons*. London: Ashgate, 2009.

Lin, Patrick, George Bekey, and Keith Abney. *Autonomous Military Robotics: Risk, Ethics, and Design*. US Department of the Navy, Office of Naval Research, December 20, 2008: http://ethics.calpoly.edu/ONR_report.pdf.

Lin, Patrick, Keith Abney, and George Bekey, eds. *Robot Ethics: The Ethical and Social Implications of Robotics*. Cambridge, MA: MIT Press, 2011.

Lucas, George. "Automated Warfare." *Stanford Law and Policy Review* 25, no. 2 (2014): 317–339.

Lucas, George. "Engineering, Ethics and Industry: The Moral Challenges of Lethal Autonomy." In *Killing by Remote Control*, edited by Bradley J. Strawser, 211–228. New York: Oxford University Press, 2013.

Marchant, Gary E., et al. "International Governance of Autonomous Military Robots." *Columbia Science and Technology Law Review* 12 (2011): http://www.stlr.org/cite.cgi?volume=12&article=7.

Riza, M. Shane. *Killing without Heart*. Potomac, MD: Potomac Books, 2013.

Roff, Heather M. "Killing in War: Responsibility, Liability and Lethal Autonomous Robots." In *Routledge Handbook of Ethics and War: Just War Theory in the Twenty-First Century*, edited by Fritz Allhoff, Nicholas G. Evans, and Adam Henschke, 348–364. New York: Routledge, 2013.

Sharkey, Noel E. "Automating Warfare: Lessons Learned from the Drones." *Journal of Law, Information & Science* 21, no. 2 (2012): 140–148, http://www.austlii.edu.au/au/journals/JlLawInfoSci/2012/8.htmlSharkey, Noel E. "Saying 'No!' to Lethal Autonomous Targeting." *Journal of Military Ethics* 9, no. 4 (December 2010): 299–313.

Singer, P. W. "The Ethics of Killer Apps: Why Is It So Hard to Talk about Morality When It Comes to New Military Technology?" *Journal of Military Ethics* 9, no. 4 (December 2010): 314–327.

Singer, P. W. *Wired for War*. New York: Penguin, 2009.

Sparrow, Robert. "Building a Better Warbot: Ethical Issues in the Design of Unmanned Systems for Military Applications." *Journal of Science and Engineering Ethics* 15 (2009): 169–187.

Sparrow, Robert. "Drones, Courage, and Military Culture." In *The Routledge Handbook of Military Ethics*, edited by George Lucas, 380–394. London: Routledge, 2015.

Sparrow, Robert. "Killer Robots." *Journal of Applied Philosophy* 24, no. 1 (2007): 62–77.

Strawser, Bradley J., ed. *Killing by Remote Control*. New York: Oxford University Press, 2013.

Valavanis, Kimon P., and George Vachtsevanos. *Handbook of Unmanned Aerial Vehicles*. Vol. 5. Heidelberg: Springer Verlag, 2014.

Wallach, Wendell. *A Dangerous Master: How to Keep Technology from Slipping Beyond our Control*. New York: Basic Books, 2015.

Wallach, Wendell. "Terminating the Terminator: What to Do about Autonomous Weapons." *Science Progress*, January 29, 2013: http://scienceprogress.org/2013/01/terminating-the-terminator-what-to-do-about-autonomous-weapons/.

9

MILITARY ETHICS AND CYBER WARFARE

We hear people referring to "cyberspace" all the time, but what exactly is it?

"Cyber" is derived from an ancient Greek noun referring to a "space" or a domain. The slightly redundant term "cyberspace" was first coined to popularity by science fiction writer William Gibson in a short story written in 1982, and afterward in his novel *Neuromancer* (New York: Berkeley Publishing, 1984), to describe "clusters and constellations" of data and their interconnections, drawn from every computer in the universe.

Cyberspace is, at first glance, a very strange place. The objects that reside there, and the events that occur in this domain, seem utterly unlike anything in the normal, physical world. If I place a normal phone call, for example, from my house near Washington, DC, to my brother in St. Petersburg, Florida, the call most likely travels as a fairly conventional electromagnetic transmission for about a thousand miles over a series of trunk lines, which are simply large copper wires or coaxial cables (or now, increasingly, fiber optic cables) that stretch along a physical route, more or less a straight line from my city to my brother's.

If I decide to email my brother instead, my message will first be disassembled into a swarm of discrete data packets, after which the system of Internet Protocol addressing will label these distinct packets and search for the quickest and least-congested Internet pathway to transmit them from origin to destination. As a result, these discrete data packets will almost assuredly travel around the world at the speed of light, perhaps more than once, and through the communication infrastructures of many countries, before they are finally reassembled at their destination. Owing to the historical evolution of the Internet as a US Department of Defense command and control project in the 1960s, moreover, the design and dissemination of the physical infrastructure necessary to support Internet communications entails that virtually all these discrete data packets, no matter where they start out or end up, will at some point pass through the Internet's physical infrastructure ("backbone") that is located within the continental United States. (This last fact has very important repercussions that we will discuss in a moment.)

Identity and authenticity are, as a result, tricky with Internet communications. When I get a conventional telephone call from my brother, I can usually verify his identity very quickly, from the unique sound of his voice. But when I receive an email from him, it may be fraudulent, *seeming* to come from him by all outward appearances, and having his name and return address. But the digital identity of the data packets may be "spoofed" to look like they came from his digital address, when in reality, this bogus email turns out to be part of what is termed a "spear-phishing" scam. Clever cybercriminals in, say, Uzbekistan, can fake my brother's (and many other users') digital identities and send many of us fake emails, hoping we will innocently open them. When we do, the email may contain a destructive virus that will destroy or steal our data, or a "worm"—a sinister software program that will download from the incoming email onto the innocent user's own computer and begin transmitting that user's sensitive information to the original sender. The recent generic term of art for such sinister software programs is "malware," and an amazing variety of these clever but unscrupulous programs have been introduced into our personal computer operating systems, stealing our credentials, identities, or credit card information, which will then be sold to criminal gangs in Russia or the Ukraine. They will, in turn, use this illicitly obtained and fraudulent information to drain our bank accounts or charge merchandise to our credit cards.

These kinds of serious pranks and crimes give rise to the need for cybersecurity. Various Internet providers and vendors may offer to protect me from such unscrupulous schemes by selling antivirus and firewall protection that will intercept and halt such attempts to penetrate and infect my personal computer and cause its software to malfunction or reveal confidential data to a criminal or prankster. Those same companies may also offer to protect me by storing my vital data and software, not on my own computer, laptop, or iPad, but instead "in the cloud," in a proprietary and presumably secure databank that only they control.

The "cloud" itself conjures up some nebulous, nonmaterial realm in which the capacity for storage is infinite, and the ownership and security of each precious item is guaranteed. Many people initially accepted this nonmaterial image that was deliberately propagated through advertisements for "cloud computing" by Internet vendors and service providers, beginning only a few years ago as the next latest thing in Internet development. In reality, however, as more and more ordinary users are beginning to discover, the cloud is spectacularly concrete.

Around 2010, a few suspicious environmental investigators began noticing the sudden appearance of enormous, windowless warehouses cropping up in the uninhabited countryside near major cities, each consuming nearly as much electricity as the cities themselves. Those investigators gradually realized that these buildings contained the physical servers, the banks of computers and computer memory, that Amazon and Google and Microsoft were using to store user data allegedly committed by their users to the cloud. But there is nothing about these physical servers that is cloud-like. Their energy use, heat out-put (the memory banks have to be cooled), and overall carbon footprint makes them vastly less efficient and more environ-mentally destructive than if all of us had just gone on stor-ing our data and programs on our individual computer hard drives. And what (apart from their solemn promises not to do so) is to prevent these commercial companies from mining all this stored data for useful information about their users?

How do we come to be mired in this confusion, uncertainty, and vulnerability with regard to this cyber domain?

From its beginnings until the mid-1980s, the Internet was largely the province of a few geeks, tech-savvy hippies, and mostly scientists, who used it to collaborate and share data from scientific and medical experiments. It had no regulation or security measures, and needed none.

Since its explosion into prominence and widespread usage, beginning in the early 1990s, advances like hypertext markup language (html) made the Web easier to use, while at the same time synergizing with advances in computer power, speed, and memory capacity to open it to a hitherto unimaginable array of applications. As a result, the World Wide Web (not to mention cell phone and GPS [Global Positioning System] networks) is now crowded with multiple users engaged in personal, private, commercial, industrial, and community enterprises, as well as engaging in the governmental, scientific, and military uses originally envisioned. Chinese government officials (reacting in anger to US criticisms of their behavior in the cyber domain) characterize cyberspace as a "global com-mons" that should be open and freely available to all without restriction.[1]

But one might reply to that analogy with a darker image, drawn from the late demographer Garrett Hardin's famous essay: "The Tragedy of the Commons." The tragedy inherent in a wholly unregulated environment, Hardin argued decades ago, was that its valuable resources, available for use without rules or restrictions, would quickly be consumed or destroyed.

A much more accurate metaphor, however, is that the cyber domain now resembles a lawless frontier, a Wild West or (in a famous political metaphor from the English philosopher Thomas Hobbes) a state of nature, increasingly crowded with multiple users whose needs and wants inevitably come into conflict. Much as original inhabitants of those once-free spaces objected to the newcomers, and to the rules, laws, and order that followed in their wake, so today's longtime users and cyber advocates would like to see everything remain unchanged, and for their interactive lives in the virtual world to go on forever, just like before.

However, political philosophers such as Hobbes also have long warned against what the original settlers in the Wild West discovered as well: in a state of nature, as in the wild, untamed frontier, life resembles one constant and insecure conflict, a "war of all, against all" in which each individual's existence is (once again, in Hobbes's famous description) "nasty, brutish and short."

It is simply *not realistic or feasible to leave the cyber domain entirely ungoverned*, especially because, just as in the actual geographical frontiers, there are some bad people and malevolent organizations who will use that freedom to exploit and harm others. And this is exactly what seems to be happening.

Furthermore, we cannot rely on the whimsical views of "Internet vigilantes" like Anonymous and WikiLeaks to afford protection, any more than frontier settlers could rely on the consistency, reliability, or fairness of vigilante justice in the Wild West. Vigilante justice, like the justice dispensed by Anonymous at present, is whimsical and unreliable and will ultimately come to pose a greater threat to safety and security than those whom they decide to persecute. The frontiers in North and South America and Australia inevitably had to become a bit less wild and so, now, also must the cyber domain.

What are some of the most important ethical challenges
that arise with our growing public presence in cyberspace?

Our growing activities within and reliance on having a presence in cyberspace poses a number of interesting, troubling,
and sometimes bewildering moral challenges for the general
public as we strive to stay abreast of these technological trans-
formations. Some of these challenges arise simply as a function
of the recent, rapid historical evolution of the cyber domain
itself, while others have to do with the unique objects and
events that exist, occupy, or transpire within that domain.

What we have been discussing so far, for example, is
"Internet-centric," and most of us think of cyberspace as consisting entirely of the Internet (e.g., the World Wide Web). But
if we are to fully grasp the nature of our challenges and vulnerabilities, it is important to recognize that the cyber domain
itself encompasses far more than the Internet alone.

The cyber domain also includes the Global Positioning
System (another U.S. Defense Department innovation, ultimately released and disseminated to the global public without
charge), as well as those once-distinct telephonic communications over conventional wires that are now controlled by
computers wired into the internet. Conventional phone calls
themselves continue to be transmitted over wires, but can be
transmitted instead over the physical structure of the internet
itself, making use of Internet Protocol (IP) to use that infrastructure as a unique (and comparatively inexpensive) mode
of data transmission in lieu of the older, original telephone and
telegraph wire and cable infrastructure.

Even more confusing to the average user is the fact that
the wireless cell phone network uses a different physical
infrastructure than the internet itself, consisting of cell phone
towers and cables that transmit telephonic communications
independently of the internet—although the two networks
can be linked, as is routinely done with smartphones—and,
of course, computers and software manage both networks.
In fact it is the linking or "networking" of all these different

systems with one another, and with the heretofore ordinary objects or "things" we conventionally use, like cars and home thermostats, which pose the greatest challenges. The resulting interdependence of everyday objects, telephones (cell phones), and computer systems and software on one another provides unprecedented convenience and productivity, but does so at the price of a greatly magnified array of serious vulnerabilities.

Without doubt, some of the most prominent ethical issues arising in the cyber domain cluster around *concerns for personal privacy*, coupled with the *anonymity* afforded to most individual users of these modes of communication.

One feature of cyber communications, for example is the ease with which malevolent users can disguise their personal identities, or "spoof" the digital identities of other users (as in the criminal case described above). This makes ordinary, good-faith users of this digital medium subject to invasions of privacy, as well as theft of sensitive information. Your smartphone accesses the GPS network to enable you to use global mapping software (like Google Maps) to find your way around—but also enables others to keep track of your movements, perhaps in a department store or supermarket, in which the cell phone camera lens may then also reveal your personal browsing and buying tendencies to cyber marketers, providing them with useful, but clearly personal and private, information about how to exploit your habits and preferences for their own financial gain.

But, of course, if commercial firms and clever cybercriminals can do this, so can governments and government agencies. Some of the most fascinating and challenging moral and legal conundrums therefore arise when governments attempt to halt cybercrime, or track down cybercriminals, or resist efforts at terrorism and espionage by other government agents, all by using massive data collection and sophisticated mathematical forensic techniques that attempt to penetrate the anonymity of those malevolent agents, but seem to do so by simultaneously violating (or, more accurately, threatening to violate) the individual privacy of ordinary users.

The ability for individuals and groups (such as the aptly-named vigilante group Anonymous) to act anonymously in cyberspace is what permits those with malevolent intentions to carry out their activities without accountability for their crimes. Espionage, for its part, is a fairly routine, government-sponsored activity that is not governed by international law. But some of the principal tactics of state espionage may involve state-sponsored agents engaging in acts like theft, trespassing, or vandalism that are themselves considered crimes within the domestic jurisdiction in which the espionage occurs (giving rise to the famous phrase in *Mission Impossible*: "As always, should you or any of your I.M. Force be caught or killed, the Secretary will disavow any knowledge of your actions.").

It would be relatively easy to stop both crime and espionage carried out by means of the Internet, therefore, simply by forcing each and every actor in cyberspace to identify themselves accurately and authentically. But critics of such proposed security precautions strenuously object that they seem eerily analogous to requiring everyone in the real world to wear or carry a personal identity card. Critics and privacy advocates equate such measures with excessive government control and fear they would lead democratic regimes to behave more and more like more oppressive regimes, wherein Internet use (for example) is closely monitored and even censored.

Is government surveillance and "big data" collection in cyberspace really a threat to each individual's privacy and freedom of expression?

This tension between security and privacy lies at the heart of the recent and highly publicized revelations of vast data collection and alleged government surveillance and massive invasions of individual privacy, as publicly disclosed by former National Security Agency contractor Edward Snowden.

Enthusiastic inhabitants of the cyber domain have come to place a premium on their largely unfettered freedom of action and personal anonymity, and sometimes conflate that extreme freedom and lack of accountability with the considerably less far-reaching privacy that most citizens in democratic, rights-respecting countries enjoy. These clusters of values constitute what we might think of as the "portfolio of individual rights" claimed by the denizens of this new domain.

Snowden's revelations laid bare to public scrutiny the ongoing programs of data collection and analysis by the NSA, carried out on a scope that he and others believed constituted a serious threat to privacy and individual liberty. NSA spokesmen, however, countered that their activities were strictly regulated by law and adversarial congressional oversight, and that no such invasions of individual privacy were either intended or transpiring. Instead, their project amounted to what might best be termed *a program of preemptive self-defense of the nation* against terrorism and state-sponsored industrial espionage. At most, some responded, what has been compromised is cyberspace anonymity rather than individual privacy.[2]

Complete anonymity, by contrast, coupled with the seemingly unbridled freedom to act, and the difficulties others have in attributing such actions to their perpetrators, means there can be mischief without accountability. Individuals, organizations, and even states can do unrestricted and indiscriminate harm to one another (in principle) without being found out and without having to take responsibility for their actions. This feature is of immense importance in understanding the main topic of this chapter: the potential advent of genuine cyber*warfare*.

We also hear a great deal these days concerning the threat of cyberwarfare. What is this, and to what extent is there a genuine threat of it happening?

The term "cyberwarfare" was first used in a RAND Corporation report written in 1992 by John Arquilla and David Ronfelt. Their report predicted a new form of conflict that would consist primarily in the disruption of the flow of data in information systems. Although the threat of this new form of conflict, also termed "information warfare," was not taken very seriously at first, concern with understanding the prospects for cyber conflict quickly grew, especially in the first decade of the 21st century, with the exponential growth in the incidence of Internet crime, online vandalism, and corporate- and state-sponsored cyberespionage.

Assessing the gravity of the threat posed by hypothetical forms of virtual conflict in cyberspace—beyond the actual crime and espionage we have become familiar with—has proven quite difficult. Part of the problem is accurately conceptualizing just what this domain itself is, and what might conceivably occur within it, that would have massive impact on persons, societies, and nations in the real world.

The wholesale lack of meaningful accountability afforded by the relative anonymity of actions in cyberspace has unquestionably fostered an exponential growth of malevolent activities in the cyber domain. Malevolent activities began in earnest during the early 1990s and rapidly evolved from relatively harmless pranks and minor vandalism into serious theft, fraud, personal abuse (both bullying and sexual harassment), human trafficking, drug-dealing, money-laundering (all of these facilitated through use of the wholly unregulated cyber currency, "BitCoin"), and the kind of widespread corporate and state espionage that we experience today. This, in turn, is what generates the fear that the scope of such malevolent activities will one day result in an all-out cyber*war*.

These threats are not purely hypothetical. In 1999, for example, two colonels in the People's Liberation Army, Quao Liang and Wang Xiangsu, published an extensive study of the US ability to project military power in the aftermath of Gulf War I. Their monograph, entitled *Unrestricted Warfare*, acknowledged that no one could stand toe to toe with the US military in the conventional sense. They recommended that the only way forward for China was to develop offensive and defensive capabilities in other areas, *principally including cyberspace,* in which the United States was itself highly vulnerable, without having achieved anything like technological dominance. China, the two PLA military theorists argued, had to be willing to use these alternative capabilities relentlessly in the pursuit of its national interests.

Thus began the unrelenting, state-sponsored campaigns allegedly carried out by a top-secret branch of the PLA, Unit 61398, based in Shanghai. These included cyberespionage and covert actions—like the planting of trapdoors and logic bombs in vital civilian infrastructure in the United States and allegedly in some European countries as well. These (alleged) acts were coupled with the massive theft of industrial and classified military technologies on an unprecedented scale that the United States, in particular, only began to acknowledge belatedly and publicly denounce during the past couple of years.

Global acts of cybercrime thus stand side by side with persistent ongoing commercial and military espionage and the massive theft of industrial and state secrets, collectively threatening the security and fundamental economic welfare of vast numbers of individuals and nations. Yet, as we noted above, efforts to counter such activities, and to provide for greater individual and state security, are strongly opposed in many rights-respecting and reasonably democratic societies. Effective, proactive (or preemptive) countermeasures to halt espionage, terrorism, or other malevolent, state-sponsored activities often involve what seems to average citizens and ardent cyber freedom advocates to be an unacceptable infringement on liberty and privacy.

Cyber analysts and prognosticators (e.g., Richard Clarke and Joel Brenner) predict that this impasse will not be overcome, short of a horrendous "cyber Armageddon": a cyberattack of a magnitude similar to the Japanese surprise attack on Pearl Harbor in 1941, or the terrorist attacks on the United States on September 11, 2001. According to these information warfare experts, a *cyberwar* could be as widespread and destructive as a conventional, or even a nuclear, war. Absent ground and air traffic control, planes filled with helpless passengers would collide in midair, while freight and passenger trains would crash or derail. Hydroelectric dams would burst and flood tens of thousands of hectares, ruining crops and drowning thousands of victims; electrical power grids would be shut down, leaving people helpless, while poisonous gases would be released from chemical factories to destroy the populations of nearby cities.

But are these scenarios of cyberwarfare really plausible? Are these fears of prominent information warfare experts well founded?

Some of these warnings may be inflated or exaggerated. Other cyber experts make fun of the very notion of warfare in connection with cyberspace. They suggest that a "cyberwar" would be something more analogous a real, physical invasion of the United States by an army from the Russian Federation—but one in which the soldiers then proceeded to threaten US citizens with being unable to renew their driver's licenses!

That dismissal of the threat is probably a bit too frivolous, however, because real, genuine, and serious harm can and has been done through cyberattacks, of a sort far more serious than the minor nuisance of being unable to renew a driver's license or log onto Facebook.

The first verifiable historical example of what might have constituted a coordinated, state-sponsored act of cyber*warfare* consisted in an intense series of distributed denial-of-service (DDoS) attacks in the summer of 2007. These were allegedly carried out by "patriotic" computer-hackers and political activists (or "hacktivists") in the Russian Federation against the citizens of neighboring Estonia. The small nation of Estonia is one of the most "wired," technologically savvy, and cyber-dependent nations, per capita, in the world. For several days, the websites of banks, hospitals, police, military, and government were shut down by the attacks. People were unable to obtain funds or conduct financial transactions, read newspapers, access medical records, or communicate via email with one another or with their employers or government agencies.

An international relations expert at King's College (University of London), Dr. Thomas Rid, argued afterward, however, that the kind of harm done in Estonia did not constitute physical harm of a serious sort, and that this attack therefore did not rise to the level of a "use of (physical) force," let alone an armed attack under international law. That would mean, if true, that whatever else it was, the Estonian episode was *not* properly understood as an act of war. In fact, Rid denied that this, or any cyber conflict, could ever conceivably rise to a level equivalent to that of an armed attack or constitute a genuine war.

If Rid is correct, the talk of cyberwarfare is strictly metaphorical and somewhat hyperbolic. At most, we are faced with a new and ongoing level of low-intensity conflict that more resembles traditional espionage and covert action, as well as criminal activity, but not actual *warfare*. We should note, however, that Rid's assertions that "cyberwar will not take place" have been seriously challenged by other experts, notably John Arquilla, the originator of the concept of cyberwar.

A separate concern has been that the "cyber Armageddon" described by Richard Clarke and others could be carried out, not just by nations, but by individuals. This could be anyone, from your next-door neighbor's 14-year-old geeky, alienated son, operating out of the upstairs bedroom, to two or three members of a small terrorist cell, hiding out in an apartment in Europe. This scenario, too, has been discounted by some (like Professor Rid), who argue that the "harm" that can be wrought in the "virtual world" of cyberspace will never, no matter how inconvenient, amount to the equivalent of genuine physical harm in our actual world.

Both extremes seem inaccurate. We have at least one instance, in 2010, in which a computer worm, labeled Stuxnet, did in fact cause serious physical damage. The worm destroyed nuclear centrifuges that were supposedly producing fissile uranium for use in a nuclear weapons program in Iran. The damage caused was fully equivalent to (although far less destructive than) what would have been achieved through a conventional bombing attack on these same facilities. This certainly constituted an act of genuine physical harm, caused by the cyber equivalent of a use of force or a conventional armed attack. Acts of sabotage, in turn, do legally constitute acts of war (should the victimized nation choose to regard them as such).

The Stuxnet case is interesting and still not fully documented, though most outside observers agree that agents of the US and Israeli governments conspired to design this fascinating and effective cyber weapon as part of a larger, multistate operation carried out against Iran. But in any case, this does not constitute the sort of program that could easily be carried out by a few terrorists or by your neighbor's alienated son, no matter how clever and determined they might all be. The resources, infrastructure, access to relevant equipment (like nuclear centrifuges), and expertise seem well beyond the capacity of even large international criminal organizations (who seem content, in any case, with much easier and more financially lucrative acts of cybercrime).

What is the upshot of all of this? Cyber *conflict*, if not cyber*war*, is nonetheless a reality. This means that the need for individuals, organizations, and nations to protect their privacy, property, commercial and defense innovations, and overall safety and welfare through enhanced cybersecurity, especially with respect to highly vulnerable civil infrastructure, is real and urgent.

Does it make any sense to talk about ethics in this kind of unrestricted cyber conflict, even if it is not technically war?

At first glance, the prospects for ethics in cyberwarfare (if there even *is* such a thing) do not look very promising. After all, adversarial nations (like China, with its doctrine of "unrestricted warfare") or Internet criminals and vigilante cyber groups like Anonymous seem to be attacking the general public relentlessly and stealing them blind, while setting traps to destroy civilian infrastructure indiscriminately, utterly without regard to who might be harmed. Under such grim circumstances, what possible sense can it make to talk about ethics and the law? In point of fact, wouldn't attention to ethics or legal governance at this point merely serve to hamper the victims or targets of these relentless cyber assaults by imposing constraints on their ability to respond to these vulnerabilities, and thereby merely grant a unilateral advantage to adversaries, who give such matters absolutely no credence whatsoever?

Initially, some very respected experts on cyber conflict and the ethics of war (such as Professor Randall Dipert, a philosopher and cyber expert at the University of Buffalo) questioned whether existing legal or moral paradigms (like the conventional just war tradition we examined in an earlier chapter) can conceivably be made to apply to the cyber domain. This is simply because, as we have noted, the objects and events in cyberspace are so unlike physical objects and events as to obviate any such comparison or extension of the relevant concepts. Others did indeed simply wonder whether any talk of law and order or of ethics in this domain wasn't just an irrelevant waste of time.

But remember that critics of all sorts have long thought that ethics and law have no place in the midst of conventional war, either. I have tried, in this book, to show how gravely mistaken and wrongheaded that view is in the conventional case.

Perhaps the cyber domain presents an entirely new theater for moral skepticism. Or perhaps, instead, we need to work harder to make sense of this new arena for serious conflict and avoid abandoning important moral and legal principles too readily in the face of technological challenges.

There are, as it turns out, at least some principles and concepts within international law and the just war tradition that can be applied to cyber conflict. Ever since the Estonian conflict, for example, a new Cyber Defense Center of Excellence (sponsored by NATO) and its staff have been at work in Estonia and at seminars throughout Europe. They are working to develop interpretations and applications of existing international law sufficient to answer questions about the conduct of conflict in cyberspace.

To be frank, the lawyers were well out ahead of the military philosophers and ethicists in recognizing the significance of this problem, and many of their most important findings in law are now published and available in a compendium known as *The Tallinn Manual*, after the capitol of Estonia, where this NATO initiative is headquartered.

Can international law (such as the law of armed conflict) really be made to apply within the cyber domain?

Despite valiant attempts and enormous effort by lawyers and scholars in international law to show how the law of armed conflict can be extrapolated into this new situation of cyber conflict, their efforts have been only partially successful.

There are several reasons for this. Legal jurisdictions are rather precisely defined, for one thing. International law is oriented toward defined geographical boundaries within which each sovereign state is delegated their jurisdiction and corresponding share of responsibilities for fighting crime or protecting the human rights of individuals. Thus, the law of armed conflict does not directly apply to the internal domestic policies regarding government use of force within states, for example. So, while international law is very state-centric and respectful of individual state sovereignty, the cyber domain knows no such boundaries. Its "denizens" do not tend to recognize or respect the authority of states or of international law—meaning that, so far as their cyber activities go, they do not seem to recognize the authority of any law whatsoever.

The other distinction that hamstrings the law is whether and how it can be applied to the classification of different kinds of activity. LOAC is addressed, for example, to opposing states engaged in conventional armed conflict. But we have just discovered that cyber conflict blurs the boundaries between war, espionage, and crime. The first and third are rule-governed, or law-governed, activities, but espionage is really not.

In addition, we noted that at least some experts doubt whether there can even *be* such a thing as a cyberwar. If they are right, then, quite literally, we can't (almost by definition) extrapolate the body of law that governs war and armed conflict between states to a situation that, by definition, does *not* involve war or armed conflict and does not explicitly involve states!

Whether or not we choose to classify the cyberattack on Estonia in 2007, or the sabotage of Iranian nuclear centrifuges in 2010 as "uses of force," or "armed conflict" or "acts of war," still it remains the case that the vast majority of malevolent cyber conflict does not rise to the level of war or armed conflict. A strictly DDoS attack interrupts, but does not physically damage, any existing infrastructure, and certainly does not directly kill or wound anyone. Instead, cyber conflict usually consists either of crime or of industrial and/ or state espionage.

International law, as mentioned, is silent on interstate espionage, primarily for simple jurisdictional reasons. As noted, almost all specific acts of espionage involve things like trespass, "breaking and entering," theft of property, and so forth. This is certainly true straightforwardly with industrial espionage. The United States accuses China, in particular, of engaging in both kinds of espionage simultaneously. But all of these activities, as straightforward criminal activities, are already punishable under the domestic law of the region in which they occur. So, technically, there is no reason to write new law or to further confuse already jumbled jurisdictional questions in the international arena.

International law has, however, scored at least one significant success in coming to terms with this new cyber world
order. Many, but not all, countries have signed onto a landmark Convention on Cyber Crime, formulated at an international summit in Bucharest, Romania, in 2001. Recognizing
the difficulties inherent in the state-centric world order in
handling criminal activity that knows no such boundaries, the
CCC (as it is now widely known) commits its signatories to
cooperate with one another to apprehend and punish cybercriminals who may operate in one domestic jurisdiction but
carry out their criminal activity in another.

Specifically, the Bucharest Convention against Cyber Crime
(as it is less-often called) diminishes state sovereignty in a
very narrow way: it requires that federal law enforcement officials of a nation within which a cybercriminal or terrorist is
engaged in fomenting crimes in other jurisdictions (the "host
state") cooperate with the agents of law enforcement who are
attempting to protect the victims of that crime elsewhere (i.e.,
within the "victim state"). So, host state authorities have to
cooperate with the victim state authorities in jointly combating
crimes that originate in the one, but affect persons and property in the other.

Specifically, the "host state" (i.e., the one found to be unin-
tentionally harboring the cybercriminal) is required both to
share information with the victim state, and also to do everything reasonably within its power to apprehend the criminal
or terrorist and put an end to his or her (or, usually, their)
criminal activities. If the host state fails to do so or refuses,
the Convention entitles the law enforcement officers of the
aggrieved victim-state to intervene or take other appropriate
action to apprehend the criminals, or otherwise find a way to
put a stop to the crime themselves. That is, once the host state
proves itself unable or *unwilling* to cooperate with victims of
crime emanating from within its borders, or to put a stop to
that crime, it incurs guilt along with the individuals perpetrat-
ing that crime.

That may seem minor, or obvious, or logical. But, in fact, it represents an enormous transformation in international relations, brought about by the oddities of cyberspace. It has never before been customary to hold states *themselves*, collectively, responsible for individual criminals hiding within their borders, let alone for the criminal actions in which those individuals were engaged. The local police were expected to cooperate in the common interests of preventing and punishing crime, but they were not *required* to do so, let alone held to account internationally for *failing* to do so.

Think, just for example, of all the German Nazi leaders who fled and hid from justice within the borders of sovereign states in South America after World War II. Technically (as we saw in chapter 7) the 1948 UN Convention against Genocide called upon nations not to provide this sanctuary, demanding instead that they apprehend such fugitives and turn them over to the appropriate authorities for prosecution. But there was no way to *compel* sovereign states to do this. Many, in fact, did not comply with the terms of this Convention—and legally, there was little anyone else could do about it.

Now, in the case of cybercriminals (or terrorists), states are *required* to cooperate with other state law enforcement agencies in putting a stop to the criminal activities originating within their borders. Host states must take the lead in arresting the perpetrators of crime. In fact, any state that refuses to apprehend perpetrators is considered, in effect, a *criminal co-conspirator*.

So, for example, if a state does nothing to apprehend a criminal organization actively working within its borders to carry out criminal activities in cyberspace, or turns a blind eye toward acts of corporate espionage (theft of corporate property and secrets, like airplane designs or pharmaceutical recipes) carried out within its borders against other nations and their industries, it thereby subjects itself to retaliation and punishment as a criminal co-conspirator. Such punishment could, in turn, range all the way from diplomatic denunciation and sanctions to (in theory at least) armed intervention across state borders to apprehend the criminals. For the first time, that is, it could turn out that a state's involvement or complicity in international crime (such as industrial espionage) would constitute a genuine act of war!

The CCC does not entirely settle the matter, especially inasmuch as many nations have rejected it (as indeed, they have rejected the interpretations of the *Tallinn Manual* itself) as constituting authoritative international law. Still, some of the contributors to the *Tallinn Manual* have noted that even if the DDoS attacks in Estonia in 2007 did not rise to the level of a use of force or an armed attack themselves, still they constituted criminal acts under the Convention. The Russian Federation's refusal to acknowledge or to take any action to stop what it characterized as the spontaneous reaction of "patriotic hacktivists" within its borders thus could have constituted grounds for some sort of military response, including a collective response by other NATO members to Estonia's plight. Such an intervention without permission of the host state, however, would itself be construed as an armed invasion and hence as an act of war.

Then how about traditional just war theory: can this offer principles of guidance for cyberwarfare?

Possibly, although the obvious dissimilarities between cyber conflict and conventional warfare mean that some new thinking will be necessary.

The basic questions are parallel to the questions that the just war tradition asks about conventional war:

- *When should we engage in cyber conflict?*
- *For what reasons?*
- *Are there limits on what we can and should do in the midst of that conflict?*
- *What do we seek to gain? What do we fear to lose?*

- *How can we conduct ourselves in better ways, rather than in worse ways, to do the best we can (and inflict as little collateral damage as possible) when carrying out otherwise-justified conflict within this environment?*

We try to employ sound moral reasoning whenever we have to address and answer such questions. Just war theory itself, in fact, is not some isolated, narrow conception of moral principles that apply only to war. Instead, the just war principles are examples of the kind of uniform results obtained from a more general kind of practical moral reasoning. JWT itself is merely one of several species of practical moral reasoning, all of which deal with "moral exceptions" or "moral emergencies" generally. Maybe reasoning in a similar fashion about cyber conflict can afford us some guidelines similar to those that we developed when confronting and questioning the morality of conventional war.

In the cyber domain, at the moment, we are clearly entering into a new frontier, a kind of Wild West situation. Cyber conflict looks for all the world like a game without rules. So let's start with that problem.

First, engaging in malevolent, antagonistic, and destructive cyber conflict is something we probably should not do ourselves, or tolerate others doing. That makes cyber conflict of a piece not just with conventional war, but with lying and deception, killing, lawbreaking, disobedience, disloyalty, and all the other kinds of things most of us normally think we should not do.

But in all these instances, there are circumstances (sometimes labeled exceptions, "moral emergencies," or even "supreme emergencies") that might allow (or even require) us to set aside these normal prohibitions, such as:

- Killing in self-defense (as a "last" or unavoidable resort).
- Lying to save a potential murder victim from his attacker.
- Breaking a law to protest the fact that it is unjust.

Perhaps cyber conflict, and cyberwarfare in particular, belongs in a same class as these other, normally prohibited activities, to which we might accord an occasional exemption if the situation were grave enough (i.e., if there were a genuine "moral emergency"). And to show that a case for cyber conflict could be made, we would have to fulfill the kinds of practical moral criteria we encounter in those other exceptional situations as well. For example:

- We would have to have a compelling reason (a just cause).
- We would have to have attempted every recourse short of a cyberattack to achieve resolution, without success.
- We would have to show that we were acting on right intentions (i.e., to defend or restore justice, punish wrongdoers, protect the innocent from harm, restore peace, re-establish good relationships, and so forth).
- We would have to demonstrate that the damage done by the cyberattack will not vastly outweigh whatever good we hope to achieve by it.

That list of important (or "necessary") conditions for the justification of our behavior in the cyber realm should seem familiar. But surprisingly, *most people, including most political philosophers who study war and ethics, don't ever seem to recognize that we apply the same or similar conditions to the doing of other kinds of things that we normally ought not to do, in addition to war.*

Thus, saying that just war criteria don't apply to cyber conflict is really kind of . . . well . . . boneheaded! *Of course* these criteria don't apply, *if* they are merely criteria exclusively governing when we may permissibly fight a conventional war.

But they are not: instead, these are the more general criteria governing when we might be permitted to do something of any sort whatsoever that we normally think we should *not* do. And we reach them through a process of practical reasoning about such moral issues that is at least as old as Aristotle.

But forget about Aristotle! Your own mom or dad probably told you when you were little that you should not kill, lie, cheat, steal, break your promise, or betray a friend. And then he or she might have added: "So if you ever *are* thinking of killing someone, or lying to them, or breaking a promise, or betraying their loyalty, let alone making war on them, you better *damn* well have a good reason, and have tried everything else first," and so forth. (And even then, you were likely in a heap of trouble, or a "world of hurt.")

But this is how basic and elementary this kind of moral reasoning is. It is the sort of thing most all of us do instinctively, whenever we face hard choices or genuine moral dilemmas. So why not use the same tried-and-true approach for thinking about something brand new and unfamiliar, like cyber conflict?

If we do, then it might occur to us to add some conditions to the list above. We might also, for example, add provisions to guide what we would be willing and unwilling to do when *conducting* or *engaging in* a cyberattack of some sort, such as these:

- Limit damage or harm solely (if possible) to those who are justifiably the object of the attack.
- Refrain ever from deliberately or indiscriminately targeting everyone, or recklessly harming innocent third parties (cyber "noncombatants").

We would also want to take care that the degree of "virtual force" used, and the damage it might do, is not altogether *out of proportion* to the political (or moral) objective of the attack itself. At least it seems reasonable, and not at all ridiculous or irrelevant, to raise these questions as considerations before we proceed.

That is to say, once we have decided upon either carrying out a cyberattack ourselves or of responding to one launched against us, if at all possible we would want to ensure that we

- Only attacked targets that were the equivalent of legitimate military objectives in conventional war (i.e., enemy
  facilities that were themselves designed to foment or
  carry out an attack against us);
- Refrained from deliberately attacking the cyber equivalent of civilians and civilian objects, such as banks, power
  plants, hydroelectric dams, and so forth;
- Took care, also, that the cyber weapons we developed
  and used damaged only their intended and legitimate
  targets, and did not "escape" or otherwise spread out to
  damage those civilian objects and infrastructure.

With respect to this last, important limitation, Peter Singer
and Allan Friedman remark that "Stuxnet may have been the
first truly ethical weapon ever developed."[3] That would be
because it *neither killed nor harmed anyone* and did no damage
to anything whatsoever apart from its intended, legitimate
military target.

Some people object, however, that Stuxnet "escaped" (perhaps when an unnamed Iranian nuclear technician violated
routine procedure, and took his laboratory laptop home to send
email) and infected other computers throughout the world.
But of course, that possibility, too, had been foreseen, even if
it seemed unlikely. Apparently by design, the cyber weapon
resided harmlessly within the operating systems of the machines
it inadvertently infected, remaining totally inert, doing nothing
to them, until it finally "self-destructed" in July 2012.

But could the weapon in the meantime, when discovered, be
studied, reverse-engineered, and replicated? If possible, that
prospect might place the weapon in the hands of terrorists or
other adversarial governments, who might not be so discriminating and cautious in their use of it. But here we encounter
something unique to cyber weapons. They are not like nuclear
or chemical or biological weapons, sitting on a shelf somewhere, to be stolen and used by anyone with the capability to
do so. They are decidedly not WMDs.

In fact, as computer scientist and cyber weapons expert Neil Rowe explains, they are one-off, single-use weapons. You get only one bite of this apple. Once the weapon is used and recognized, experts will study and try to reverse-engineer it. Meanwhile, everyone knows it is out there, and how it works, and has erected various improvised, new cyber firewall defenses against it. No truly effective cyber weapon (as apart from annoying generic viruses and worms used for theft or vandalism) *has ever been replicated and reused successfully* . . . not, at least, to anyone's knowledge.

Given these criteria for cyber conflict, how do we assess the attack on Estonia?

The dispute, and the ensuing attacks, erupted over a controversy in 2007 about where to place a Russian war memorial statue. It was moved from a place of honor in the center of Tallinn to a nearby military cemetery. That is not an insignificant diplomatic affront, but hardly seems to rise to the level of a cause for a state-sponsored (or tolerated) cyberattack. It certainly could not justify an attack launched massively and indiscriminately at anyone and everything in Estonia. What if people who had had no part and no interest in where that statue was placed had somehow lost their lives as a result, perhaps because they couldn't gain access to their bank funds to buy food or to their medical records to seek urgent care?

Apparently no care or concern went into thinking about who or what ought properly be attacked and with what degree of virtual force. That is, in the language of both law and morality, these attacks were utterly and wholly *indiscriminate*. They were also *entirely out of proportion* to any harm to which they were a response.

Taken with the weak justification or cause, that suggests that the attacks were illegal and criminal. And if they were permitted or tolerated (let alone encouraged, or even ordered) by the host state government, then, under the Bucharest Convention, that state and its government could be held accountable and punished for those attacks, along with those who actually carried out the attacks.

These attacks were, in effect, "cyber war crimes," recklessly and indiscriminately directed at civilians and civilian objects (as well as against agents of the Estonian government who might have ordered the removal of the war statue). This indictment holds true even if, fortunately, no one was in fact seriously injured, nor was property or important infrastructure seriously damaged.

There are a number of other instances of cyberwar-like altercations that experts like Clarke, Singer and Friedman, and others describe in detail, carried out (allegedly) by Russians, Israelis, Iranians, and the United States, among others. (These do not include the ongoing theft of military and industrial secrets by the PLA Shanghai unit, five members of which were finally placed under symbolic criminal indictment for these actions.) Ethical analysis of these incidents would proceed along this same line of reasoning.[4] Some look much more justified, and properly conducted, than the attack on Estonia.

In your assessment of Stuxnet, you omit the fact that it was used preemptively, before any actual harm had been inflicted by Iran. But didn't we learn that it is wrong, according to just war doctrine, to launch an attack before you yourself are attacked?

One additional interesting feature of the Stuxnet attack on the Iranian nuclear weapons facility is that it challenges our understanding of a concept sometimes termed "preventive self-defense." Preventive use of conventional force violates just war doctrine in two important ways. First, if the only *justified* cause for the use of force is suffering aggression in the form of an armed attack, then Stuxnet violated the principle of just cause (since no attack had first been launched by Iran, nor was such an attack imminent or soon likely to occur). Second, by definition, a preventive use of force (no matter how justified or unjustified it may otherwise seem) by definition violates the principle of last resort.

If we raise the last-resort objection, we are merely copying from the final list of just war criteria governing conventional war, rather than deriving a set of new necessary conditions from scratch (using the same underlying procedure of reasoning) for cyber conflict. But, for the sake of argument, let's assume that we have already carefully shown this same principle also applies in cyberspace, to cyber weapons and warfare. Then we seem to have a serious problem. *The Stuxnet attack (undertaken by whomever) then appears to have lacked a just cause and was not a "last resort."*

I tend to think that this is where the prospects for cyber conflict and cyber weapons constitutes a moral dilemma on the frontier of military ethics. The principle of last resort, for example, requires that efforts short of engaging in morally prohibited behavior (in this case, an armed attack) first be attempted, and that ample warning be given an adversary: there should be a kind of "public declaration" to leave off the illegal and threatening behavior, or suffer the consequences.

But such warnings were, in fact, given to Iran, which ignored or derided them. Numerous attempts at solving the nuclear proliferation problem had already been attempted and failed. We thus confront the question that the last-resort principle always presents, even in more familiar situations: *When has enough been done? When is there no alternative but to attack?*

This is especially problematic in the case of cyberattacks and calls for an additional provision to govern our decisions regarding when to engage in, or refrain from, undertaking them.

- Is the cyberattack a substitute for a conventional attack?
- Will the cyberattack incite a conventional counterattack?

In the Stuxnet case, prospects for a conventional attack had been looming in the ongoing tensions between Iran and other nations. There was good reason to fear that the nation most threatened by the Iranian nuclear program, Israel, would attempt to do there what it successfully did in Syria in 2007, and earlier in Iraq in 1981: that is, launch a conventional bombing raid to destroy or degrade the nuclear weapons facility under development before it could be brought fully online and made operational.

Given the ability of the Israelis to undertake such a mission successfully, the prospects for widespread regional conflict erupting in its wake were a grave concern. So in this case, the use of a cyber weapon at precisely this juncture was, shall we say, fortuitous. It obviated the need for the Israelis to attempt a daring and dangerous and destabilizing conventional attack. The use of the cyber weapon, in sum, appears for the moment to have avoided something much worse.

Does that qualify as a "last resort?" Within the paradigm of traditional just war doctrine, the cyberattack would technically be a next-to-the-last resort. And in this particular kind of situation, we might conclude that, given the choice between a cyber weapon and a conventional weapon in an otherwise justified conflict, the less destructive alternative may (or indeed, even must) be attempted first. And, we might also conclude that this version of the principle of "last resort" to cyber weapons also licenses, on very rare and restricted occasions, their use in this "preventive" fashion, *if doing so will prevent an even greater and more destructive use of conventional force* by one of the adversaries.

What challenges does the advent of this new form of warfare present for ethics in the military profession?

In the preceding chapter, and in an earlier one on private contractors, the problem of ethics and military professionalism was seen to be twofold: could we replace military personnel, as members of the profession of arms, with robots or with private contractors? If so, then the idea of a "military profession" seems quaint and outmoded. But if not, then it must be that the professional has some virtues beyond pure skills and capacities that cannot be emulated in robots or relied upon in contractors (working for personal profit in the private sector). Principal among those properties were *situational awareness and prudent moral discernment.*

Here the problem is a bit different, somewhat more akin to the kind of professional transformation that replaces human pilots in a fighter jet cockpit, for instance, with a "virtual" warrior, running a control station in a remote location thousands of miles away. Does the safety and security of the desk job, in the case of the fighter pilot, transform the profession? Or does it require *a carryover of professional attitudes and legal restrictions into the new environment?*

If "virtual" cyberwar now promises (or threatens?) to replace conventional war, or to supplant it in the sequence of events leading to conventional war as a last resort, does this transform the profession of arms or somehow alter the persons who join that profession? Does it change their core values or alter any of the bedrock moral principles by which they previously guided their activities?

Certainly one troubling transformation is the supplanting of conventional combat personnel with intelligence, espionage, and covert personnel. The latter used to play a subordinate role to the former in events leading up to, and into, war, as well as in offering strategic and tactical advice to civilian authorities. Now those roles are inverted: in cyber conflict, the "intel community," so to speak, is driving the ship.

They are also designing and deploying the weapons. Why should this matter, especially since many in the intelligence community came to those jobs from regular positions in military service? As cyber expert Neil Rowe objected several years ago, the weapons and tactics being proposed for cyber conflict involve the tacit commission of war crimes, in that the most effective weapons and tactics are directed against civilian infrastructure. That this is, or was being done, so far as anyone can tell, without a thought, comes from the basic background and cultural assumptions of the intel community versus the conventional combatant community.

The latter at least know of, understand, and see themselves as constrained by the law of armed conflict (LOAC). The former, quite to the contrary, do not. And under normal operational circumstances, they are not constrained. There are regulations internal to services and agencies, of course, that dictate appropriate action and differentiate between activities that are permissible and impermissible.

But the deep underlying difference stems from the understanding of what is termed "low-intensity conflict," like espionage and covert actions that fall short of war, and "hot" or "high-intensity" or "kinetic" conflict that involves conventional weapons. It is the latter kind of conflict that is governed by LOAC, and by a customary code of the warrior, encompassing the concerns for proportionality, discrimination, accountability, and economy in the use of deadly force, for example.

But when we think of espionage and covert action, we think of deception, dirty tricks, theft of state secrets, assassination, and intrigue—in short, we think of activities either outside the boundaries of law and morality, or else of actions that are conventionally considered illegal within the domestic regimes in which they occur. What happens when, all of a sudden, people accustomed to operating according to one particular regime of rules and principles are suddenly put in charge of the virtual equivalent of armed conflict, something that falls under an entirely different regime? Clearly, persons placed in such a new situation might initially fail to recognize that the relevant rules have changed, and that, unless careful, they may find themselves engaged in developing tactics and in proposing the use of weapons in a manner that would, in a conventional conflict, constitute clear-cut war crimes.

Much of this exemplifies the confusion, once again, at the dawn of a new era, when we are trying to figure out how to navigate, and to govern our thoughts and behavior, in a totally new and unfamiliar realm. All along we have seen that the initial approach to this new cyber realm is to see it as a domain in which anything goes and in which there are no discernable rules and constraints. We have seen, however, that the relevant rules, principles, and laws emerge with time and are recognized by practitioners as necessary to bring a degree of order, regularity, and predictability to their complex activities that is necessary for their ongoing success. We might characterize ourselves, in the cyber world, as inhabiting the steep upward slope of a "learning curve," with much lying before us to learn and master, in order to operate comfortably in this realm.

When it comes to conducting war in this realm—as well as, for that matter, conducting a great many other complex operations in, say, commercial competition (as well as interstate conflict), the fighting of crime, and the protection of innocent individuals from undeserved harm in this realm—we do indeed have a long way to go and a lot to learn about how to conduct ourselves, and to reign in the most extreme and destructive impulses of others.

Colonel James Cook, a US Air Force pilot with a PhD in philosophy, who now teaches at the US Air Force Academy, likens the development of a rulebook for the cyber realm to the kind of evolution that occurred over millennia in seagoing navigation (where the rules, regulations, and customs were built up over time), as well as to the dawn of aviation just over a century ago. The rules for operating craft in the air in three dimensions were consciously developed in analogy with seafaring navigation (which, apart from submarines, took place in two dimensions). It took time to figure out how to adapt the customs of the maritime environment to the aerial environment. Indeed, the very term "aviation" was an acronym coined from "navigation," simply replacing the Latin root for "sea" with that for the sky.

Hence, Cook argues, we will in time inevitably develop a handbook for "cyberation," the adoption of rules from conventional conflict to apply to this new realm of cyber conflict.

Likewise, we will one day learn to regulate and order the behavior of all the new kinds of private, commercial, and state-centered activities that take place daily in this realm, as they now do on sea, land, and air (and even space) without undue confusion or lack of accountability. Cook's observations on this matter seem precisely on target.

In addition, we likely need the formulation of a new code for the cyber warrior, grounded in the code of the conventional warrior that we find in the just war tradition and international law. Our new generation of "virtual" warriors will need to learn to respect individual privacy and dignity of persons whose cyber trails they inadvertently come across in the pursuit of adversaries. They will need our trust to pursue criminals and terrorists, and to protect our lives and property from adversaries, while we count on them to respect our individual liberty and privacy.

Future cyber warriors need to be made aware of this, and prove themselves worthy of this trust, just as conventional combatants have to train hard to prove themselves worthy of their exclusive right to bear arms and use deadly force for purposes of legitimate security (rather than for abuse or oppression of the individual citizens they have sworn to serve). This new generation of cyber warriors will need to rein in their customary instincts, as intelligence operatives, to engage in conflict that deliberately targets the lives, privacy, and property of citizens, including even citizens of adversary states, as they pursue conflict with the "virtual combatants" of that adversary state.

If such indiscriminate behavior was ever acceptable conduct in the course of espionage, it is no longer acceptable in cyber conflict, especially when it involves the thoughtless and unreflective targeting of entire populations with cyber weapons designed to destroy or seriously degrade their lives and welfare. Such conduct is no better than the "terrorist" ("strategic") bombing campaigns of World War II, including the use of indiscriminate nuclear weapons against enemy civilian targets that characterized the latter phases of that war (to our enduring shame and regret).

We cannot carry over the worst, most unjustifiable excesses of conventional combat, which we learned to understand as constituting unacceptable professional practice in war, and still pursue such tactics in the cyber realm. But that is how we started out. And that is how cyber pundits like Richard Clarke fear it may end: in the cyber Armageddon that threatens to lay waste to all we have managed to achieve with our new technologies.

Such a miserable outcome is less likely, however, if our cyber warriors are helped, by the rest of us, to recognize the professional principles of best practice inherent in the moral justification for their enterprise. We will, that is to say, need to respond to change and new challenges in warfare with a new sense of professionalism, and of professional ethics, to accompany this, and all future developments that transform the profession of arms in the coming century. That is truly something about which all of us need to know

Notes

1. David E. Sanger, "Differences on Cybertheft Complicate China Talks," *New York Times*, July 10, 2013; www.nytimes.com/2013/07/11/world/asia/differences-on-cybertheft-complicate-china-talks.html.
2. Readers will find these details more extensively narrated and analyzed in my recent article, "NSA Management Directive #424: Secrecy and Privacy in the Aftermath of Snowden," *Journal of Ethics and International Affairs* 28, no. 1 (Spring 2014): 29–38.
3. This was Singer's comment during an NPR interview shortly after, and concerning, the publication of this new book. There he is quoting my earlier evaluation of this feature of Stuxnet, made shortly after it was discovered. I agree with the thrust of Singer and Friedman's argument, as do others, that if one were going to design and use a cyber weapon, it would need to perform much like this one did. See P. W. Singer and Allan Friedman, *Cybersecurity and Cyber War: What Everyone Needs to Know* (New York: Oxford University Press, 2014), 98.

4. I've done a good bit of this analysis already, beginning shortly after the discovery of Stuxnet itself. See, for example, *"Jus in silico*: Moral Restrictions on the Use of Cyber Warfare," in *The Routledge Handbook of War and Ethics*, ed. Fritz Allhoff, Nick Evans, and Adam Henschke (New York: Routledge, 2013), 367–380. I will present a more detailed summary of this argument in my forthcoming book, *The Ethics of Cyber Warfare* (New York: Oxford University Press, 2016).

Further Reading

Arquilla, John. "Cyber War Is Already Upon Us." *Foreign Policy*, March–April 2012: http://www.foreignpolicy.com/articles/ 2012/ 02/27/cyberwar_is_already_upon_us.

Arquilla, John. "Ethics and Information Warfare." In *The Changing Role of Information in Warfare*, ed. Zalmay M. Khalilzad and John P. White, 379–401. Santa Monica, CA: RAND Corporation, 1999.

Arquilla, John, and David Ronfeldt. "Cyberwar Is Coming!" *Comparative Strategy* 12, no. 2 (1993): 141–165.

Brenner, Joel. *America the Vulnerable: Inside the New Threat Matrix of Digital Espionage, Crime, and Warfare*. New York: Penguin, 2011.

Carr, Jeffrey. *Inside Cyber Warfare: Mapping the Cyber Underworld*. 2nd edition. Sebastopol, CA: O'Reilly Media, 2011.

Clarke, Richard A., and Robert K. Kanke. *Cyber War: The Next Threat to National Security and What to Do about It*. New York: HarperCollins, 2010.

Cook, James. "'Cyberation' and Just War Doctrine: A Response to Randall Dipert." *Journal of Military Ethics* 9, no. 4 (2010): 411–423.

Council of Europe. "Convention on Cybercrime." Budapest, November 23, 2001: http://conventions.coe.int/Treaty/EN/ Treaties/html/ 185.htm.

Denning, Dorothy. E. "Cyberwarriors." *Harvard International Review*, Summer 2001, 70–75.

Denning, Dorothy E. "The Ethics of Cyber Conflict." In *Information and Computer Ethics*, edited by K. E. Himma and H. T. Tavani.

New York: Wiley, 2007. Available at http://faculty.nps.edu/deden-nin/publications/Ethics%20of%20Cyber%20Conflict.pdf.

Denning, Dorothy E. *Information Warfare and Security*. Reading, MA: Addison-Wesley, 1998.

Dipert, Randall R. "The Essential Features of an Ontology for Cyberwarfare." In *Conflict and Cooperation in Cyberspace: The Challenge to National Security*, edited by Panayotis A. Yannakogeorgos and Adam B. Lowther, 35–48. Boca Raton, FL: Taylor and Francis, 2014.

Dipert, Randall R. "The Ethics of Cyber Warfare." *Journal of Military Ethics* 9, no. 4 (December 2010): 384–410.

Dipert, Randall R. "The Future Impact of a Long Period of Limited Cyberwarfare on the Ethics of Warfare." In *The Ethics of Information Warfare*, edited by Luciano Floridi and Mariarosaria Taddeo, 25–37. Amsterdam: Springer, 2014.

Dipert, Randall R. "Other Than Internet Warfare: Challenges for Ethics, Law and Policy." *Journal of Military Ethics* 12, no. 1 (2013): 34–53.

Dunlap, Charles J. "Perspectives for Cyber Strategists on Law for Cyberwar." *Strategic Studies Quarterly*, Spring 2011, 81–99.

Graham, David E. "Cyber Threats and the Law of War." *Journal of National Security Law* 4, no. 1 (2010): 87–102.

Liang, Quao, and Wang Xiangsu. 1999. *Unrestricted Warfare: China's Master Plan to Destroy America*, Panama City, Panama: Pan American, 2002. Selections available at http://www.cryptome.org/cuw.htm.

Libicki, Martin C. *Conquest in Cyberspace: National Security and Information Warfare*. New York: Cambridge University Press, 2007.

Libicki, Martin C. *Cyberdeterrence and Cyberwar*. Santa Monica, CA: RAND Corporation, 2009.

Lucas, George. "Can There Be an Ethical Cyberwar?" In *Conflict and Cooperation in Cyberspace*, edited by Panayotis A. Yannakogeorgos and Adam B. Lowther, 195–210. Boca Raton, FL: Taylor and Francis, 2014.

Lucas, George. "*Jus in silico*: Moral Restrictions on the Use of Cyber Warfare." In *Routledge Handbook of War and Ethics*, edited by

Fritz Allhoff, Nicolas G. Evans, and Adam Henschke, 367–380. New York: Routledge, 2013.

Lucas, George. "NSA Management Directive # 424: Secrecy and Privacy in the Aftermath of Snowden." *Journal of Ethics and International Affairs* 28, no. 1 (Spring 2014): 29–38.

Lucas, George. "Permissible Preventive Cyber Warfare." In *The Ethics of Information Warfare*, edited by Luciano Floridi and Mariarosaria Taddeo, 73–83. Amsterdam: Springer, 2014.

Rid, Thomas C. "Cyber War Will Not Take Place." *Journal of Strategic Studies* 35, no. 1 (October 2011): 5–32.

Owens, William A., Kenneth W. Dam, and Herbert L. Lin, eds. *Technology, Policy, Law, and Ethics Regarding U.S. Acquisition and Use of Cyberattack Capabilities.* Washington, DC: National Research Council / American Academy of Sciences, 2009.

Rid, Thomas C. "Think Again: Cyberwar." *Foreign Policy*, March–April 2012: http://www.foreignpolicy.com/articles/ 2012/02/27/ cyberwar.

Rowe, Neil C. "Ethics of Cyber War Attacks." In *Cyber Warfare and Cyber Terrorism*, edited by Lech J. Janczewski and Andrew M. Colarik, 105–111. Hershey, PA: Information Science Reference, 2008.

Rowe, Neil C. "The Ethics of Cyberweapons in Warfare." *Journal of Technoethics* 1, no. 1 (2010): 20–31.

Rowe, Neil C. "Toward Reversible Cyber Attacks." In *Leading Issues in Information Warfare and Security Research*, edited by Julie Ryan, 145–158. Reading, UK: Academic Publishing, 2011.

Rowe, Neil C. "War Crimes from Cyberweapons." *Journal of Information Warfare* 6, no. 3 (2007): 15–25.

Schmitt, Michael N. "Computer Network Attack and the Use of Force in International Law: Thoughts on a Normative Framework." *Columbia Journal of Transnational Law* 37 (1999): 885–937.

Schmitt, Michael N. "Cyber Operations and the Jus in Bello: Key Issues." *U.S. Naval War College International Law Studies* 87 (2011): 89–110.

Schmitt, Michael N., ed. *The Tallinn Manual on the International Law Applicable to Cyber Warfare*. Tallinn: NATO Cooperative Cyber Defence Center of Excellence, 2013.

Schmitt, Michael N. "Wired Warfare: Computer Network Attack and *jus in Bello*." *International Review of the Red Cross* 84, no. 846 (2002): 365–399.

Singer, P. W., and Allan Friedman. *Cybersecurity and Cyber War: What Everyone Needs to Know*. New York: Oxford University Press, 2014.

Tallinn, 2012. *The Tallinn Manual on the International Law Applicable to Cyber Warfare*. Michael N. Schmitt, ed. (Cambridge: Cambridge University Press, 2013).

Whetham, David and George Lucas. "The Relevance of the Just War Tradition to Cyber Warfare." In *Cyber Warfare: A Multidisciplinary Analysis*, edited by James A. Green, 160–173. London: Routledge, 2015.

Yannakogeorgos, Panayotis A., and Adam B., Lowther, eds. *Conflict and Cooperation in Cyberspace*. Boca Raton, FL: Taylor and Francis, 2014.

EPILOGUE

Reconsidering Ethics within the Profession of Arms

The core of this book is an account of military service itself, and of military personnel in each and every country of the world, as *the members of a profession*, traditionally labeled the profession of arms.

If this label represents anything other than a meaningless honorific title, however, it has to be made to encompass the idea that military services and their personnel, like the members of every other recognized profession, are held to basic principles of common practice that apply to every single member of the profession, regardless of race, nationality, religion, or culture.

To many readers, perhaps even some military readers, that may have seemed like a very strange and unfamiliar idea. But it is an important idea to grasp, inasmuch as many of the basic principles of professional practice in the military (perhaps more than in any other profession) are *moral principles*, setting forth the core values and elaborating the ideals and best practices of that profession; of equal importance, defining professional identity, demeanor, rectitude, and probity; and establishing the boundaries of acceptable professional practice.

Collectively, these moral principles constitute the ethics or the code of ethics of that profession, and serve both to define it and to set it apart from other human communities or social organizations (with their own, equally distinct practices).

It was precisely in this sense that this was, finally, a book about military ethics. I attempted to describe the *ethics* of the military *profession*, or what members of the US Army, at least, sometimes term the "professional military ethic."

This is a concept that has proven extremely elusive, even among members of the profession who believe it exists and is vital to their performance and self-understanding. Perhaps that is because it requires all of us to understand who individual military personnel themselves *are*, and what they understand themselves to *be about* in the wider world. This, too, seems to be a topic that everyone, but *especially military personnel themselves*, need to know.

In other professions, such as medicine or law, such discussions of professional ethics and the boundaries of acceptable professional practice are carefully discussed and debated among the members of the profession. The resulting consensus views are then taught to new initiates into the profession, and often codified in a code of ethics, or an oath of commitment to the profession—an oath to which all members are required to swear allegiance or commitment.

What have we learned about the military profession in these respects? Recall that the book opened with a quotation from *On War* written by the great 19th-century Prussian general and military strategist Karl von Clausewitz, who, following service in the Prussian and Russian armies during the Napoleonic Wars, served as rector of the Prussian Military Academy in Berlin for 12 years prior to his death. His famous treatment of military strategy, even after nearly two centuries, is still widely admired, cited, taught, and studied by military personnel and international relations experts. Clausewitz's famous axiom, that war itself represents nothing more or less than political ends pursued through nonpolitical means, is all but ubiquitous, and probably known to virtually every high school student who has ever taken a course in history or social studies.

In this quotation, taken from the third volume of this classic work, Clausewitz describes the military itself as constituting a guild, or what we might now term a profession. He speaks of "professional pride" as playing a vital role in fostering what he also terms the "military virtues."

The passage that I quoted is, in turn, located precisely at the center of a lengthier discussion by Clausewitz of military virtue. Clausewitz appears to say that, despite the necessity of recruiting military personnel from all walks of life, and despite the growing desire in his time (as enshrined in the American Constitution, for example) of seeing a national military force as a militia of citizen-soldiers, the fact seems to be that those military personnel *themselves* invariably see themselves—and indeed, Clausewitz seems to be saying that *it is vital* that they come to see themselves—as members of what we now call a "profession," set apart from society by shared skills, respon-sibilities, and what Clausewitz termed "military virtues." Indeed, he connects the origin and cultivation of military vir-tues, whatever those might be, with the interesting phrase, "professional pride."

The things that Clausewitz terms virtues are what we now often term "best practices": that is, forms of excellence, and ideals of behavior toward which each member of the profes-sion must strive, and which each must to some degree embrace or embody in order to maintain membership in the profession. If the military itself is a profession—as Clausewitz seems to imply, and as many contemporary military personnel also strongly believe—then it must collectively espouse high ide-als of professional behavior, promote "best professional prac-tices," and also take great care to foster the responsible exercise of professional autonomy by its individual members, as well as define the limits of acceptable professional practice for those individuals.

It is essential to the survival, health, and proper function-ing of the profession that its members each understand these foundational moral obligations, as well as believe them and practice them. Accordingly, the central purpose of this work was to provide a description of the essential features of regular, professionally trained military forces, focusing, in particular, upon both the legal and the moral constraints under which they operate and some of the core ethical values that define their profession.

These are all matters about which every citizen should know, no matter what his or her nationality, culture, and religion. These are also matters about which there should probably be more knowledge and consensus among individuals who presently serve on active duty in military organizations than there seems to be at the moment. It is therefore my sincerest hope that the effort we have engaged in together will go some distance toward addressing that need.

ADDITIONAL EXPRESSIONS OF GRATITUDE AND RESPECT

This book will prove useful only if understood, not as a compilation of my own personal views, but as a reflection of all I have learned, and all that has been bequeathed to me through the lifelong experience of growing up with the guidance of, and ultimately working alongside, some wonderful, intelligent, dedicated, and inspiring people.

From the eminent and generous philosopher Alasdair MacIntyre, arguably the most accomplished and original moral philosopher alive today, I long ago came to realize that "ethics" is largely a discussion of norms and values, and of "right and wrong" behavior, elicited from the members of a common community of shared practices, primarily as a result of the community members' own reflections on the better and worse ways of carrying out those practices in striving toward a commonly-held conception of "the Good" toward which they tended. MacIntyre's own exemplar of this method was Aristotle, living in the midst of his own city and cross-examining it and his neighboring cities about their varied forms of political organization and their individual beliefs, habits, and customs.

This examination of Aristotle's was part of a quest to discern an ideal form of political and social organization—and, even more, a quest to discern more precisely those virtues, excellences, and habits of heart most likely to bring about human flourishing, and point individual human beings toward those ends and goals that collectively embodied their shared conception of the "good" and worthwhile human life.

Somewhat in contrast to Aristotle's rather elevated view of his own role in all this, however, I came also to realize that, in that activity, *the philosopher is little more than an observer, a handmaiden and stenographer*, and perhaps, at least on some occasions, a sympathetic therapist, helping those concretely engaged in the profound complexities, and wrestling with the wrenching moral ambiguities, of their shared endeavors, to narrate their own experiences and the valuable lessons they themselves have learned through those experiences, more effectively. Philosophers speak of this process as "helping to tease out the *normative dimensions* of professional practice." That is what I hope this book has achieved.

Over the past 20 years, I helped develop and build a core curriculum and a small academic department ("section") devoted to teaching ethics, military ethics, and case studies, alongside military lawyers and psychologists, and a large cadre of junior and senior naval officers assigned to teach leadership, seamanship, and navigation in what was then the "Professional Development" division of the Naval Academy. These and other officers "around the Yard" (campus) were my tutors, mentors, colleagues, and friends. I learned much from them and about them, and am deeply indebted to all of them, as well as to successive classes of midshipmen whom I had the privilege of teaching over those years.

It was likewise a special privilege to collaborate with our visiting holders of the Distinguished Leadership Chair: in succession, Admiral Leon "Bud" Edney, Admiral Henry "Hank" Chiles, Vice Admiral Michael Haskins, and, currently, Marine Lieutenant General John Sattler. Navy Captains Bill Craft, Denny Whitford, Todd Hundley, Elizabeth Holmes, Mary Jo ("MJ") Sweeney, W. "Rick" Rubel, Mark Clemente, "Corky" Vazques, Lee Geanulias, and countless other captains and commanders in the Navy, and Marine Corps colonels (such as then-Colonel John Allen, Commandant of Midshipmen) were assigned by a succession of superintendents of the Academy (Admiral Charles Larson, and Vice Admirals John Ryan, Rod Rempt, and Mike Miller, and now Ted Carter) to work with our civilian department to teach the core ethics course. And, in light of the dramatically increased role of US Special Forces after September 11, 2001, I became especially close to Navy Captain Robert (Bob) Schoultz and Master Chief Will Guild of the Navy SEALS, who taught for several years in our ethics program. These are the two SEALs whose classroom teaching techniques for the SEAL Team10 case I especially admired.

Bob was a captain with over 30 years in the service. In the case of SEALs, that sort of longevity is not easy to attain, if you catch my meaning. Gentle, thoughtful, and graciously modest almost to a fault, his last years on active duty were spent reading philosophy, particularly the works of Søren Kierkegaard, with midshipmen aspiring to join the Special Forces. Will, for his part, was the Navy's senior or "Command" Master Chief. After more than 30 years of service, it was appropriate that he was also the first (and still, so far as I know, the only) member of the Navy or Marine Corps enlisted ranks ever appointed to teach alongside senior officers in the core ethics course.

Will was an imposing figure with enormous experience. There was probably not a bone in his body that hadn't been broken at one time or another (which caused him to suffer considerable and constant pain). Quite surprisingly—especially to the large number of midshipmen who admired him as a teacher and military professional—Will held an undergraduate degree in philosophy, obtained from the same university in Virginia that Secretary Robert Gates and I had attended, all at nearly the same time. Will's life goal, whenever the SEALs would permit him finally to retire, was to attend Harvard Divinity School to study theology.

During the final years leading up to my retirement from the Naval Academy in 2012, I was appointed to the Distinguished Chair in Ethics in the Vice Admiral James B. Stockdale Center for Ethics and Leadership. Once again a Marine colonel, Arthur J. Athens, was director of that center and the best supervisor I ever experienced. Meanwhile, officers were then "rotating in" from multiple tours in Iraq and Afghanistan to teach at the Academy. Whenever possible, I encouraged them to write up their experiences as ethics cases for publication in what was the first volume of military case study literature ever compiled, edited by Captain Rick Rubel and myself. Our companion coedited textbook, *Ethics and the Military Profession: The Moral Foundations of Leadership*, went through four editions and for a while was the most widely used textbook on this topic in the world.

Over the same period, I began volunteering to teach ethics for students in some of the programs at the Naval Postgraduate School (NPS), where I often encountered former Naval Academy students, returning after a decade in the fleet to obtain a master's degree. I moved to NPS full time in July 2010, where I continued to teach and write in the field of military ethics, working especially on the ethical problems arising from new modes of warfare and technology, such as cyber conflict and robotics. It was those midcareer students, both from US services and international military services, who helped me so much at the end of the road. They are acknowledged in the opening of the book.

These shared experiences taught me to care about understanding this subject more deeply, and also to try to communicate what I learned from all those great friends and acquaintances back to the military communities whose individual members had helped me learn it, as well as to the general public.

INDEX